Cavana - Fuller + bruz

THE STOCK PICKER

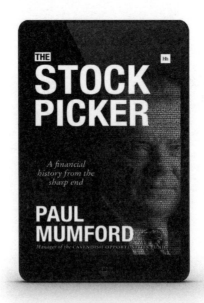

THE STOCK PICKER
A financial history from the sharp end

Paul Mumford

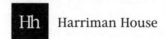 Harriman House

HARRIMAN HOUSE LTD
18 College Street
Petersfield
Hampshire
GU31 4AD
GREAT BRITAIN
Tel: +44 (0)1730 233870

Email: enquiries@harriman-house.com
Website: www.harriman-house.com

First published in Great Britain in 2016.

Hardback ISBN: 978-0-85719-554-8
eBook ISBN: 978-0-85719-555-5

British Library Cataloguing in Publication Data
A CIP catalogue record for this book can be obtained from the British Library.

Set in STEMPEL GARAMOND and DIN Pro.

To Stephen and Betty Mumford

My wonderful parents, to whom I am indebted and who will forever be in my memory

CONTENTS

ABOUT THE AUTHOR

Paul Mumford is one of the longest-serving fund managers in the UK, with 50 years' experience in the markets as a stockbroker and fund manager. He runs the Cavendish Opportunities Fund, AIM Fund and Select Fund, having launched the first in 1988 as the Glenfriars Opportunities Fund. He is a stock picker who aims to find shares in undervalued companies and often ends up swimming against the tide and buying unloved shares. Paul has three daughters and two granddaughters. His outside interests include bridge – he has obtained the rank of Life Master – supporting live music at local venues, and following two football teams as a season ticket holder.

Acknowledgements

Top of the list I would like to thank Alison Hyde, manager of the Cavendish Technology Fund, who checked my spelling and punctuation. After she had finished her work on each draft chapter, there was a raft of red crosses over the pages.

Ron Bullivant, manager of the Cavendish Japan Fund, also read the corrected draft and added comments on points that I had overlooked.

Ben Lewis, the chief executive officer of River Island, kindly reviewed the chapter regarding the origins of the Lewis Trust Group and helped add part of the history of which I was unaware.

A History of the London Stock Market 1945–2007 by an ex-colleague, George G. Blakey, helped me to remember various dates and events, and *The Property Boom* by Oliver Marriott, published in 1967, was used to refresh my memory of the events leading up to my speciality in asset valuation. Otherwise Wikipedia provided additional background information, but for the most part I used material gleaned from company accounts and press comment.

Introduction

"Most stock pickers are complete morons"
– Peter Hargreaves

This book is the story of my life rather than an investing 'how-to'. It is, in many ways, a very personal book. I never wished to write anything else. However, I hope there are chapters that will be interesting and useful to fellow investors, and that the rest will be enjoyable for anyone who likes to look back at how the stock market and indeed the wider world has changed over the years. I write about how to find investing bargains, what makes for a robust company and all the most important lessons I have learned as an investor – but also about the musical world of the 1950s and 60s, my time as a schoolboy bookmaker, and the time I took an art course and painted trees that looked like lollipops. I think the latter (and many other experiences I touch on) all played a role in making me who I am as a stock picker. Nevertheless, while I do make those connections between the personal side of my life and investing in the stock market, I do not try to labour the point; the book is a collection of memories rather than a manifesto.

At first the thought of writing around 4,000 words per chapter seemed daunting, but I found sufficient material and soon discovered that I could cover a whole range of topics without padding. It was exciting to delve into the past and pore over information on bygone investments and historic events. One of my objectives was for the reader to come away saying, "Gosh I did not know that" (and hopefully to do so more than once). An overriding goal was to make each paragraph and every chapter as interesting as possible and to throw some light on the ups and downs of a stock-picking approach to investment.

Are most stock pickers complete morons? In a headline to an article in the *FT Adviser* that seemed to be Peter Hargreaves' verdict. Curiously, though, he has built up Hargreaves Lansdown plc on the basis of being able to choose and recommend to his followers the most successful active investment managers. The firm became a FTSE 100 company because of its ability to *pick* the right investment funds for its clients. From a humble beginning to having a market value of £6 billion is some going. Was his tongue-in-cheek definition of the stock picker correct? Perhaps it is best to form your own judgement.

PART I

School Days and the Stockbroker Years

I

Bleak Prospects

"At present, his prospects of success look bleak."

The headmaster came out with this comment to conclude a pretty poor end-of-term school report for my final summer term in 1962 at Dorking County Grammar School. He went on to state that, "Much more concentration on work is needed." My bleak prospects were partly responsible for my later move into stockbroking and eventually fund management.

Compared to today, the world in 1962 was very different for a young lad aged 17 seeking a career. On the positive side there were many more choices open to a school leaver. Did you wish to go into banking, insurance or accountancy? Perhaps you had skills in carpentry, metal work or engineering? Maybe you could sing, play a musical instrument or had some artistic flair for painting or design? Another option might be the armed forces or the dizzy heights of an airline pilot. A medical career as a doctor or surgeon was also an option; and sport was a further possibility.

On the other hand, you were Paul Wilfred Mumford, who had three times failed to pass his General Certificate of Education English exam and whose headmaster refused to give you a reference.

Fifty-plus years later I have had a career spanning 25 years as both a fund manager and stockbroker. I am known as a 'stock picker', an approach which has developed over time. I am still learning and every day presents exciting new opportunities and sometimes challenges. This is the story of a journey through the ages picking up investing techniques along the way. Thank heavens for my headmaster's negativity – otherwise I might have ended up in a boring job.

Destiny is a funny thing; I am a strong believer in fate. I got into the headmaster's bad books for being the first sixth former to get the cane. My education was varied as my parents moved from Bristol to Hinckley to Eastbourne and, finally at the age of nine, Dorking. Dorking is a small town in Surrey situated near the Mole Valley at the bottom of Box Hill (famed for providing a gruelling cycling section at the 2012 Olympic Games). Its most famous citizen was the composer Ralph Vaughan Williams. Its most redeeming feature when we moved there was that the population of around 10,000 was serviced by 30 pubs. Its focal point was and is St Martin's church, which has a 210ft tower.

Largely as a result of my poor English, in 1955 I failed my eleven-plus exam – the test which determined who would get a grammar school education. Consequently I was obliged to attend Sondes Place County Secondary School. It consisted of several huts built just after the Second World War and looked like a concentration camp (without the barbed wire and sentry towers). Today it is a perfectly respectable comprehensive school but in the 1950s it was a tough establishment fed by the eleven-plus failures from the various junior schools in the district.

The first day was like being in a spaghetti western as the two 'hard nuts' who had joined from Powell Corderoy and St Martin's infant schools, respectively, fought a brutal battle in the lunchtime break. Inevitably neither won but, having fought to a standstill, became allies, much to the discomfort of the rest of us. The area's infant schools were then, and remain, first-class establishments and I had attended St Martin's.

The 1950s was the Teddy Boy and rock 'n' roll era. As well as long draped jackets in various bright colours with black lapels and cuffs – not to mention tight black jeans and luminous yellow, green, orange or red socks, ideally slipped inside 'brothel creepers' (blue suede shoes with crepe soles up to an inch thick) – the Teddy Boys often went around armed with flick knives or knuckle dusters. Even more unpleasant as weapons were iron bars and bicycle chains.

Fortunately the Teddy Boy phenomena did not particularly penetrate Sondes Place and 'gang' rivalry was all but nonexistent once the two putative leaders in our year had resolved their differences. Nevertheless the school was fairly tough.

The fact that both of my parents managed the two local cinemas in Dorking did not help my standing. Today these cinemas do not exist. It became uneconomic to have one let alone two cinemas in a town the size of Dorking. However, in the 1950s the industry was thriving. Few people owned televisions and there were no such things as personal computers or mobile phones.

Both cinemas could attract good-sized audiences and would show the main film together with a second film termed a B-movie, often a cheap budget western or science fiction film. Between films there was a newsreel known as *Pathé News*, which kept audiences up to date with news topics. Sadly this was discontinued in February 1970 due to increased competition from television, but we have to thank it for footage of historical events such as the Second World War or even earlier in the days of silent movies.

On a Sunday one of the cinemas showed different films in two performances, but the highlight for the under-12s was Saturday morning kids club. This would consist of two or three cartoons followed by one or two short films. Typical comedies would feature Abbott and Costello, Laurel and Hardy and, of course, The Three Stooges – all good slapstick stuff. Westerns included *The Cisco Kid*, Gene Autry's singing cowboy movies, *Hopalong Cassidy* and *The Lone Ranger*. Last, but not least, were the classic science fiction series of *Buck Rogers*, *Flash Gordon* and *Superman* in glorious black and white.

As my parents managed Dorking's cinemas, I got in for free – but the downside was that a lot of my school contemporaries had been thrown out or banned. On one notable occasion I came to the rescue of my father when he was trying to eject a rowdy youth and helped him throw the offender out. Unfortunately, we found trouble waiting for us after the show. The Embassy Cinema was directly opposite a coffee bar and on this particular day a gang of about 20 youths had assembled outside it. The group included the rowdy customer who had been thrown out earlier. Things looked grim. I decided that the best course of action was to bluff. In true Western style, I crossed over the road and said "Had you been in my place wouldn't you have gone to your father's defence?" Furthermore, "I will take on anyone who has a problem with that." Much to my relief and surprise they stood down and I seemed to have earned some respect.

At school there was only one thing worse than being the son of a cinema manager and that was being the son of two cinema managers. My mum would stand no nonsense from rowdy patrons. After all, this was the one area of recreation for all age groups and a potential courting place for young couples. On a Sunday the back row was always filled with heaving bodies. One well-known Casanova, over several weeks, even managed to create a double seat by using a hack saw to remove the arm rest.

I managed to survive at Sondes Place but my parents wanted me to have a better education. Their jobs were not well paid and private school was out of the question. Progress could be made by passing the thirteen-plus examination, designed for those who failed the eleven-plus exam and was a route back into a grammar school education. Fortunately (as it eventually turned out) I failed this exam too. The failure was mainly due to lack of concentration – a problem correctly identified by my headmaster in my school report five years later.

The examination took place at Dorking County Grammar School and I would have fared better had it not taken place on the second floor of the main building overlooking the tennis courts and playing fields. Several of my friends attended the school and it was an inspirational place when compared to the mission huts at Sondes Place. I was keen to pass the examination, but did not reckon on the railway line.

Sad to say, I was an avid trainspotter. It was the era of the steam train and each locomotive carried its own name or number. I spent many happy hours sitting on a draughty railway station ticking off these numbers in specially published books – and yes, I had a spotty face to complete the stereotype.

As luck would have it, the railway line ran adjacent to the school playing fields and my examination desk afforded a grandstand view. Once a day, at about noon, an express train called the *Birkenhead Express* passed the school. It ran from Birkenhead (near Liverpool) through Oxford, Reading and Redhill to Dover and was often pulled by steam engines from other regions of the rail network. The service was for the South East and Central Region, whose initials were also affectionately said to stand for the 'Start Early and Crawl Round' service. This was to be a one-off chance to collect an unusual train number and I spent half the exam looking out of the window for this green monster, and the other half noting numbers of other trains on the local service.

Much to my parents' and my own disappointment, I failed the thirteen-plus examination.

So what now? Fortuitously, the government was experimenting with a completely new idea – the comprehensive system. About ten miles from Dorking there is a town called Merstham, which has been around since pre-Roman times. After the Second World War it was decided to build a new town there and this included Albury Manor County Secondary School, one of the first new-style comprehensive schools.

Pupils attended from the ages of 11 to 16, with mixed classes of boys and girls. Classes were graded from G down to U. G was the grammar stream where GCE grades could be obtained. This was followed by A to E, descending in merit, where lower-grade exams were taken. These classes concentrated more on technical skills such as metal work, woodwork or technical drawing. Class U was an unrated class containing those with little academic potential; pupils here would spend half the time doing the garden or shovelling coke for use in the school boiler system. Maybe I should have been put into class U, but my parents actually managed to get me into the grammar stream.

I found the school very refreshing as there were no gangs and everybody got on well. In my class the worst one had to face was an initiation ceremony called ducking. In the lunch break, an individual child was chosen and then had their head plunged into a basin of cold water. I cannot say the experience was very original or pleasant but it was all taken in good spirit. It turned out to be a good bonding process. Several individuals on the receiving end of this treatment ended up having distinguished careers. One of them became the British ambassador to Antigua. Indeed the school produced a number of successes. Fifty years later a student from a lower form, having run a very successful paintball business, attended a school reunion flying his own helicopter. Possibly the crowning success was the form-U pupil who ended up owning an extremely profitable landscape gardening company.

Merstham was ten miles away from Dorking and I had to catch the eight o'clock bus every morning. By that time I was also doing a morning paper round which meant getting up at six – I have been an early riser ever since. My parents provided me with the bus fare which I eventually saved by hitch-hiking home in the evening. The money thus saved was put to good use: my first experience of trading. The bus fare was 11 old pennies; I would buy five weights cigarettes for nine old pennies and sell them onto the school's smoking community (known as the 'behind-the-wall' brigade) at three pence each. Unfortunately, as you pass through the years, you end up behind the wall yourself, forced to purchase from younger budding traders.

Albury Manor had its own playing fields plus a modern gym and was renowned for its sporting activities. I was not good enough for its very strong school football team, but played in goal for my house against such notable players as Derek Possee and Phil Beal, who both had professional careers with Tottenham Hotspur. The most torturous exercise was to do one and a half circuits of the running track and for the rest of the class to chase you home for the last two hundred yards. I did not enjoy it, or excel at it.

I think that team-bonding is important in life. I was in the strange situation of having two sets of friends, ten miles apart. After-school activities included regular visits to the local billiard hall in Redhill, a little over two miles from the school. In Dorking, apart from cinema visits, weekends were spent playing football or cricket on the local recreation ground using jackets as goalposts and a concrete fence post as a wicket. Needless to say there were multiple arguments on whether a goal was scored or a wicket taken.

Another pastime was fishing in the River Mole. This stretch of water provided plenty of quantity but little quality; the largest fish I caught was a minnow all of two inches long. In those days sports shops also sold air guns, air rifles and bows and arrows. My parents' three-up two-down terraced house had a long garden in which I erected targets on an upturned table for target practice. I once aimed my air rifle at a blackbird on our apple tree and hit it straight between the eyes. To see something alive one moment, happily chirping away, and the next lying prone on the ground, I found very upsetting – and I never took another shot like that again.

My two sets of friends would occasionally meet at the Market Hall in Redhill, a Saturday night live-music venue. Some of the more notable musicians to play the Market Hall included Tom Jones, who had just cut his first record, Johnny Kid and the Pirates, and Screaming Lord Sutch. The venue has long gone, replaced by a Sainsbury's, but the bouncing wooden floor remains forever in my memory. Music had become an important part of my life.

The year 1957 introduced me to rock 'n' roll through the cinema and a series of films, most notably *Jamboree!* and *The Girl Can't Help It*. The three piano players, Fats Domino, Jerry Lee Lewis and Little Richard made an immediate impact, and I started buying their records after one of my aunts bought me a record player. This was a mechanical device which had a handle to wind it up after each play. My paper-round money and cigarette dealings enabled me to buy one record each week – I still have 60 singles purchased at this time, including all of the early releases by Elvis Presley.

Things moved on and I was determined to buy a tape recorder so that I could record songs played on the radio. For my birthday in 1960 my parents gave me £6 which I used as a deposit to purchase one for £29. In those days £6 was about one week's wages and far more than I would normally receive as a birthday present. I was extremely grateful as it made me appreciate the value of money and taught me how to save. However, I did begrudge the extra cost of having to buy on hire purchase and disliked being in debt.

The following Christmas I was given my first electric gramophone. It had three speeds, enabling me to play my collections of 78s, 45s and 33 1/3s (the numbers representing the revolutions per minute of the record turntable). It was great to have this extra choice, but music was nearly the death of me. Rather stupidly, I decided to listen to a record while having a bath. I reached across to change the record and felt a tremor in my finger. The shivering moved up to my arm and soon my whole body was shaking. Things went black and I found myself looking at my body and moving away towards the ceiling. It may sound silly but I prayed for help. My mother was downstairs and heard an almighty crash. She rushed into the bathroom, grabbed the record player away from me, and went to telephone the ambulance service. She was convinced that I was no longer alive. Then she heard me snorting and gasping for breath.

A powerful electric shock had entered through the joint in my middle finger and exited through my toe. Luckily the shock had not passed through my heart. Being six foot four in height, my foot had not been in the bath water. I was in shock for several days after this, during which any sort of buzzing noise would make me jump out of my skin. The one consolation to arise out of this experience was that I know there is life after death. As to religion, I do believe that there is substance in most.

As well as music, horse racing later became very important to me, impacting even more directly on my subsequent investing career. At

Albury Manor, I was first introduced to this world: one of my fellow pupils ran a betting book. Each day he would bring in the back page of the *Daily Mirror* pinned to a piece of cardboard. The school punters would have an old penny to win or a penny each way on the horse that they fancied. I followed this with interest but was too involved in my cigarette trading to participate (but immersion in that world would come later). Other things were occupying my mind – such as the lunchtime card school. In the fifth form we were allowed to stay in the classroom for lunchtime break and would play three-card brag, a watered down version of poker. Being a good bragger, I invariably won. To prevent cheating we used different tokens each day to represent money. These had to be cashed in at the end of play but one of my friends often forgot and walked around with an assortment of matchsticks, paper clips and wooden *Monopoly* houses and hotels in his top pocket.

Life at Albury Manor was good; I even scraped through some O-level examinations, though I failed English Language and English Literature. The school did not have a sixth form so I would have to move elsewhere to take A-levels. Again, somehow, my parents came up with the goods and managed to get me a place at Dorking County Grammar School – the school I had previously failed to get into. Trouble occurred on day one. I had several friends at the school and we were walking down the drive when a car driven by the woodwork teacher approached from behind. My friends told me that he could stand a joke and everyone called him Fred. As the car passed, I bent over and said, "Hello Fred" through the driver's window.

Some friends!

My cheerful greeting to the woodwork teacher went down like a lead balloon. Being sent to the headmaster's study on the first day was not amusing. It was how I became, as mentioned earlier, the first sixth former at Dorking County Grammar School to be given the cane.

My time at the grammar school was bearable but I found that there was a degree of snobbery regarding those children with a secondary school education – a very strange and uncomfortable feeling after experiencing a school where there was full integration of educational levels. By the time I started in the sixth form, Sondes Place had become a respectable school with a good reputation. Members of the 50s generation had left to be replaced by less troublesome children.

I was born in November and therefore changed schools in the run-up to my 17th birthday. Life changed completely due to drink, driving and betting. This is not as bad as it sounds.

In the late 50s, it was common to frequent coffee bars. Dorking had two: the *Ronda* and the *Tyrola*, both of which are long gone. My friends frequented the former, which was slightly more upmarket and where you could make a cup of cappuccino last for several hours. The *Tyrola* was used by motorbike gangs and was not a place for the faint-hearted. At the age of 17, teenagers would graduate to the pub, where most landlords would turn a blind eye. In Dorking, the motorbike gangs congregated in a pub called The Sun, which closed several years ago. There were many pubs in Dorking and, during our late teens, we would patronise several of these, but kept well away from The Sun.

In those days money was scarce and it was only occasionally that we would have a skinful to drink. A typical weekly evening schedule was darts practice Monday, darts match Tuesday, card school Wednesday and pub crawl followed by a Chinese meal Friday. On most Saturdays there was either a party or a gig at one of the village halls. We were not proud and were happy to attend functions at the Young Conservatives, Young Labour, Young Liberals or even Young Communists. Best of all was an organisation called '18+' which was a non-religious, non-political group. Sunday lunchtime consisted of darts practice and sometimes cards in the evening.

Driving took the form of a BSA Bantam 150cc motorbike. I was attracted to this mode of transport from my hitch-hiking days. One day, coming home from school, a motorbike ridden by a girl with long brown hair stopped to offer me a lift. I had not been on a motorbike before and she told me to either put my arms round her waist, on her shoulders or to hold on to the luggage rack. Not sure what to do, I put my arms on her shoulders and had the most exhilarating ride for the next 15 minutes. There was no thought of wearing a crash helmet. It's an exciting image – but remember that this glamorous female motorcyclist would now be at least 80 years old.

I worked in a variety of jobs – in a fish shop, in a timber yard, in a construction company – and saved £40 to buy the BSA Bantam I had spotted in the (now sadly defunct) motorbike shop in Dorking. It was a modified model with drop handle bars, chromium mud guards and a long racing saddle. When I collected it a mechanic showed me how to start the engine but I was perturbed because one of the brakes failed to work. He informed me that it was not a brake. It was the clutch. He then gave me a lesson on how to change gear. Off I rode into the sunset with no crash helmet, little instruction and conking out about three times on the half-mile journey home. The big upside was that it now enabled me to do a country paper round of six miles, earning £4 a week, a lot of money in those days.

As I touched on earlier, during my Albury Manor days I had learnt a lot about horse racing. Now at the age of 17, I started to profit from this knowledge by spending my Saturday afternoons in a smoke-filled betting office situated on the first floor of the Dorking Halls (still the local entertainment venue). I hated to lose and was very prudent with my selections and stake money. Of course, despite such caution, I undoubtedly lost over time. Fortunately, this was more than made up for by my own bookmaking activities. At the grammar school, I started to offer betting facilities to those in my year and the year above. It all worked well until the running of the Lincolnshire Handicap in 1962.

The Lincoln, as it is now known, is a handicap race run over one mile in March. At the time it was held at the Lincoln Racecourse, but moved to Doncaster Racecourse when the former closed in 1964. On the particular day in question, the race featured a local colt called *Sable Skinflint*. It had a starting price of 40/1 and was tipped to win by local connections to the stable. Word spread like wildfire throughout the school and a flood of money descended on it. The race was timed to start at 3 pm and I needed to skip a class in order to lay off the wagers at the local bookmaker. This meant crossing the playing fields, sneaking under the school fence, followed by a brisk walk into town.

While I was preparing to make my getaway, a voice bellowed, "Mumford, what are you doing?" I turned about. It was the housemaster. "You are supposed to be in the house football team," he continued. This was followed by the immortal words, "And I would like two bob each way on *Sable Skinflint.*"

How could I refuse? Two bob is the equivalent to ten pence in modern money, but was five times the normal bet. Due to the high odds, everybody backed the horse each way, and because of the number of runners, it paid 10/1 for finishing in the first four. The total staked was £4, and, not having been able to lay off the wagers, I now stood to lose £160 if it won or £40 if it was placed in the first four places. Remembering that £6 was an average week's pay package, I cannot recall such a miserable cold, wet muddy March afternoon. To make matters worse, my house football team lost 6–0 with me in goal. Happily the horse finished down the field and I came home wiser and considerably better off. After this scare I gave up my budding bookmaker's career.

With so much going on, my homework and revision was pushed to one side; it is little wonder that the headmaster ended up making pointed reference to my lack of concentration. So far as the exams were concerned, I managed to fail the English O-level twice but did pass a minor English examination. My A-level results were little better, failing Applied Mathematics, Pure Mathematics and Geography, but achieving O-level grades. I was not allowed to stay for a further year. My future really did look bleak.

2

Animals in the Zoo

Although I did not distinguish myself at school, I learnt a number of things that would help in later life. Most important were financial meanness and the ability to survive on limited resources. I lived at home and therefore had a roof over my head plus food. However, I needed money for cigarettes, petrol, entertainment and, occasionally, clothes. My paper-round money would provide for these living expenses but when I left school I wanted to go on holiday. In those days air travel was too expensive, so I arranged to hitch-hike to Ireland with a chum. To raise the required funds, I obtained part-time employment with the construction company building the Dorking bypass.

Day one of my ventures always turns out to be disastrous. I was asked to make the tea for the construction crew. I did not drink tea and had no clue how to make it, but was too embarrassed to own up. Consequently I made a foul-looking brew by putting both the tea leaves and milk into the kettle. The Irish foreman was not amused. He found it staggering that someone with a grammar school education could not do such a simple task. And to get his own back, he allotted me a job from hell.

The road needed to traverse a small stream called Pipp Brook. It required a bridge on concrete supports. These were constructed by building a frame with metal shutters into which concrete was poured.

The shutters were like giant tin lids about three-foot square fixed to metal girders to form a box-like structure. When the concrete set, the square shutters and frame were removed to leave a free-standing wall.

There were three problems. First, the concrete had to be strengthened, which involved having a steel mesh set into it. Secondly, the air bubbles in the concrete needed to be dispersed. Finally, to overcome this problem, somebody had to climb inside the frame with a pneumatic device to mix the concrete while it was being poured. I was the poor unfortunate blighter given a pair of wellington boots and assigned to the task. It was a bit like working in quick sand. To keep its consistency the concrete was poured at an alarming speed and my mixing job was made more difficult by the metal mesh. I often wonder how many bodies might be found encased in similar structures.

I survived the summer and finished with sufficient funds for the Irish holiday. My friend and I hitched lifts to Fishguard in Wales and caught the ferry to Wexford in Southern Ireland. We managed to obtain a lift along the coast to Dublin where we visited the Guinness Brewery and stayed for a couple of days before making the return journey. We both ran out of money and had to sleep in bus shelters on the way home.

Back in England it was decision time as I needed a job. As well as my experience in the construction industry I had taken other jobs in the school holidays. Unloading planks from the back of lorries for a timber company was hard work but not as unpleasant as working in a local fishmonger, which involved moving fish in and out of a walk-in freezer and plucking chickens. Less onerous was serving behind the counter at WH Smith, though it was tiring on the feet. Cleaning rust off wheelbarrow frames on an assembly line in a factory was well paid, but dirty and tedious.

I concluded that manual labour was not for me and decided upon a desk job. As I found written work boring, it had to involve mathematics. Unfortunately even in those days most insurance companies, accountancy firms or banks insisted on an English qualification. Much to my surprise, I passed an English exam at night school. This was the Certificate of Secondary Education (CSE), designed for secondary school students who did not take the General Certificate of Education (GCE). However, this exam was not recognised by most employers and the fact I had taken other GCEs highlighted English to be a problem subject.

Youngsters today will confirm that being without a job can be very stressful. I was not too concerned because I could survive on my paper-round money and enjoyed pitting my wits against the local bookmakers. Nevertheless, a series of unsuccessful interviews was disheartening. By the end of September I had given up looking, but at the beginning of December 1963, with Christmas fast approaching, I recommenced my endeavours.

Two of my secondary school friends, who did not have any GCE O-level qualifications, left school at the age of 16 and were working for a 'jobbing' firm in the City of London. A *stock jobber*, commonly termed a *jobber*, and now known as a market maker, traded stocks and shares. They were not allowed to deal directly with the public and could only buy and sell shares to a stockbroker. The jobber would quote a two-way price. His profit would be made through buying at the lower price and selling at the higher one in much the same way that I had traded cigarettes at school. A stockbroker could only act for the public or institutional investor and had to deal through a jobber. Money was made by charging the client a commission on these transactions.

I applied for a job as a settlement clerk with a firm of stockbrokers. At the time I had no idea what a stockbroker or a settlement clerk was. The firm was based over two floors in an office building, just off Moorgate in the City of London, fairly close to the Stock Exchange and Bank of England. The partners of the firm were situated on one floor of the building and the general office occupied space on the floor below.

The general office could best be described as the engine room of the firm. A 'bought transfer department' dealt with the receipt and registration of shares purchased for clients. Similarly, a 'sold transfer department' handled the delivery of shares sold by clients. Other departments included those dealing with accounts, client settlements, shares in overseas companies and dividends. In overall control was the office manager who reported to the partners of the firm.

As I had been on numerous interviews, I felt quite relaxed as I rang a bell on the wall in a small reception lobby. A serving hatch sprung open and I was faced with a formidable-looking lady in her late-50s with a fag hanging out of her mouth. She had the ability to talk without removing the cigarette, which by the time I arrived had half an inch of ash on its end. As she talked the cigarette moved up and down, but, magically, the ever-growing length of ash remained on its tip. It was strangely unnerving.

I was marched through an open plan office and shown into a glass partition room in which there were two facing desks where the office manager sat opposite the firm's cashier. These two were like characters from a Charles Dickens novel. The portly office manager was bald on top with wisps of silvery grey hair on the side of his head; a pair of pince-nez glasses and a kindly smile gave him a pixie like appearance. On the other hand, the cashier had a nervous twitch of his shoulders and looked more daunting. He was six feet tall, slim, and had the appearance of a monk – sporting a small amount of short black hair.

The office manager did all the talking, first asking about my school qualifications. I said that I had taken GCE A-level examinations in Applied Mathematics, Pure Mathematics and Geography. When asked, I explained that Applied Mathematics was similar to Physics in that it was practical maths used in science and engineering dealing with such things as force, acceleration, velocity and pressure. On the other hand, Pure Maths dealt with conventional subjects such as algebra, calculus and trigonometry but in an abstract way. When asked about Geography, I explained that the subject was broken down into regional and physical geography. The former was about countries and populations whilst the latter covered climatic and geological features with a wide range of topics from cloud formations to volcanos, rivers and rock structures.

So far, I had progressed further than most of my other job interviews and the next question I was asked was whether I had any practical experience which could help in the client settlement role. I said that two summers ago, I had had a holiday job working in the head office of Key Markets, a supermarket chain formed by Fitch Lovell in 1960. It eventually became Gateway, then Somerfield and is now part of the Co-op. The company owned a number of stores in southern England and all orders were passed through the head office. Those were the days before computers and even calculators. Consequently, any bookwork had to be done manually.

In my interview I did not confess that, initially, I had found that job very difficult. Each of the supermarket branches would order goods on a daily basis. Invoices were passed to the head office for completion and I was placed in the department which dealt with these. It was the days before decimalisation so calculations were made in pounds, shillings and pence, where 12 pence equalled one shilling and 20 shillings one pound. To make matters worse, the currency contained half pennies.

Although at the time I was studying mathematics at a reasonably high level, it had been a while since doing basic addition and multiplication sums. An invoice could cover a number of pages with orders such as two dozen bananas at three and a half old pennies or seven cases of washing-up powder at one pound two shillings and six pence a case. The figures had to be accurate before the order was confirmed, passed and entered into the head office books. Much to my embarrassment, virtually all of my early calculations were littered with mistakes. I now confess to being the only young man who was completely outshone by the young women, all of whom had had a more basic maths education. Eventually, my calculation abilities improved – and I can still quickly add a column of figures with accuracy. The trick, known as pairing, is to look down the column and to pair those numbers equalling ten, i.e. seven with three, two with eight, and four with six, etc.

After manoeuvring through these questions my heart sank when the office manager asked why, with my qualifications, I had not found work in the last six months. I explained that I had failed my A-level exams. He said that that did not matter as I was clearly knowledgeable about these subjects and some people are not good at taking exams. Similarly, I confessed to only having a CSE pass at English rather than the GCE qualification, which everybody recognised as the main yardstick. Again he said that, as far as he was concerned, this was a sufficient qualification for a job.

Having come within sight of the finishing post I came up against the final hurdle when asked to provide a written reference from the headmaster of Dorking County Grammar School. I had to admit that he was not prepared to give me one. Rather taken aback, the office manager picked up the telephone and asked the operator to get hold of the school. As luck would have it, he was put through within a couple of minutes. There followed a heated argument, with the headmaster sticking to his guns, only to be told that it was a disgrace to treat an ex-pupil in this manner. When the headmaster refused to give a verbal reference, the office manager slammed the phone down on its cradle and said that the job was mine; could I start on Monday at a wage of £6 a week plus luncheon vouchers? Needless to say I accepted with surprise and delight.

The name of the firm was Norris Oakley Bros. It was established in 1880 and was known for its specialisation in the iron and steel industries, where it published an annual industrial handbook. By the time I joined it was also the leading stockbroker in investment trust shares. There were six partners, each with a personal assistant and secretary. The back office consisted of 20 clerks plus six girls who typed the firm's ledgers on massive machines which were capable of adding up numbers to produce running balances and statements.

The woman I had first encountered on the day of my interview turned out to be the chain-smoking 'Mrs A', who ran the post department. This was a very responsible job as it involved managing the messenger boys, who were usually 15-year-old school leavers. In the days before the internet, fax machines, photocopiers, automatic payments and computers, everything was done manually. For shares to change hands a transfer form had to be completed. As the name suggests, this was used to transfer shares from the seller into the buyer's name. Cheques were drawn to settle sales or received in settlement of purchases. Dividends also had to be claimed or paid depending on whether the buyer or seller was entitled to them. A messenger spent long hours delivering documents to various firms throughout the City of London. It could lead to the promotion from the back office – many a messenger boy went on to a successful career in finance.

I was fortunate to walk straight into a back office job in client settlements and was to work alongside the head of the department and his assistant. As luck would have it, the assistant obtained a position with another firm shortly after I joined, which left me with extra responsibilities. The department head was also due for a varicose vein operation. Consequently, having joined at the beginning of December 1963, I found myself running the department two months later.

As the name suggests, the client settlement department dealt with the payment and receipt of money from clients. In those days the stock market operated a two-week accounting system. Dealings commenced on the first Monday of the period and continued until the Friday of the second week. Settlement of all transactions occurred on the next but one Tuesday. This system allowed investors to buy or sell at any time in the period without putting up any cash.

Clients comprised individuals and institutions. Settlement for private clients was expected to take place on the account day. In the case of purchases, payment was due against a statement showing the deals. Similarly, on sales, the broker would pay the client on account day. Where there were both sales and purchases, settlement was made on the outstanding balance.

In the case of institutions, the transactions were much larger, and settlement was made against each individual trade. With a large-sized purchase there might have been several sellers and the institutional buyer would not be expected to pay for shares until they were delivered. Often there were delays in delivery, which might not take place until several days or even weeks after the account day.

Those were the days before electronic settlement. Companies would issue share certificates showing details of the shareholder and number of shares held. When selling, these share certificates had to be surrendered to the company. Selling shareholders would also have to sign a transfer form and deliver this, plus the share certificate, to their stockbroker. These documents would then be delivered to the broker who acted on behalf of the buyer. The buyer's details would be entered on the transfer form which would, together with the share certificate, be sent to the company registrar who would register the shares in the new name.

The two-week dealing system enabled share speculation to take place. Investors could buy a share in the hope that the price would go up and sell at any stage in the two-week accounting period without paying for the purchase. Short selling – selling shares not owned in the hope of buying back at a profit during the two-week period – was strictly forbidden under the prevailing stock exchange rules.

Sometimes the system led to dishonesty. Norris Oakley Bros employed a chartist who would keep charts of various share prices. He was so successful that one of the partners entrusted him with a client portfolio worth £150,000. The idea was to manage the portfolio based upon the predicted share price movements as indicated by the share charts. Nobody monitored the deals and a huge number were transacted in every two-week accounting period. He even broke the stock exchange rules by selling shares he did not own. To make matters worse, a large number of these unlawful sales were not bought back in the same two-week stock exchange account. This gave a false illusion of the value of the fund. As no money was taken out of the portfolio, the situation was not picked up for several months. By that time, most of the original capital had been lost and had to be made good by the partners of the firm.

My role in the client settlement department was to send out statements and pay in cheques from private clients and draw cheques to settle balances in credit. With institutional clients, transactions were settled on an individual basis. Usually this involved delivering or receiving share certificates against payment to the institution. Included amongst these clients were clearing banks, merchant banks, insurance companies, pension funds, unit trusts and investment trusts. Tuesday account days were the busiest and there was always a rush to complete the settlements before the banks closed at 3 pm. Accuracy was important and I had to audit the accounts every two weeks.

I managed to run the apartment without a major problem due mainly to the training provided by the person whom I was replacing. His only annoying habit was to sing the same song repeatedly. Some Christmas songs are catchy and others make you cringe. I am not sure where this one featured on that scale. Originally released by Bing Crosby, it was covered by 22 artists including Frank Sinatra. The version by Big Dee Irwin and Little Eva was the most well-known and in November 1963 reached number seven in the UK hit parade. 'Would you like to swing on a star?' was a classic of its kind and years later some of the words seemed appropriate for my career choice.

The song makes the case for self-improvement. It asks whether one would like to swing on a star and carry moonbeams home in a jar or end up one of several creatures: a stubborn mule who hates to go to school, a careless and lazy pig, a slippery fish who nevertheless ends up getting caught, or the kind of monkey not found in a zoo.

Quite by chance I had managed to land a job that I enjoyed, otherwise I might have turned out to be a mule or even a pig. I did not wish to be a fish. The last thing that I wanted was to be a monkey.

I wanted to swing on the stockbroking star.

3

Under Starter's Orders

After being with Norris Oakley Bros for just two weeks, I received my first pay packet which, much to my surprise, contained six weeks' wages. It was explained that the firm gave everyone two extra weeks' money for both Christmas and prior to annual holidays. Suddenly I felt very rich, especially as I was still earning money from the paper round. Even in such a short period, I had become fascinated by the world of stocks and shares and decided to make my first venture into the stock market.

There are certain things I remember in life such as my first love, where I was when President John Kennedy was assassinated... my first purchase of shares is one of these things. The shares were in an Irish travel company called Ryan Tourist. One of the Norris Oakley Bros partners was buying shares in this company for all of his clients. I am not sure what was behind the partner's investment decision but I decided to join the herd as the name sounded good. Following my purchase, the share price fell sharply and remained depressed for a couple of years. Eventually, I was able to scramble out at a small profit.

I actually think of Ryan Tourist as one of my best purchases as an investor. It taught me not to follow others blindly and to do my own research into a company's investment merits.

In those days, partners of a stockbroking firm consisted of those with money and those with ability. That is not to say that those with money did not have ability, but as in all walks of life, people have different talents. A wealthy, well-connected person would have well-heeled friends who could become clients. These individuals would also move in affluent circles, leaving a substantial hunting ground for the budding stockbroker. All that was needed was integrity and some competence. Wealthy partners were also the ones to inject working capital into a stockbroking firm, for even in those days the London Stock Exchange strictly monitored the financial strength of member firms.

Under the prevailing stock exchange rules, a stockbroking firm was only allowed to make money from commission charged on share deals. Turnover from a private client portfolio was relatively low and the total income from this source would not be sufficient to cover the running costs of a firm. Consequently, there was a reliance on business from institutional investors. Some of these passed orders through the old boy network – colleagues from the same school, university or even City club. On a more professional basis, stockbroking firms that generated original ideas and research would be rewarded with orders from institutions based on those recommendations.

Norris Oakley Bros was noted for its specialisation in the iron and steel industries. In order to produce its annual handbook there was a need to keep up to date with company and industrial trends. Steel was something of a political football. Capacity was increased just after the Second World War and the industry was nationalised by the Labour government in 1949 only to be denationalised by an incoming Conservative government in 1952.

When I joined Norris Oakley there was a considerable amount of activity in this sector of the market. It was in the run-up to the next general election, which occurred in October 1964. Those looking for the Conservative Party to return to power bought shares in steel companies while those backing Labour reduced their holdings. Tory policy was to leave the industry in private hands while the Labour Party was strongly in favour of nationalisation. The election looked set to be a close-run affair – in the event, Harold Wilson won the election for the Labour Party, but with an overall majority of just four seats. This would prove to be unworkable and a snap election was called in March 1966 with the Labour Party being returned to power with an overall majority of 96. The scene was set, and nationalisation occurred once again when, in 1967, 14 steel companies were amalgamated to form the British Steel Corporation. Subsequently, this company was privatised by the Thatcher government in 1988 and, one year later, renamed Corus after merging with the Dutch steel producer Koninklijke Hoogovens. Corus was acquired for around £6 billion by the Indian company Tata Steel in March 2007. Cheap imports from China led to the industry's demise and, in 2016, Tata Steel offered the company for sale, but felt it had very little value. A one-time leader in the industrial revolution was fast becoming a dinosaur having always been treated as a political football.

Up until steel nationalisation by Labour in 1967, the level of business in shares of the six quoted steel companies was huge and Norris Oakley handled a substantial proportion of the turnover. One particular overseas institutional investor seemed to have a bottomless purse and took the view that the compensation terms of nationalisation would be favourable. On the other hand, a substantial number of UK institutions did not like the political gamble and wished to lock-in their profits. Norris Oakley undertook the purchases on behalf of the overseas buyer and this created a considerable workload for the back office. The busiest time would be in the run-up to the Tuesday settlement day. Share certificates together with transfer forms would be delivered to the office from a number of stockbrokers whose clients had sold steel shares in the stock market. To complete delivery, and receive payment, we had to enter the buyer's registration details in the appropriate space on the transfer form. This task was undertaken manually by members of the back office at double the normal hourly pay rate.

On the settlement side, I had to handle claims and payments on purchases and sales in a timely manner. Due to the large amounts of money changing hands, Mrs A had her work cut out when organising the messengers (amazingly, yes, the ash always remained on the end of her cigarette). She sent messengers scurrying round the City of London between the stock exchange settlement department, clients of the firm and the banks. Woe betide the messenger who failed to meet the delivery deadline – they would feel the lash of Mrs A's tongue. However, fear did not always work. One day a bundle of documents was discovered at the bottom of a lift shaft where, rather than facing the wrath of Mrs A, they had been discarded by a hapless messenger.

My official hours were 9.30 am–5.30 pm for five days a week, on pay which worked out at three shillings an hour. On most days there was one hour overtime to be had, with an extra hour on the Monday prior to settlement day. My overtime pay at six shillings an hour was a minimum of 30 shillings or, in today's terms, £1.50 – which might not seem much. To put this in context, we were issued with daily luncheon vouchers with a face value of three shillings. There was a basement restaurant in London Wall called Bettafood, which we affectionately called Grotty Grub. Here a three-shilling luncheon voucher would buy a main course, dessert and a cup of coffee. It was good healthy stuff such as sausage toad or shepherd's pie with chips and baked beans followed by the likes of treacle pudding or jam sponge with custard.

With my various earnings I was able to save enough money to build up a small share portfolio. I did not really know what I was doing but managed to make a reasonable profit. It was fairly difficult to follow share price movements. Dealings between stockbrokers and stockjobbers were carried out in the stock exchange in Throgmorton Street. The dealing area was known as the dealing floor, where the jobbers stood in allocated places called pitches and the brokers would circulate in order to find the best dealing price. In many ways this is similar to bookies at a racetrack. At 3.30 pm the firms would leave the stock exchange floor and return to their offices to undertake dealings over the telephone.

Before the days of internet and electronic trading, share prices and company news flow was transmitted to stockbroker offices via a ticker tape. A reel of paper, very similar in appearance to a toilet roll, was linked to a printer. Extel, a leading news agency, provided the information fed over the tape. Share prices were obtained by the Extel staff directly from the jobbers in the stock market and fed into the system continuously throughout the day. Abbreviated company results, as and when they were released by the stock exchange, were periodically published over the system. The paper roll containing this information would be produced from a printer about the size of a bedside table. On the walls adjacent to the printer, at about shoulder-height, were a series of hooks from which the printed rolls of information would be hung.

To me this was manna from heaven: I could track share prices and follow results. After my disappointment with my investment in Ryan Tourist, I decided that I would make my own selections. At that time, I knew absolutely nothing about profit-and-loss accounts or balance sheets and relied entirely on chairmen's trading statements. Fortunately (though it was frustrating at the time), I had to save money from my earnings so I could only purchase a fresh holding every six weeks. This taught me to be highly selective in my choices of investment.

An important lesson I had learnt from my school horse-racing exploits was not to gamble. Nevertheless, lessons can be ignored and rules can be broken and one day, as a young man, I could not resist doing both. At 4.15 on a Monday afternoon on the first day of the two-week stock exchange account, Thorn Electrical produced shocking results. The share price dipped from 50 shillings to 49 shillings and six pence. I was convinced that the results would get adverse coverage in the morning newspapers. Acting quickly, I sold 25 shares at 49 shillings, with a view to buying them back more cheaply the next day. (You will have noticed that this was the same as shorting, and was prohibited at the time – but as I said, I was breaking the rules!) Strangely, though, the next day's opening price was a little over 50 shillings and it proceeded to edge higher during the day. Not to worry, I had nearly two weeks in which to close the deal and buy back the shares. However, the share price kept moving higher over the ensuing days. Eventually I had to pay 60 shillings and six pence. The loss hurt more than my pride – it was more than two weeks' wages.

It was intensely stressful seeing the price moving ever higher on the ticker tape, especially as I did not want to be caught selling shares that I did not own. It did a lot of good in teaching me about share price behaviour, something I would use to good advantage throughout my career. A well-known financial expression is that 'it is often better to travel than arrive'. In the case of Thorn, the share price had fallen in *anticipation* of bad results, but these (while bad) were better than expected – hence its recovery. Later I was to learn that share prices often predict situations before they occur.

Norris Oakley Bros had its senior partner to thank for the important source of business that was steel shares. Of equal importance was its specialisation in investment trusts, which was down to Ernest Guy Libby, who discovered (or rediscovered) the art of value investing in the UK. Looking back to the mid-1950s there was no such thing as practical value investing in Britain. Gold was traded at a fixed price, whilst oil, property and equities were considered less attractive than the high-yielding preference shares of companies in those sectors of the market. Similarly, investors were only interested in the preference shares of investment trusts. Maybe, after the Second World War, investors were more attracted to income than capital growth – but things were to change as the 'equity cult' emerged.

The first investment trust was Foreign & Colonial, formed in 1868. By the start of the First World War there were 90 in existence, with a total stock market value of £90 million. Today there are about 400 investment companies with a value in excess of £100 billion.

In 1955, Guy Libby was 27 years old. He had joined Norris Oakley from Cambridge University where he had been a rugby blue.

His potential was soon recognised and by the time I joined the firm in 1963 he had been made a partner. Guy felt that it was a nonsense that ordinary shares in investment trusts traded at a discount to the underlying value of the assets, when unit trusts changed hands at a price based on net asset value. He shared his thoughts with the investment manager of the London and Manchester Assurance Company and they spent many happy hours studying hundreds of investment trust accounts spread out over the office floor, with the aim of finding those investment trust shares which represented the best value.

This was truly a stock picker's paradise – you could discover bargain investment trust shares selling at huge discounts to asset value. (Of course, taking into account other factors such as geographic spread, market sector allocation and level of prior charges was also essential to avoid making poor investment decisions.) Everyone likes a bargain and investors are no exception. Using all this information, Guy approached Norris Oakley's institutional client contacts and soon built up a profitable investment trust speciality – identifying attractive investment trusts that were ripe for investment and advising the sale of shares in those with less potential. By the time I joined Norris Oakley there was a separate research department specialising in the sector and a substantial number of additional institutional clients.

I was doing a job I enjoyed and was extremely happy when, after three months, my salary was raised to £8 a week. Due to an increasing interest in the stock market, I was anxious to advance my knowledge. The partners of the firm had personal assistants who were either university graduates or (more frequently) sons or relatives looking to be brought into the partnership. After being with the firm for about two years I became restless and felt that I was capable of filling a personal assistant role. I applied for this position in another larger firm. The interview went well and to my astonishment I received a letter offering me the job a week later.

Before accepting the offer I handed in my notice only to find that Norris Oakley did not want me to leave. I was offered a job in the bank department, which was seen as a training ground for budding young stockbrokers. It was an opportunity too good to turn down and I accepted on the spot. Much to my surprise, I was then asked how much the other job paid. I did not seek an increase but my salary was immediately adjusted to that higher level.

In 1966, banks were not allowed to give investment advice to their customers and were obliged to use the service provided by stockbrokers. The bank department of Norris Oakley acted for a number of branches and customers of Barclays Bank and Midland Bank (the latter is now part of HSBC). Occasionally there was a telephone query from one such customer, but mostly requests were made in writing. The work of responding to these was quite varied, from suggestions for where to invest money to giving an opinion of shares or reviewing customers' share portfolios.

Apart from myself working in the bank department, there was the head of the department, his deputy and two secretaries. My initial task was to give an opinion on certain shares. Information would be obtained from statistical cards produced by Extel and Moody, competing news service providers. The cards would contain an abbreviated balance sheet and a profit-and-loss account, together with the chairman's statement and company announcements. The updated cards arrived daily in packages and had to replace the old ones. This suited me well and I would happily file the new cards and keep the ones that they replaced to read.

One of my first jobs when joining the department was to produce letters about individual shares where a bank customer had asked for an opinion. In the case of buy queries, it was not too difficult to form a view. Sometimes a share was clearly high-risk due to balance-sheet weakness, a poor trading performance or the speculative nature of the business. Blue-chip shares could be readily recommended, but the majority fell between the two types. It was more difficult when a customer asked if a particular share should be sold. Often the share price had already collapsed – or, alternatively, increased several fold. We were not allowed to contact other stockbrokers for an opinion but could ask our dealers to obtain a view from the jobbers. Having gained as much information as possible, I would dictate a letter to the bank giving a summary of the company fundamentals followed by a conclusion.

Some weeks after starting in the bank department, I was given my first portfolio to review. This involved preparing a valuation and making comments on the various holdings. Portfolio reviews would be undertaken every three or six months and there would usually be some changes to make. Often the customer would have been with Norris Oakley for years and have formed a fairly close relationship. Others would be new clients who might have changed banks or become disillusioned with their previous advisor. The final part of the equation was the construction of a share portfolio for clients with a sum of money available for investment.

When I left school, due to my liking of mathematics I could envisage myself being involved in the accountancy profession, but it was difficult to imagine spending most of the time writing letters to clients. Looking back, I believe that the reason I did not thrive at English Language was sheer boredom with the subject. The bank department role meant that I was actually writing on a variety of interesting subjects. At first, my written reports and letters were closely scrutinised by the head of the department and had to be rewritten on several occasions. One of the reasons for this was because I did not give a balanced view. As the banks were culpable we had to cover their backs. For example, a buy recommendation would have to cover the risks attached to the shares and a portfolio review would need to include a comment on stock market risk. Within a fairly short space of time I was producing unsupervised work.

As part of my training, Norris Oakley Bros sponsored me for the stock exchange law and practice examinations. I was enrolled as a part-time student at the City of London College (now London Metropolitan University) in September 1965 and completed the two-year course in June 1967. It covered one morning and two evenings a week and opened my eyes to a whole new world.

The first year consisted of three subjects:

- 'Principles of accounts' covered basic accounting standards, some of which I was familiar with through my client settlement role, but it also delved into profit-and-loss accounts and balance-sheet construction.

- Economics was very wide-ranging and extremely interesting for somebody with no knowledge of the subject. Concepts such as laissez-faire, elasticity and inelasticity of demand were completely new to me, but the thing that I remember most was the lecturer saying that there were no hard-and-fast rules in economics. Provided an answer was well-argued, it was difficult to prove it wrong. Over the years I have found this to be true, not least when many economic arguments used by governments have blown up in their faces.

- 'Stock exchange practice' was the most involved subject, covering basic aspects of the workings of the stock exchange. It had a three-hour written examination while the others were only 90 minutes in duration.

It must be said that the first year whetted my appetite, with the second year putting the icing on the cake. This time it covered four subjects, which meant an extra morning tuition session:

- 'Company accounts and prospectuses' went into some detail and introduced me to a whole new exciting area of investment. As well as the basic information from the Extel and Moody cards, I now had access to greater information on companies. Strangely, the written examination was only 30 minutes long.

- 'Monetary theory and finance' would be daunting for some, but I found it a fascinating follow-up to the first-year economic course. The topics involved were more specific, covering money supply, exchange control, the function of the Bank of England and other practical measures relevant to finance and management of the UK economy. The examination time was set at two hours, which seemed too short bearing in mind the amount that could be written when answering the questions.

- 'Investment' basically covered portfolio construction, financial instruments such as options and general investment information and theory. The written examination lasted for 90 minutes.

- Finally, 'stock exchange practice' continued to cover all aspects of the stock exchange including back office procedures, accounts and various investment strategies. As the subject was involved and wide-ranging it again required a three-hour written examination.

I found both years of courses stimulating. From a practical point of view, it helped in my job as it enabled me to have a more informed opinion on shares of individual companies. There were a large number of candidates sitting the stock exchange examinations, a pass being necessary to become a member of the London Stock Exchange or a partner of a stock exchange firm. I do not know the exact number who took the exams, but 33 received a merit award of £10. Much to my surprise I had the third-highest mark over the two years and received an extra £10. Needless to say, I bought shares with the proceeds.

By this time I was keen to use my knowledge and move on to better things and kept an eye on the appointment column of the *Financial Times*. An advertisement appeared for a fund manager from a unit trust management company saying, "Sharp shooter required to manager UK investment portfolio". I replied under the heading, "Have gun – will travel" (the name of a popular cowboy series starring Richard Boone). After a lengthy and thorough interview I was offered the job. My two years of looking after client portfolios might have helped and certainly the stock exchange examination result did no harm. Who knows – I might have been the only applicant.

Before accepting, I decided that it was only fair to inform my employers. As before, I was offered a promotion into a quite unexpected role. Once again I was happy to stay and take up the fresh challenge and, as before, to my embarrassment my salary increased without me asking. One way or another, my career looked likely to move forward, but there was still a lot to learn on the stock-picking front.

4

Gigs, Gee-Gees and Trees

Undoubtedly a number of factors have influenced my outlook and career as a stock picker. Perhaps it is hard to make a case for the influence of music. Nevertheless, it was an important part of my life, particularly up till the time I started work – and there are some striking parallels between the two worlds. In 1955, popular music and modern equity investment were both in their infancy and I was fortunate to be around at the time. My career in the investing world has provided me with excitement and a similar buzz to that once obtained from music. And both music and investing involve discovery, a search for originality.

So I make no apology for sharing my early experiences in the music world in this chapter. I'll also look at horse racing and painting and even try to elaborate on exactly how all of these formed my outlook as an investor. They are the other half of the picture to everything I was learning at Norris Oakley at the time.

My parents had purchased their first television in the late 1950s. It had a nine-inch screen, increased to 11 inches with the addition of a magnifying glass. In 1957, the BBC produced the first televised pop music show, *Six-Five Special*, named after its showing time. The show appeared at peak viewing time for teenagers, and featured mainly young British artists. It was produced by Jack Good and broadcast live in front of a teenage audience. By 1958 the show was looking a little jaded and Jack Good left to join a commercial channel to produce 40 episodes of a show called *Oh Boy!* This was also a live show with a young audience and was the basis of a career for the likes of Cliff Richard and Marty Wilde who were among several resident artists.

Ready Steady Go! was produced for the commercial channels between August 1963 and December 1966 but the most successful weekly programme was *Top of the Pops*, first broadcast by the BBC in January 1964. One of the problems with these programmes was that a large number of artists mimed to their records. On the plus side, they included performances by American artists.

In the late 1950s and early 60s I was lucky enough to attend a number of gigs. There were some stormy acts. Most memorable was Little Richard, a black American rock 'n' roll performer who played a grand piano standing with one foot in front of the other and screaming into a microphone. The first time I saw him was at a theatre in Kingston, Surrey. He came on to the stage balancing a kitchen chair in his mouth; threw it across the stage; rushed to the piano and started singing 'Long Tall Sally', one of his bestselling hits. After several other frantic numbers he leapt on top of the piano whilst performing another classic, 'Tutti Frutti'. To the horror of the audience, he collapsed on the stage and the band stopped playing. Three of the band members rushed to his aid, leaving everyone in shock. Suddenly he started screaming out his song from the point he left off. The audience went wild, partly due to immense relief.

Little Richard was not just a frenzied entertainer but also a songwriter. His real name was Richard Penniman and, having been born on 5 December 1932, was in his mid-20s when fame struck. In 1962, the Beatles supported him on a British and German tour. I saw him perform again towards the end of 1963 at the Hammersmith Odeon (now the Hammersmith Apollo). On this occasion the supporting groups included the Rolling Stones. The only other time I have ever seen the Rolling Stones was on 14 December 1963 at the Epsom Municipal Baths. The 100-foot-long swimming bath was covered by maple flooring with a stage at one end. I obtained a ticket in the spectators' gallery which surrounded the pool area. It was a time when the Rolling Stones were beginning to become popular, having had two hits – 'Come on' and 'I wanna be your man'. I have never seen the Beatles but they and the Rolling Stones acknowledged Little Richard to be a major influence on their careers.

Another performer to equal Little Richard's showmanship was Jerry Lee Lewis, who also played the piano but was not noted for writing his own material. His UK tour in 1958 was abruptly terminated when the press discovered that he was married to his 13-year-old cousin. I was too young to see him perform at that time but attended shows in the early 60s. His act was full of exciting moments and included him kicking the piano stool across the stage and hitting notes with his foot on the piano keyboard.

A third influential piano player and prolific songwriter was Fats Domino. He was born on 25 February 1928 and started his career in 1948, cutting his first record one year later. I saw him in concert at the Royal Albert Hall in the early 1960s. As his stage name suggests, he was quite tubby, something he used to good advantage when beginning a performance by pushing the grand piano across the stage with his stomach. During the show his New Orleans band marched round the auditorium playing their instruments in true Mardi Gras style.

Besides Elvis Presley, the best-known artist in this genre of music was Bill Haley, who was born on 5 July 1925 and made records in the 1940s. His record 'Rock Around the Clock' from the film *Blackboard Jungle* (1955) was credited as the record that launched the rock 'n' roll era. I was lucky enough to attend two of his concerts. The first at the Royal Albert Hall ended in a riot with fights in the audience and seats thrown. The second was some years later at a London club and an altogether calmer affair.

The final all-round entertainer, and in my opinion the most gifted songwriter of all, was Chuck Berry, born on 18 February 1926. He inspired many young British musicians with his brand of music, which became known as rhythm and blues. Certainly, all of the local village hall bands when I was growing up would play several of his songs – they were ideal to dance to. I never tired of watching his live performances. His trademark was the 'duck walk', which involved moving across the stage in a squatting position whilst playing the guitar. Both the Beatles and the Rolling Stones recorded several of his songs.

By the mid-1960s, a lot of the true wild men of rock 'n' roll were no longer popular and music was becoming more melodic, a lot of it influenced by *Top of the Pops*. I lost interest. You could say that television helped kill my interest in music for about 30 years.

I was also getting more interested in horse racing at this time. In some ways it simply displaced my interest in music. Harking back to my school days, I was more concerned with making than losing money. It did not take rocket science to appreciate that, if gamblers could consistently win, bookmakers would not survive. However, I did not want to part with my hard-earned cash; I wished to save my earnings to invest in the stock market. I set about trying to overcome this contradiction. My experience of short-selling Thorn shares had taught me to avoid gambling. Was it possible to 'gamble' on the horses in a way that avoided all or many of the pitfalls?

An important influence in the horse-racing world at the time was a 1960s newspaper called the *Daily Herald*. It was first published in 1912 and was in the same stable as the *Daily Mirror*. There were close connections to the trade union movement, which sold its controlling interest in 1930. By 1933, it was reported to be the world's bestselling newspaper with a circulation of two million copies. In subsequent years its readership declined sharply and, in 1964, the TUC disposed of its minority interest, after which the newspaper was relaunched as the *Sun*. It was considered to be extremely left wing and continued to lose readers to the *Daily Mirror*. By 1969, the circulation had more than halved and the newspaper was making substantial losses. International Publishing Corporation decided to sell and it was purchased for £800,000 by Rupert Murdoch through his company News Corporation. The rest of the story is well known.

When I started work at Norris Oakley, I continued with my paper round, which enabled me to read the newspapers as I walked from house to house. In those days, the *Daily Herald* did not have a City page but had easily accessible horse racing coverage on the back page of its broadsheet format. My paper round was in an affluent area where only two houses subscribed to the *Daily Herald*. Luckily one of these was at the end of a long drive, which enabled me to take an extended look at the racing page on a daily basis. Good news sells newspapers, and a tipster using the name Supernap was a star for the *Daily Herald*. He would recommend one or sometimes two bets daily, and consistently produced profitable results. To capitalise on this he published a book, *Betting to Win*, which I purchased with a view to discovering the secret of his success. To my surprise the system he described worked. It gave me a way to gamble without gambling too recklessly – indeed it taught me a kind of discipline that I could also apply to stock exchange investment.

Horses are introduced into racing at the age of two and their form is most consistent in that first year of racing. It is even more reliable over short race distances. Consequently, under the Supernap system, wagers were only made on races for two-year-olds over five or six furlongs. The official flat racing season started in March and it was not until June that it was possible to accumulate sufficient information on form. The theory was that the fastest horse should win over a short distance. Each race was electronically timed and every race course had an average time per race, which could differ significantly. For example, the average time on the downhill slopes of Epsom or Bath would be much faster than on other courses.

Getting slightly technical, there was a formula which gave each horse in a race a 'speed factor' that related the time of the winner to the average time of a race. Thus a horse finishing first at the average time for a race would merit a speed factor of 100. The speed factor would be less on slower-run races and higher when the average time was beaten. Once the rating of the winner was calculated it could be adjusted to give a figure for the other runners (using a three-point benchmark deduction for each length finished behind the winner). The speed factor assumed that each horse carried nine stone and an adjustment would be made if one carried a different weight. In a handicap race, an expert handicapper would allot weights to the runners so that, in a perfect handicap, there would be nothing to separate the horses at the finish, known as a dead heat. Consequently, as well as ruling out races greater than six furlongs, all handicap races would be ignored for betting purposes.

There were other factors to take into account. For instance, race courses should be split into three categories. Tracks such as Ascot, Newmarket and Epsom would attract better quality horses than, say, Lingfield Park or Windsor. Northern courses such as Hamilton or Carlisle might be further down the scale. Races themselves were bracketed into different types. Groups one to three were the highest category, followed by listed and then classes one to seven. Even if a horse had a high speed factor it would be most unusual for it to win in a better class race. Equally, a racehorse that ran moderately well in a large field at Royal Ascot might be expected to perform well at a lesser-known racetrack. A further point to take into account was the state of the ground. There is little point in expecting a horse that finished with a fast time on firm ground to reproduce that form on heavy going.

Making a horse selection was similar to stock-picking in that a lot of work had to be undertaken before putting your money down.* Generally, at a race meeting, two out of six races featured two-year-olds. In the early part of the season all races were over five furlongs, with six furlong races introduced in June, followed later by seven furlong and one-mile races. Handicap races, known as nurseries,

---

* Nor is that the only way the two worlds of horse racing and investing overlap. In some respects jobbers – who made their money by buying and selling shares to stockbrokers, profiting from buying shares at one price and selling at a higher – were similar to bookmakers in that share prices and horse-betting odds could both be influenced by the amount of money invested. The profit or loss would be magnified in the event of a share price movement when they had a position in the shares.

were introduced in the early summer months. At the beginning of the season there was more choice of races to bet on. In the days before computers, records had to be kept by hand – a time-consuming process. Each day, using the racing results published in the morning newspaper, I would calculate the speed factor for the first three finishers in each of the relevant races. On a Friday I purchased a publication called the *Sporting Chronicle Handicap Book*, which had details of the first six to finish. From this I could calculate the ratings of those horses occupying places four to six. Typically, I would spend a minimum of half an hour a day, plus at least two hours at weekends, calculating and compiling the information. The morning train journey to work would be used to examine the daily runners with a view to identifying a winning horse.

When it came to betting, you would stake an equal amount to win on each horse that fulfilled the strict requirements referred to above. At the beginning of the season a racing bank or kitty of 40 units would be employed with the objective of turning it into 100 units. First bets were made in June and the final ones at the end of August, at which stage the number of runners per race increased and the weather deteriorated. In 1963 I started with a racing bank of £20, which was based on a stake of ten shillings (equivalent to 50 pence) per bet. Results exceeded expectations and at the end of the 1965 season I had accumulated £400 and was prepared to bet in £10 units. A calamity then occurred: the Labour government introduced betting tax. The effect on margins would have meant turning a 40-unit bank into 60 units – unacceptable given the amount of time being expended. I immediately stopped the activity. Gordon Brown removed betting tax in 2001 and it would be possible to operate the system today – though, of course, my time is now better employed elsewhere.

My next move during this period of my life was into the world of art. At each of my junior schools we had art classes using horrible powdered paint which looked like gravy granules when dry. I was pretty hopeless at drawing and derived most pleasure from mixing the paints into a muddy mess. At my secondary schools there were classes in technical drawing, which involved the production of accurate plans for objects such as machinery parts or wood joints. Some drawings were three-dimensional while others were conventional front and side elevations. We were issued with wooden drawing boards, pencils, compasses, set squares and a 'T-square' – a T-shaped ruler used for drawing straight lines. The top of the T is run down the side of the drawing board to enable the user to draw any number of horizontal lines. Even in this form of straightforward drawing I managed to produce a horrid end product, with paper covered with smudges due to the heavy use of a rubber. Several of the more gifted members in these classes went on to have successful careers in engineering or architecture.

Despite my lack of natural artistic ability I felt that deep down inside there was a great painter waiting to emerge. My father was gifted at pen-and-ink sketching and my grandmother at watercolours and I was determined to see if I had inherited their talent. The answer was to enrol in a night school course and to choose oil painting, where mistakes could be covered up. I bought a box of oil paints, pallet, pallet knife, charcoal and a variety of brushes. I was advised to paint on an artist's board rather than canvas. This turned out to be sound advice as my talent had yet to be proven and a canvas frame was fairly expensive. With my school experience in mind, I purchased a white apron, white spirit and several rags to clean up any mess.

The first potential masterpiece was a still-life painting featuring a brass jug standing beside an orange, lemon, banana and a couple of apples. In the initial class, I completed a charcoal sketch which vaguely represented the arrangement – but disaster struck. I arrived for class two to find that somebody had eaten one of the apples and the banana had turned from yellow to a shade of brown. To make matters worse I was seated at a different desk and had to view the still-life arrangement from another angle. It took three lessons to complete the painting and I was pleased with the finished product, only to be brought down to earth when I saw the paintings produced by other class members.

Maybe landscape painting would be my forte. We were told to paint a picture from a photograph or a postcard. I thought this was a great idea: everybody would be painting a different scene. This time I decided to use a blank canvas that I had purchased at the beginning of the course. My choice of subject was an autumn view of a Scottish lake surrounded by a large variety of different trees with various coloured leaves. Even though I say it myself, it was not a disaster. It was a *complete* disaster. The colours were difficult to reproduce; the trees looked like a line of lollipops. I was so embarrassed that I sneaked the painting home and resigned from the class.

Needless to say, that was the end of my aspirations to become a famous artist. The major positive to come from this art adventure was that I was able to see and view things in a new light. The still-life experience made me appreciate shapes, shadows and reflections. Landscape painting gave me a view of perspective, colours and distances. And it helped me better admire nature. After looking at my lollipop trees, I appreciated more than ever all the complex and beautiful ways in which real ones are not simply coloured blobs.

So what parallels can be drawn between pop music, betting and art to the world of investment and a career as stock picker? In the case of popular music we have seen that it emerged in the mid-1950s in a rather basic form. It appealed to the younger generation and became more sophisticated over the years. Groups led by the Beatles wrote their own material and were at the forefront of the music revolution. While this was happening the equity cult was emerging in the stock market. And the art of modern investment developed over the years. Having appreciated the music revolution I was able to relate to a changing investment world. Both my leisure and working lives were filled with the excitement of a world going through a technical transformation.

The challenge of horse racing was to make money consistently against the odds. As far as I can tell, there has perhaps only ever been one professional gambler who always made a profit. His name was Alex Bird and he was thought to have 500 consecutive winning bets over a 20-year period. His success was attributed to betting on the result of a photo finish. Before modern technology, the outcome of a close finish of a horse race was determined by a photograph taken at the finishing post. It could take up to five minutes to develop the film and an active betting market would materialise. The bookmakers' pitches were usually situated a little distance from the finishing line and, geometrically, this would give the illusion that the far side runner had the advantage. To gauge the true result, Alex Bird would watch every race in a position adjacent to the finishing post, close one eye and look across the imaginary finishing line. Once he knew the result he would place his bet on the certain winner.

I had not heard of Alex Bird at the time he was making these betting coups, otherwise I might have retired early to take up this no-risk way of earning a living. As it was, I had accumulated a useful amount of money in my own fashion. Bearing in mind that my first two-up two-down house in the centre of Dorking cost £3,000 in 1970 (now selling at nearer £300,000), my racing bank of £400 was not to be sniffed at. Selecting horses was similar to picking stocks. In both cases one was trying to avoid losers to gain a return by achieving a spread of interests, rather than betting the bank on a small number of perceived winners. Racing also taught me to devote time and patience to the management of money and not to be too greedy.

Art taught me that it is worth trying something that appeals but not to persevere if unsuccessful. My painting lessons taught me to look at scenery in fine detail in much the same way that an investment should be considered from as many angles as possible. Stockbroker research is not always rounded but based more on the conclusion as to whether a stock should be bought or sold. Some companies are difficult to understand. If they have the appearance of a lollipop tree, look for greater detail elsewhere.

5

Boom Boom

When the Labour Party gained an overall majority in the March 1966 election, steel nationalisation was destined to take place. As we have seen already, the two-way business in steel shares would cause a surge in commission income earned by Norris Oakley Bros. Unfortunately for the firm, the market in steel shares would completely disappear after nationalisation. Another worrying factor was increased competition in the investment trust market. Norris Oakley Bros was still considered the pioneer and one of the leaders in the sector; it had a large number of institutional clients and close connections with the specialist jobbers. However, other stockbrokers were producing research and taking market share. There was a need to produce a new income stream.

One of the solutions was to merge. In 1967, the firm amalgamated with Richardson and Glover to become Norris Oakley Richardson and Glover. The combined firm had 20 partners, including Lord Ritchie of Dundee, who was on the board of the Port of London Authority and, until 1965, chairman of the London Stock Exchange. Richardson and Glover had a reasonable-sized private client business with good Far Eastern contacts, including clients such as Hong Kong and Shanghai Bank, Bank of India and Standard Chartered Bank. I was made a trustee of the joint pension fund, a move I later regretted.

In some respects the merger was almost a reverse takeover in that the incoming team assumed the key positions in the firm. My big disappointment was that our office manager had to step aside, but some consolation was that he was approaching retirement age. Needless to say, nobody was brave enough to replace the formable Mrs A, who continued to run the messenger department. Guy Libby remained the driving force behind the enlarged partnership and took me under his wing for his new venture. He was looking for the next big thing after investment trusts and it turned out to be commercial property.

Property companies have had phenomenal growth over the years. The largest quoted property company is Land Securities Group plc, which was formed in 1931 and was acquired by Harold Samuel in February 1944 when it owned three houses in Kensington together with some British government stocks. Three years later the decision was made to concentrate on commercial property situated in and around the West End of London. By 1950, Land Securities owned 17 London properties, including some in Regent Street and Oxford Street. These were included in the balance sheet at a cost figure of £2.4 million, compared to a market value of £7 million for the equity shares of the company.

Further West End assets were acquired in the 1950s and a subsidiary was formed to deal with the regeneration of shopping centres in cities that had suffered bomb damage in the Second World War. These included Hull, Exeter, Plymouth, Bristol and Coventry, and elsewhere covered town centre developments in several 'new towns' which were springing up. A decade later the company added industrial property to its list of activities. Today, Land Securities owns a 25 million square foot property portfolio worth in excess of £13 billion. It is a FTSE 100 company having a stock market value north of £8 billion.

An even older company is British Land, which was established in 1856 to buy and trade land. At the beginning of the last century it started to invest in income-producing properties situated mainly in and around London and the south of England. In 1950, the property portfolio was worth just £371,000 and the company had a stock market value of £360,000. The most significant growth occurred from 1970 when Sir John Ritblat came on board. As we will see later, he was a canny operator who was adept at making money. Under his guidance, the company built a substantial property portfolio which today includes 7.9 million square feet of offices and 25 million square feet of retail properties. The value of its property portfolio is over £12.8 billion and the company is also in the FTSE 100 index with a stock market value of around £7 billion.

Hammerson is another company now included in the top 100 quoted companies. It was established in 1942 as a residential property developer but moved into commercial property in 1948. It was made public in 1954 and is best known for developing Brent Cross, which opened in 1976 to become the first covered shopping mall in the UK. Unlike Land Securities and British Land, the company invested in overseas properties. As early as 1960, interests were taken in Australia, New Zealand and the US, to be followed by Canada and Europe a decade later. An important expansion into France occurred in 1985. More recently, it sold its London office portfolio with a view to focusing on retail property, such as the partnership with Westfield in the £1 billion Croydon town centre regeneration project. Its property portfolio is worth around £6.8 billion and the company has a value of a little over £4 billion.

In 1939, at the start of the Second World War, London offices had an estimated floor space totalling 87 million square feet. Bomb damage reduced this by 9.5 million square feet. Under planning rules, building licences were required by property developers, but the elimination of these in November 1954 resulted in a boom in property development. It was fuelled by access to cheap bank borrowings which meant that often the developer only had to outlay 20% of the construction costs. Fortunes were made on the basis that, when completed, a building would be worth at least 50% more than it cost to construct. It is therefore little wonder that London office stock increased from 115 million square feet in 1960 to 140 million square feet by 1962.

Socialism has largely been anti-property investment, and rather bizarrely, the Labour Party was responsible for the boom in commercial property values. By 1964, supply and demand for London offices were imbalanced, but in November of that year George Brown imposed a ban to stop any further increase in supply. This involved two important measures. First was the banning of a change of use. Each location was zoned as office, commercial, industrial, residential, retail or a combination of these and change of use would not be permitted. The second change in legislation involved the introduction of the plot-zoning ratio, which designated how much gross floor space could be developed on a site. A plot-zoning ratio of one would mean that the whole site could be covered by a single floor or half the site by a two-storey building. Similarly, a plot-zoning ratio of five meant that the new building could have an area of up to five times the size of the site. To further complicate matters, an office development permit had to be acquired before development could commence.

The impact of the planning restrictions and delays cut the supply of London offices at a time of rising demand, and the net effect was a huge rise in office rents. In simple terms, the value of a freehold property is based on the income yield it could secure for the owner. For example, a modern building which provides £100,000 of rental income would be worth £20 million on the basis of a 5% yield or £10 million when valued on a 10% yield. The yield would be partly dependent upon the type of property, its condition, and more importantly, location. It would also depend upon its potential to produce a higher income at the time of a rent review or lease expiry. A further factor would be the quality of the tenant; a building leased to a blue-chip company would be classed as having a good covenant. A building in the City of London, where there is usually strong tenant demand, would command a higher value than an identical one in a provincial town. Equally, offices would be valued on a lower yield than industrial property. Shop property in a prime location would be expected to change hands at an even higher price.

Because of the structure of a lease, the rise in rents was not immediately apparent in the accounts of a property company. There was no requirement for regular valuations of properties which, in those days, were allowed to be included in the balance sheet at cost. Properties were often let on 21- or 42-year leases with rent reviews every seven years. This meant that the huge rise in rentals was not immediately reflected in the profit-and-loss accounts of property companies. Equity shares of property companies had the same undervaluation as those in investment trusts ten years earlier. Guy Libby proved yet again to be an innovator when he instructed an individual from the BBC *Money Programme* and me to learn how to value property.

The idea was to produce schedules of the properties held by property companies in order to show their current market value. Once this was established we could then approach our institutional clients to persuade them to invest. It proved a very successful enterprise and, although work on an individual company could take several weeks, the research would provide the firm with a significant flow of orders. Unlike today, where most stockbroker research is freely available, we would use it highly selectively. Thus, at any time we would only have one client buying shares in an individual company. In this way, large holdings could be accumulated without disturbing the share price. Eventually, a revaluation, or rise in profits, would give the client a substantial capital gain.

So here I was with a clear mandate to become proficient in the valuation of property assets held by property companies, when I knew absolutely nothing about the subject. My colleague also had no experience in the field, but had a contact at Edward Erdman, an estate agency which specialised in commercial property and City of London offices. Rental levels are determined by supply and demand and planning restrictions led to central London being the area where the most spectacular growth was to emerge. It was, therefore helpful to have this contact who could guide us on the London property market as well as the property valuation process.

The first step was to identify which properties were owned by a property company. In the case of those companies which came to the market in the 1950s, it was a matter of starting from the original prospectuses, obtaining back copies of the annual accounts and interim reports from company registrars, and adjusting for changes to the property portfolios. For old established companies, such as British Land and Land Securities, the starting point was from *Skinner's Property Share Annual*, which published financial information plus details of the principal property holdings.

The next step was to obtain accurate details of the individual properties. All companies are legally obliged to file audited annual financial returns to which the public is entitled access. In those days these records were kept at Companies House which, before moving to Cardiff, was based in London. All subsidiary accounts were also freely available and included in these was a wealth of material. For our investment process, the most valuable information was to be found in mortgage deeds. These would show full details of each property: areas, leases and lettings.

Properties can either be freehold or leasehold. The owner of a freehold property owns both the land and the building whereas, in the case of leasehold, the holder occupies the building for a set period of time. Historic leases were often over a 99-year period or, in some cases, 999 years at a fixed rent. The leasehold properties could then be occupied by the holder of the lease or sublet to a tenant. If these details were not available from the information stored at Companies House it would require us to contact the tenant. When handled properly, it was possible to acquire the necessary data from a simple telephone call.

Another part of the job was to visit the local authority planning office. This was mainly to determine the zoning of a site and to see whether there was any possibility of a change of use. The public have access to files which give details of any planning permissions in the offering. A further source of information was the Guildhall library, which stored large-scale maps from which site sizes could be measured. These were essential where the size of a building was not available. It was possible to estimate the letting area by visiting the site, calculating how much was covered by the building, multiplying the number of floors and deducting an amount for corridors, lift shafts and other open areas. A site visit was essential to identify the tenant and type of occupancy. A banking hall or shops on the ground floor would command a higher rental and accordingly greater valuation than the rest of a building. Similarly, the age and condition of the building would need to be assessed. The final destination would be a series of estate agents to determine current rental levels for the properties.

Once the information had been assembled, a valuation could be carried out. It is fairly obvious that an office property let at a current market rent of, say, £10 per square foot would be worth far more than an identical building with an historic rent of £1 per square foot, but without the benefit of a rent review for ten years. Equally, a similar building with, say, two years until the next rent review, would have a value closer to the open market value. To value a building, the current rent received will be valued on a yield basis, and the rent expected after the rent review would be valued on a similar basis, but discounted to give it a current value. We were able to compile detailed valuation tables, which were then used to prove the asset value of property companies to potential investors. As most property companies employed borrowings to finance their operations, the gearing effect meant that the underlying net asset value could be greatly in excess of the share price.

Part of my new role was to present our property research to the institutional clients of Norris Oakley. These included household names such as Barclays Unicorn, Brown Shipley, Hill Samuel, M&G, Rothschild, and Schroders. As it involved recommending shares in each company to only one institution at a time, the bulk of my work was devoted to producing property valuations. Even though our research was highly detailed, it did not take too long for other stockbrokers to produce recommendations based on less-sophisticated assumptions. This was prompted by the huge rise in property values which were being evidenced by actual transactions taking place in the property market. Eventually the property share sector had a sharp rise and several share prices reached asset value. In the direct property market, yields were driven down and property values inflated. It got to the stage where a development plot was valued at an unrealistic figure. This assumed that a building had been completed, financed and let, to give a present-day site value after applying a discount factor over its estimated period of construction.

Life moves on. We now decided to look at asset situations in other sectors of the stock market. In many ways this was a much easier task since I was valuing assets owned and occupied by trading companies. These properties were valued on an open market basis using current rentals and yields. As there were no tenants involved, a vacant possession value would be obtained. It involved valuing unusual assets such as hotels and garages. In the case of the latter, I approached a well-known firm, Conrad Ritblat, a firm of estate agents which specialised in commercial property, to find out how to value filling stations. I was ushered into an office where I explained to a man sitting behind a desk that I was employed by a stockbroking firm to produce research on asset-backed companies and could he tell me how to value garages? He was extremely interested in our approach to investment and seemed willing to help. The sting in the tail came next when he wanted to discuss fees. I said that we were not prepared to pay for the information and was promptly kicked out of the office. His approach was understandable, but it was the first time that I had encountered such a situation. The person in question was John Ritblat and it was no surprise that he used his entrepreneurial skills to build British Land into a FTSE 100 company.

Another firm of estate agents was more helpful. It turned out that a filling station was valued on the basis of a charge per gallon of petrol throughput, plus a value for showroom, retail and engineering space. In those days, there were several quoted motor companies and valuations were done on Frank Gates, Henlys, Kennings and Perry Motors. Several of these owned valuable London sites, some of which could be developed for alternative use. In fact, at the height of the property boom, I valued one site in Uxbridge at £500,000 against a book value of £200,000. I discovered from the planning department that the site was zoned for offices and, in my opinion, could be worth £2 million. The directors of the motor company which owned the property disputed both values, but sold the property a little while later for £3 million.

By 1971 I had built up an extensive library of properties and, in May of that year, published a booklet containing brief financial details of 29 asset situations in 17 sectors of the stock market. The final paragraph stated that it was

"not the intention to focus attention solely on the takeover prospects of the companies included. Bids, and bid hopes, will no doubt continue to enliven the shares of many of them, but the longer-term benefit of shareholders may best be served by directors capitalising on the built-in asset advantage that they have, to improve the company's trading prospects, instead of seeing their company swallowed up by a larger group and the subsequent trading improvement diluted. However, while it is clear that, in theory, a shopkeeper owning freehold ought to have a competitive edge over a newcomer to the business who has to pay the going rent, the fact that very often this is not true in practice, suggests that established management is either unwilling, or unable, to utilise its advantage. It is only in such cases that a bid may be the best solution."

Eventually, all bar three of the companies featured in the report were taken over.

The largest company mentioned in the report was National Westminster Bank, which had a market capitalisation of £374 million on 23 April 1971. It was acquired by the Royal Bank of Scotland in 2000, but retains a separate identity trading under the name NatWest.

For the year to 31 December 2015, it made an operating profit of more than £1 billion before impairment charges. The question arises as to whether shareholders would have been better placed if the bank had remained independent.

Another company in the report was J. Lyons & Co, which had been established in 1894 and had diverse activities ranging from food manufacture to the operation of hotels and restaurants. Its London hotels covered the Regent Palace, Cumberland, White's and the Strand Palace. Subsequently, it developed the Tower Hotel at London Bridge and purchased the Dunkin' Donuts and Baskin-Robbins brands. The company was taken over by Allied Breweries to become Allied Lyons and merged with Pedro Domecq in 1994 to be renamed Allied Domecq. It was acquired by Pernod Ricard in 2005. The following year Dunkin' Brands was sold to a US private equity firm for US$2.43 billion. In 1971, J. Lyons had a market capitalisation of £60 million and one wonders how much value might have been achieved for shareholders had it remained an independent company.

Five years after J. Lyons was incorporated, construction started on the Savoy, one of London's landmark hotels. The Savoy Hotel was family-controlled, but the shares were listed on the London Stock Exchange with a 1971 market value of £13.8 million. At the time it was rebuilding the 300-bedroom Berkeley hotel and owned Claridge's and Connaught hotels, as well as Simpson's-in-the-Strand and Stone's Chop House. The company was acquired in 1998 by private equity and changed hands in 2004 with the Savoy and Simpson's being sold shortly afterwards for a reported £250 million. The three remaining hotels are held in the renamed company, Maybourne Hotel Group. This company has a value of about £550 million but based on a rumoured approach from the Abu Dhabi State Pension fund could be worth up to £1.6 billion!

The most successful company featured in our report was Whitbread. In 1971, its equity shares had a value of £157 million on the London Stock Exchange. At the time, it owned 20 breweries plus a large portfolio of public houses and 70 hotels, having more than 1,900 bedrooms in total. It sold the brewing interests in 2001 and the pubs were hived off one year later. Today its principal activities are Premier Inns, the largest budget hotel company in the UK, and Costa Coffee. Premier Inns owns a chain of 650 hotels containing 50,000 rooms, while Costa Coffee has more than 2,800 outlets in 30 countries. Whitbread is now one of the top 100 quoted companies in the UK, with a market valuation in excess of £7.5 billion.

Two more companies that featured in the report and which are still quoted are Development Securities and Johnson Group Cleaners (now named Johnson Service Group). In 1971, the former had a market value of £8 million and the latter £5 million. Their respective market capitalisations are now around £280 million and £220 million.

It was exciting to be involved in the property boom, but another boom was happening at the same time. It occurred in Australian mining shares, with the ASX All Mining Index increasing fourfold between 1964 and 1969. UK investors became involved after publicity associated with a company called Poseidon. In the late 1960s, industrial disruption in the Canadian mining industry and increased demand due to the Vietnam War caused a spike in the nickel price. In 1969, the price of nickel on the London market rose from under £2,000 per ton to a peak of £7,000 per ton in November. Poseidon announced the drilling result of its Windarra drilling prospect at the end of September 1969. During the month, the share price had risen from AUD (Australian Dollar) 0.80 to AUD1.85 and jumped to AUD6.60 on the announcement of a nickel discovery. The share price doubled two days later when it was disclosed to be a major find. Another drilling report emerged in the middle of November 1969, by which time the share price had touched AUD60. A month later, the share price reached AUD175 and eventually peaked at around AUD280, which valued the company at AUD700 million.

The dramatic rise in Poseidon shares captured the public imagination and prompted speculative buying of shares in a large number of Australian companies. A company named Tasminex was also a well-known star of the period. It was a pure exploration company investigating leases at Mount Venn in Western Australia. Some traces of metal deposits, thought to be nickel, were rumoured to have been discovered and the share price jumped from AUD2.80 to AUD3.30. More rumours surfaced and the next day the price closed at AUD16.80. Following publication of an interview with the chairman, the share price peaked at AUD96 in the London market. A scandal arose when it was discovered that he had realised a substantial profit by selling shares at an enhanced level and no commercial deposits were found.

Both of these stock market booms were interesting in their separate ways. Property was an asset which I understood, but Australian mining share prices reached levels which looked grossly overvalued. Owing to my conservative approach – ingrained because of my horse-racing ventures and losing money on Thorn shares – I was not tempted to buy any of the speculative mining shares. It amazes me that a company such as Poseidon, which was yet to mine or make profits, was valued at 1/3 of the value of BHP, Australia's largest company. I might have missed potentially large profits, but at least I slept at night.

6

What on Earth is Going on?

Undoubtedly, the most influential event to shape my stock-picking approach was the 1973–74 stock market crash. The UK benchmark at the time was the FT 30 Share Index which, as the name suggests, comprised an index of the 30 largest UK quoted companies. It reached a peak of 516.2 in December 1972, to virtually halve by July 1974, only to continue falling and to, finally, bottom at 146.2 in January 1975. From its peak to its trough, the index fell by a staggering 72% and caused investors to lose huge amounts of money before eventually creating eye-watering investment opportunities.

Most leading stock markets had major setbacks in that period and the US Dow Jones Industrial Index fell by 45%. Even worse, the Hong Kong Hang Seng Index fell from 1800 to 300. The world had moved into a sharp global recession, with US GDP falling from plus 7.2% to minus 2.1% and inflation, as measured by the Consumer Price Index, rising from 3.4% in 1972 to 12.3% in 1974. By comparison, UK GDP moved from plus 5.1% to a negative figure of 1.1% and inflation, measured by the Retail Price Index, more than doubled to reach a peak of 24.9% in 1975.

The 1973–74 crash might be better thought of as a prolonged bear market. It was brought about by several factors. The starting point might have been the devaluation of the US dollar when it moved away from the gold standard. At the end of the Second World War, the US adopted the Bretton Woods system, whereby the US dollar was pegged to gold which had a fixed price of US$35 per ounce. In turn, overseas currencies were pegged to the US dollar. International pressure forced the US government to abandon the Bretton Woods system at a time when the country needed substantial expenditure to finance the Vietnam War. As the currency no longer needed to be backed by gold, there was a build-up of money being issued into the system. The increase in money supply was inflationary and the cost of financing the extra debt devalued the currency. The new Smithsonian agreement reached between ten countries in 1971 (abandoned two years later), pegged their currencies to the dollar and led to it being devalued by about 8%.

In the US, unemployment was rising, which increased the cost of social welfare, and the economy was running large budget deficits. The pressure on the US dollar meant that, in 1971, the US federal government imposed price and wage controls, but interest rates were reduced in order to boost the economy ahead of the election. It worked initially, but the effect was a huge rise in inflation which, at the start of 1973, was 3.6% and ended the year at 8.3% before eventually peaking at 12.2% by the end of the following year. Under such circumstances, it is little wonder that the US stock market fell sharply and that global investors in US Treasury Bills felt the impact. As often happens, there was a knock-on effect on overseas stock markets. As the old adage has it, 'when America sneezes, everyone else catches a cold'.

In the UK, the situation was slightly different in that sterling was fairly stable against the US dollar, but inflation had started to rise sooner. Part of this can be attributed to the property boom. The Retail Price Index increased from 2.5% in 1967 to 7.9% in 1970. Worse was to come with the Retail Price Index hitting double figures in 1973, peaking at 24.9% in 1975. In the early 1970s, growth in credit might have exaggerated the problem with two major events occurring. First was the deregulation of the mortgage market, which allowed the high street banks to undertake mortgage business.

Previously only building societies were allowed to undertake this lending to home buyers. Secondly, the introduction and mass use of the credit card boosted consumer spending at a time when Anthony Barber, the Conservative chancellor of the exchequer, introduced large tax cuts. House prices were rising sharply. For example, the value of the house that I purchased for £3,000 in 1970 had doubled in value by 1973, and was eventually sold for £11,300 two years later. The availability of cheap credit also created demand for motor cars and other goods such as colour televisions.

Global economies were in no state to take a shock, but this came in the shape of an unexpected oil embargo by the Organisation of Arab Petroleum Exporting Countries (OAPEC). It was in response to American involvement in the 1973 Yom Kippur War, where Egypt and Syria launched an attack to regain territories occupied by Israel since 1967. The embargo lasted from October 1973 to March 1974 and included Canada, Holland, Japan, the United Kingdom and the US. After an initial 70% spike, oil prices increased from US$3 per barrel to nearly US$12 per barrel over that period. In 1970, the Conservative government under Ted Heath had reversed the pro-Israel stance taken by the previous Labour government. As a result, the supply of oil to the UK was not too badly affected, but the rise in oil prices fuelled inflation and accelerated development of the North Sea reserves.

The two main concerns facing the Heath government were the increasing rate of inflation and a weakening pound which, in 1972–73, depreciated by 20% against a basket of other currencies. To make matters worse, a five-week coal miners' strike at the beginning of 1972 caused a declaration of a state of emergency followed by the imposition of a three-day working week to conserve energy. Simultaneously, dock and rail strikes were settled at high levels, forcing excessive wage demands in other industries at a time when unions had a strong bargaining position. In order to stabilise the pound, interest rates more than doubled from 6% in June 1972 to 12.75% in 1974. A further miners' strike at the beginning of 1974 prompted another three-day week and a general election when the Labour Party, led by Harold Wilson, was returned to power.

By early March 1974, the FT 30 Share Index had fallen to just above the 300 level, but worse was to come. Under Denis Healey, the Labour chancellor of the exchequer, the basic rate of tax was increased by 3% to 33%, the top rate from 75% to 83%, and to 98% on investment income. Corporation tax increased from 40% to 52% and it was no surprise that the index fell to 267.4 by the end of the month. It is little wonder that the background situation led to a secondary banking crisis. Lending to property companies had got out of hand and a fall in inflated asset values would cause several secondary banks to become insolvent. To solve the problem, the Bank of England, together with the clearing banks, formed the 'Bank of England Lifeboat', which would advance funds to banks that were experiencing financial problems. By mid-January 1974, £200 million had been advanced; the bailout figure peaked at £1.3 billion in March 1975.

The Labour government was unable to persuade the trade unions to accept pay restraints and wages were increasing at an annualised rate of 19% at a time when there were strict price controls. Company earnings were being affected by increasing costs and higher taxation, which provided a gloomy outlook for the equity investor. To make matters worse, the global outlook was not improving. In the United States, the Dow Jones Index fell 100 points to 656 on the news of the resignation of President Richard Nixon. Harold Wilson called another election for October 1974 and was returned to power with a majority of three. The Budget that followed did little to help confidence and share prices slumped towards their lows.

A major shock to the stock market was the suspension in trading of Burmah Oil shares at the beginning of January 1975. Burmah Oil was a profitable company with production interests in Burmah and stakes of 21.6% in BP and 2% in Shell. It made the mistake of acquiring two US companies financed by US$650 million loans. One of the businesses was a large-scale tanker operation which suffered from the slowdown in trade as a result of the oil embargo. Burmah Oil moved into loss at a time when its holding in BP had fallen in value from about £440 million to £182 million. The Bank of England agreed to bail out the company by guaranteeing the American loans but the price was high as, in return, it was forced to relinquish its interests in BP and Shell together with 51% of its North Sea assets. Bizarrely, the FT 30 reached its low of 146.3 one week later and within three weeks the Bank of England had made a profit of £86 million on its newly acquired holding in BP shares.

I was fortunate enough to live through this two-year bear market, but at the time it was a painful experience. I owned no personal investments as I had sold these to raise funds for a deposit on the house that I purchased in 1970. However, I looked after my parents' modest share portfolio which had been inherited from my grandmother. By that time they had both retired and needed dividend income to supplement their state pension. It was painful for me to go through a period when dividends were being cut and share prices were collapsing. Not much money was involved, but the responsibility was huge.

The protracted decline in the stock market had a marked effect on stockbroker profits as the fall in values gave rise to smaller trade sizes and, hence, lower commissions. Investors were not happy to sell shares at a loss and therefore stock exchange turnover fell sharply. At the time, I was earning a basic salary to which a 25% share on commissions generated from my personal clients was added. Happily, through two bits of luck, I became one of the higher commission-earners for the firm.

My specialisation in asset situations helped me to cover most sectors of the market and one of those was shipping. There were few specialists in the sector and no one else studied it from the asset perspective. The *Investors Chronicle* was updating its publication called *Beginners Please* and I was asked to produce a comment on shares in the shipping sector. Rather than the cruise line or super tanker companies, I saw the greatest value at the smaller end of the market. There were several tramp shipping companies which owned small vessels used to transport bulk cargoes between various destinations. Sometimes these ships were operated by the owner but, more often, were chartered to other companies over a set period. The charter rate can be likened to property rental and the value of a ship can depend on its earnings potential together with its age.

London and Overseas Freighters, which owned a mixed fleet of tankers and dry cargo vessels, was the largest tramp shipping company. It had a chequered history. In the mid-1990s it avoided liquidation before eventually amalgamating with Frontline in 1997. Not so lucky were shareholders of Lyle Shipping and Reardon Smith, which both went into liquidation in 1985/6 due to a downturn in world trade. A smaller company – Turnbull, Scott & Co – sold its last ship in 1990 to become a specialist company in security hardware such as underfloor safes. James Fisher remains as a quoted company on the London Stock Exchange but has become a diverse support service business. I had been contacted by the managing director of a small merchant bank who had read my comment about the shipping sector. He had a client wishing to invest in these companies and I was able to acquire substantial holdings for the bank in the two-year bear market.

Once again, I had to thank Guy Libby for my second stroke of luck – an introduction to the Lewis Trust Group. The company's origins can be traced back to 1948 when Bernard Lewis partnered with a colleague to sell fruit and vegetables from a shop in North London. In the early 1950s he and three brothers decided to move into the knitwear market and opened their first shop in East London. The family had always been innovative and decided to capitalise on a changing trend in women's clothing. During the Second World War, many women enlisted in the armed forces and became accustomed to wearing uniforms rather than dresses and skirts. The Lewis brothers latched onto this and started selling coordinated skirts and jackets under the name Lewis Separates.

Further innovation occurred in 1965 when the group had expanded to 70 UK stores. It was decided to concentrate on younger fashion and a shop called Girl was opened on the King's Road in Chelsea. This part of London became associated with 'pop' culture and, as an experiment, a shop trading under the name Chelsea Girl was opened by the firm in Leeds. It was a successful rebranding and grew to become a highly profitable fashion chain, foremost in the creation of a shopping experience for the younger age group. A menswear chain called Concept Man was launched in the early 1980s and the two merged to become River Island in 1988. It had moved from being one of a number of 'value' retailers to a more upmarket fashion chain which employed its own young designers. Today, River Island has more than 350 stores in the UK and is represented in 18 countries. Website sales are made to over 100 countries and fashionable kidswear has been added to the clothing range.

The Lewis Trust Group has become one of the largest UK private companies, with interests covering investment property, hotels, travel and finance. It had direct exposure to the 1970s secondary banking crisis through having deposits with a small bank called Consolidated Credits and Discounts Ltd. Rather than let it be rescued by the Bank of England, the Lewis Trust Group bought the bank. Consolidated Credits Ltd was a successful acquisition, but was seen as non-core and recently ceased its operations. At the time, it seemed a brave move but the Lewis family have always had an eye for a bargain and were happy to bet against the crowd. For this reason, in 1973 when the stock market had halved in value, they decided to purchase a portfolio of stocks and shares.

Fortunately for me, the Lewises hired an employee of Norris Oakley Richardson and Glover to look after the investment. He turned to Guy Libby who then appointed me as the firm's representative to handle the account. The initial investment was £1 million, a considerable amount of money when considering that an average house would be worth around £8,000. My brief was to select shares in all sectors of the stock market and to search for outstanding value. At that stage, I considered that this was a great opportunity as there were so many attractively priced shares. A portfolio of around

30 shares was assembled in a relatively short space of time. I was the sole stockbroker involved and would make recommendations for approval. This was really a formality and, over the years, a strong relationship was built up with the client.

Although the stock market had halved in value, worse was to come when it fell by a further 50%. The portfolio had outperformed the market, but its value was still well under water. My parents' portfolio had also declined, and to make matters worse, one of the companies had gone into liquidation leaving the shares worthless. With a three-day week, high interest rates, strikes, power cuts and an uncertain political situation, the outlook seemed grim. When an investment meeting was called in December 1974, I feared the worst, but the outcome was unexpected: we were instructed to invest a further £1 million in the stock market. There was a directive to throw caution to the wind and concentrate on the riskier sectors of the market. It was too late to sell my parents' shares and I thought that anyone committing further funds to the stock market was stark staring bonkers.

It was thought afterwards that the stock market recovery was staged by a group of institutional investors who met for lunch at the Prudential Assurance Company and decided to commit funds to equities. Certainly shares looked incredibly cheap; the FT 30 share index had a dividend yield of nearly 13.5% and was selling on a price–earnings ratio of just 3.8×. These values suggested that the economy was in complete meltdown and companies had little intrinsic value. Investors were fearful of the future and wanted to hold cash despite the fact that its spending power was being sharply eroded by double-digit inflation. Like everyone else at the time, I was fearful that company profits would evaporate and that bad news would drive share prices still lower.

Once the intention to invest the extra funds was received and a high risk/reward strategy was put in place, it was a question of identifying and purchasing appropriate shares. An obvious starting point was the banking sector. The price of National Westminster Bank shares had fallen below 100p having been at 411p when I produced my booklet on asset situations in May 1971. The shares produced a dividend yield of 12%, were selling at less than two years' earnings and the company was valued at just £175 million. In an example of how grave the situation had become, the Bank of England issued a statement to say that the bank had not asked it for financial support. This was pretty scary stuff and it was little wonder that bank shares had fallen so much. We bought holdings in Barclays Bank, Lloyds Bank, Midland Bank and National Westminster Bank.

Part of the problem with the banking sector was the huge amount of property lending to which it was exposed. In 1970, the Bank rate was reduced from 7.5% to 5% and credit was more freely available. In the next three years, bank lending to the property sector increased from £343 million to £2.8 billion, with property growing at an annual rate of more than 14%. Remembering that property is valued on the basis of a yield on the present rents and future income it is expected to produce, this growth could not continue against a background of double-digit interest rates. In fact, in order to halt a run on the pound, interest rates were hiked from 6% in June 1972 to 12.75% in 1974. This occurred at a time when property companies had invested in property developments that were not income-producing and were seeing a fall in rents on the back of declining demand. My old friend British Land became a penny share, as did Capital & Counties and Town & City Properties. Under our investment brief, we purchased shares in these companies in preference to Hammerson, Land Securities and MEPC, which were considered to be the blue-chip companies in the sector.

Outside of the financial sectors there were many bargains to be had. Imperial Chemical Industries was considered to be the bellwether for the stock market. At its low point the shares provided investors with a dividend yield of 14% and were priced at just 3.5× earnings. Even better value were BP shares which could be acquired at a little over 2.5× historic earnings and yielded nearly 13%. Some shares, such as those of the hotel companies Grand Metropolitan and Trusthouse Forte, were on similar ratings, but had dividend yields which were in excess of 20%. These, and shares in numerous other companies, were purchased on equally tasty valuations.

The instructions from the Lewis family directors, and the timing of the share purchases, were outstanding. In just seven weeks, the FT 30 Share Index more than doubled. In April 1975, Denis Healey produced a tough budget which included a 2p rise in the standard rate of income tax. Inflation was running at 24% and the aim was to reduce it to single figures by the end of 1976. Surprisingly, the chancellor persuaded the trade unions to accept an immediate 10% voluntary pay restraint, which would fall to single figures over the same period. A referendum in June won a two to one majority for the UK to stay in the EEC and this removed an area of uncertainty. Over the first six months of 1975, the Lewis Trust's £2 million investment had increased in value to £3 million and would grow to £8 million over the next three years. The higher-risk shares purchased with the second tranche of funds became the star performers.

There were several lessons to be learned. Perhaps the overriding one was to treat the market dispassionately. This can be difficult, as I discovered when looking after my parents' small share portfolio, where every downwards lurch in its value caused a feeling of guilt and anguish. It would have been bad enough to see notional losses on my own portfolio, but even worse where my parents were concerned. They did not follow the movement of individual share prices, but would have been well aware of newspaper reports on major stock market changes; "millions wiped off shares" hardly inspired confidence. My father kept records of purchase and sale transactions and incoming dividends, but fortunately did not have access to share prices. Both my mother and father had been honest hardworking people, which added more stress to the situation. From my point of view, the fact that the Lewis family were undertaking a large share-buying programme somehow had a mitigating effect.

The second lesson was that stock market behaviour can be governed by fear or greed. In that extraordinary two-year bear market, investors had completely lost confidence. In some cases this might have been justified in view of the unfavourable economic background, but once faith has been lost it is difficult to restore. It eventually reaches the point where there are only sellers of shares coupled with very little buying interest. The situation might have been worse at that time, as the stock market jobbing system led to a great level of share price volatility. A jobber was obliged to quote a two-way price in a definite number of shares and, for this reason, often became a forced buyer. After purchasing unwanted shares, the jobber would mark the share price lower in order to attract a buyer and to avoid purchasing additional shares at the same price.

A third lesson was that share prices can reach unrealistic levels before stock markets turn. In the 1973 bear market we have seen how the FT 30 Share Index reached an attractive level in terms of dividend yield and its price–earnings ratio. The mirror effect will apply at the top of a bull market. Shares such as Poseidon in the Australian mining boom or UK property shares at the height of the market were examples of this overvaluation.

This leads to the fourth lesson, which was not to follow the crowd. It was right to track the Lewis family and buy when others were selling. The initial timing might not have been perfect, but shares had been acquired at half their peak levels. At the time, the second forage into the stock market was brave, but proved to be a master stroke. I also found it interesting that this was the first time that the Lewis family had ventured in the stock market. Later events vindicated their judgement; a shrewdness also shown in other decisions they were to make to build their group into one of the most successful private companies in the UK.

Finally, we come back to the 'lollipop' factor – it is best to acquire shares in companies that are easy to understand. Equally important is to comprehend the fundamentals. Back in 1974, on paper, banks and property companies appeared to rank amongst the riskiest of investments. However, it was inconceivable that the government would let the former go bust, as it would signal the collapse of the financial system. Equally, property companies owned proper assets, the values of which would recover at some stage in the future. In the years ahead I came to love bear markets as they created many anomalies together with opportunities for the stock picker. That is where fortunes can be made.

7
The Final Throw

Norris Oakley Richardson and Glover was a partnership consisting of 25 partners. The equity partners contributed capital for running the business and shared its profits or losses in proportion to their interest. Our firm was an unlimited partnership which meant that the equity partners were personally accountable for all liabilities. Some of the partners had no equity interest and were paid a salary plus a bonus or share of commission. In these cases, they did not share in any distributable profits and had no personal liability for losses.

During the two-year bear market, Norris Oakley Richardson and Glover was going through a difficult period; revenue was falling and 75% of the partners were approaching retirement age. Some partners were involved purely to provide working capital and brought little business to the firm. It was therefore understandable that, in view of the poor market conditions, there was considerable nervousness about the mounting losses that were being made.

I was unaware that there were concerns about the future facing the firm. Perhaps I might have had a clue in my role as one of the trustees to the firm's pension fund. The benefits were extremely favourable: members of the scheme, on retirement, were entitled to an annual income amounting to 50% of their final salary. With the wage inflation of the early 1970s, it did not take a rocket scientist to calculate that the fall in the stock market could create a huge deficit which would have to be made good by future partners of the firm. To make matters worse, it was a non-contributory scheme, where the firm paid the annual premiums. In order to rectify the situation, it was proposed to fundamentally change the terms in regard to benefits and contributions.

One day, an official-looking paper was thrust in front of me to sign. I did not need to be an actuary to see that the document radically changed members' entitlements. As I was not a partner in the firm, and had the best interests of pension trust members at heart, I refused to sign. This would have jeopardised the new agreement, but the firm came up with a neat solution: they dropped me as a trustee and appointed another, more cooperative, member of staff in my place.

In the middle of 1974, the outlook for a stockbroking firm looked dire, and the partners decided to retrieve their capital by merging with two other firms. At that time, my annual wage was £4,000 and commission earnings increased it to £7,200. This meant that I was providing the firm with gross commissions of £12,800 from my own clients. In addition, I serviced clients of the firm who were supplying it with a substantially larger commission contribution. Since I was the most profitable source of income outside of the partnership, I was invited to join in the merger.

There were two major obstacles. First, they required me to be a salesman or an analyst, but not both. I was not happy to split the role because an analyst does not get the satisfaction of selling his great idea while a salesman has to sell other people's recommendations, whether good or bad. The second problem was that my salary would be a flat £5,000, thereby substantially reducing my annual earnings. Faced with this dilemma, I handed in my notice. Guy Libby generously offered to make up the difference in pay from his own pocket, but the job specification that I wanted could not be accommodated in the enlarged firm's corporate structure.

As luck would have it, one of the other partners of the firm heard of my decision and informed me that he was in a similar position to myself and was considering not joining in the merger. He was also a large commission-earner for Norris Oakley but, unlike Guy Libby, could choose his own destiny. (Guy was a key member of the firm, and the merger would not have gone ahead if he had opted out.) Two others joined us to form a research-based team searching for a new home.

As we were a profitable unit, a number of opportunities became available. However, several of these were in firms with a poor reputation or that were financially unstable. The one stockbroking company that stood out a mile was R. Nivison & Co. It was a family-owned stockbroking firm established in 1886, run in a responsible and conservative manner. The company, alongside Mullens & Co, was arguably one of the two most prestigious stock exchange firms. Mullens acted for the British government while Nivison numbered Canada, New Zealand, South Africa and Northern Ireland among its brokerships. Nivison was also the official stockbroker for National Westminster Bank and several UK local authorities.

In those days, local authorities financed their operations by a weekly issuance of bonds, which were repayable in 12 months. These local authority yearling bonds ranked just below gilts in terms of security and Nivison was an issuing house for them. It was also involved in the management of local authority pension fund portfolios. Apart from family and friends, there was little private client business. Nivison produced no internal equity research and its widespread institutional contacts created an amazing opportunity for a team such as ours. Much to my delight, we were accepted into the firm as a research team that would be rewarded by a share of the commissions generated from our clients. Looking back, it seems a brave move considering the two-year bear market that had gone beforehand.

We joined in November 1974 and, in the event, our timing could not have been better; the FT 30 Share Index began its recovery in January 1975. It continued to rise and breached the 400 level by the beginning of 1976. Confidence had quickly returned on the back of positive news. Company profits were recovering sharply and inflation, at a mere 15%, looked to be under control. Interest rates even fell to 9% in March 1976. However, all was not a bed of roses and dark clouds appeared on the horizon. Sterling fell from an average rate of US$2.22 to the pound to below US$1.80, trade figures deteriorated, unemployment started to rise and Harold Wilson suddenly resigned to be replaced by James Callaghan as prime minister.

Worse was to come as interest rates were hiked to a peak of 15% in October 1976 and sterling was to fall to US$1.57 to the pound. Several rights issues dampened demand for equities and the net result was that the FT 30 Share Index fell to 265.3. Volatility was the order of the day and from this low in October the FT 30 Share Index finished the year at 354.7. Prospects improved in 1977 mainly due to the increasing revenue from North Sea oil, which allowed interest rates to fall to 5% in September 1977 and the FT 30 Share Index to reach a new high of 549.2.

I had learnt from my experience in the 1973 bear market and was able to take advantage of the rollercoaster ride in the stock market during the early years at Nivison. Admittedly it was difficult to persuade investors to buy equities in a falling market, but my ideas were generally asset-based which provided some comfort. By the same token, it was hard for investors to accept taking profits in a rising market. The asset-value approach at least provided a means of measuring intrinsic values. One factor that I had not faced before was that my earnings would depend entirely on the commissions that I generated. Thus, no client dealings meant an empty pay packet. Thankfully, without rent to pay and no back office costs, the only overheads were salaries for our two secretaries. I could therefore be fairly relaxed about the level of business that was generated.

There were two approaches that a self-employed stockbroker could adopt. The first was to make daily calls to as many clients as possible using a scattergun approach on the hopes of picking up random orders. This was not our style. We followed the second approach, which was to contact clients only when we had original news, ideas or added-value comments to share. Linked to this was our generation of unique research to be presented to our institutional clients on an individual basis. A change of emphasis occurred following the introduction of SSAP19, a company law compelling companies to provide shareholders with a fair value of their property assets. I now had to look elsewhere for value and decided to specialise in smaller companies.

My specialisation in asset situations still brought in recurring revenue from existing clients and one major advantage of joining Nivison was the fact it was a financially robust organisation and, as such, had the support of most institutional clients. Barclays Unicorn became one of my most important clients. It was an investment management subsidiary of Barclays Bank, dealing exclusively with its suite of unit trusts. My contact was through the fund manager who looked after the Barclays Unicorn Capital, Financial and Extra Income funds. He had the same philosophy as the Lewis family and in November 1974 decided that the property sector had an extraordinarily attractive valuation. For each of the funds, he purchased holdings in British Land, Capital & Counties Property, Great Portland Estates and Land Securities. This seemed a courageous move at the time, but proved to be exceptionally rewarding. A little later, the same fund manager did equally well by investing in shares in the oil and gas sector.

Fund managers in those days followed the same process that I adopt today, namely to have complete control of their investment decisions, and to pass orders directly to the broker who came up with the recommendation. Today, fund management companies have become so large that orders are passed through centralised dealing desks. I believe this process can harm the broker/fund manager relationship and is inefficient. Most people on the institutional sales desk prefer to talk directly to the fund manager, who can make a quick decision and pass them the order. Under the centralised dealing system, the order will not necessarily be placed with the stockbroker who originated the idea. Investment timing is important and the best price is often achieved by the first to deal on an announcement.

From my point of view, having direct access to the top managers of leading fund management groups was an important business relationship. Looking after my parents' portfolio made me appreciate how painful a wrong decision could be. Consequently, I was very selective when choosing shares to recommend. Some up-and-coming fund managers, such as Anthony Bolton, 'kicked the tyres' and would seek out company visits, but the majority relied upon advice provided by stockbrokers. I learnt at an early stage, that, over a period, the policy of making sound recommendations paid off. A relationship of trust was built up and often the reward was recognised by being given random orders.

Although the stock market had recovered, the political and economic background remained alarming; 1978–79 was famously termed the winter of discontent. A government guideline of 5% for pay increases was in place, but when workers at Ford Motor Company were offered this they immediately went on a strike that lasted seven weeks. The final 17% pay settlement prompted miners to seek a 40% increase and engineers one of 33%. A strike by lorry drivers in the new year forced the government to declare a state of emergency, which enabled troops to maintain essential services. The fact that there was uncollected rubbish in the street and services were being disrupted demonstrated to the public that the Labour Party was unable to control the trade unions. A general election was scheduled for 3 May 1979 and a change of government was expected. For this reason, the stock market remained near its peak level.

The leader of the Conservative Party was Margaret Thatcher, MP for Finchley since 1959. She was appointed to the cabinet as secretary of state for education in 1970 by Edward Heath, whom she deposed on 11 February 1975. The Conservative manifesto promised to reform trade unions, cut taxes, control money supply and make sure that pay bargaining returned to a sensible level without government interference. By comparison, the Labour Party sought for further control of industry, to impose a wealth tax, abolish public schools and exert further control over prices. In the event, the election result exceeded expectations and the Conservatives were elected to power with an overall majority of 43 seats.

Back to reality, wages were rising at just over 14% and there was a £1 billion trade deficit in the first quarter of the year. Against this background, in his first budget the chancellor of the exchequer cut income tax from 33% to 30%, increased the 40% tax threshold from £8,000 to £10,000, and lowered the top rate of tax for those earning more than £25,000 to 60% from 83%. These moves were balanced by increasing VAT to a uniform rate of 15% and imposing higher excise duties on drinks and tobacco. Public expenditure cuts of £1.5 billion were promised and a series of asset sales announced. Interest rates, which had been cut to 12% by the previous government just before the general election, were raised back up to 14%. A further interest rate increase, to 17%, occurred in November 1979, a level which was to persist over the next 12 months.

In the first year of the newly elected government, the FT 30 Share Index fell by 12%, but the much more broadly based FT All-Share Index actually managed to rise by 4.2%. Under these circumstances, investors were seeking investment opportunities away from the largest companies and a stock-picking approach worked well. By this time, I was able to cover all sectors of the stock market, but overlooked gold-mining shares. This may well have been due to nervousness following the events of the earlier Australian mining boom and the lessons learnt from the Poseidon episode. Due to instability in the Middle East, the gold bullion price increased from US$300 to US$526 an ounce and the FT Gold Mines Index was up 90%. Missing this golden opportunity showed that not all lessons I had learnt from past experience worked out well. Nevertheless, I had neither real regrets nor sleepless nights, even though the gold price reached US$800 an ounce in 1980.

By 1982, interest rates were down to 9% and price inflation and wage increases were below 7%, but oil prices drifted lower and sterling depreciated to below US$1.60 to the pound. It had been a tough period for the government and a general election was called for

9 June 1983. The Conservative Party was returned with a majority of 144, helped partly by victory in the Falkland Islands conflict. Maybe the Labour Party was expecting to lose, but its election manifesto seemed suicidal. At a time when the CBI survey was forecasting a substantial recovery in business confidence, the Labour Party was proposing withdrawal from the Common Market, renationalisation, exchange controls, the repeal of industrial legislation and a £7.5 billion increase in public expenditure.

In January 1984, the London Stock Exchange launched a new index to be known as the FTSE 100. It comprised the 100 largest UK companies and was weighted by size so that the larger the company, the greater the proportion of the index it occupied. Almost immediately, the FTSE 100 Index, which had a base of 1,000, replaced the FT 30 Share Index, now at around 900, as a yardstick for the UK stock market. It was a good year for investors and both indices advanced by around 23%, despite dock workers' and miners' strikes which lasted for more than 23 weeks. The US dollar was strong and in February 1985 sterling fell to just over US$1.05 to the pound, which prompted interest rates to again reach 14%. Despite this, the stock market still looked cheap, selling at around 11× earnings and yielding 5%. From a stock-picking perspective I was finding plenty of opportunities and my client base was expanding.

A transformational event was to occur in the mid-1980s. The stock market was deregulated to meet the conditions of the modern world. The move became known as Big Bang due to the expected increase in stock exchange turnover. Previously the London Stock Exchange had been owned by its members, but after the rules changed on 27 October 1986 it became a private limited company (obtaining a quotation on the main market in 2001). The minimum scale of commission charges was abolished and stockbroking firms were allowed to make markets in shares. Rather than the traditional face-to-face trading on the floor of the stock exchange, transactions would now be over the telephone or through computer terminals. Stock exchange firms could now be owned by outside corporations.

The main economic event of 1986 was the collapse of the oil price. Having been around US$27 a barrel in 1985 it fell briefly to US$9 a barrel before stabilising at US$14 a barrel. The correction was attributed to a fall in demand from industrial nations. Most UK companies would benefit from lower oil prices, but North Sea oil revenues would fall. In the budget ahead of the May 1987 general election, the basic rate of income tax was reduced from 29% to 27% and interest rates were cut to 10.5%. Mrs Thatcher was returned to power and by July the FTSE 100 Index had reached 2443 and the FT 30 Share Index was 1926. It seemed too good to be true and I advised my clients to capitalise on the rise and lock in some profits.

Most of my day was spent talking to clients on the telephone, leaving little time to produce research notes, so these were prepared in the evening and at weekends. With the reduction in commission charges following Big Bang, my earnings suffered and I decided to move into fund management. In order to produce original ideas, I had concentrated my research on smaller companies where there was less competition. The idea now was to launch a smaller company unit trust in which my institutional clients might become investors. Coincidentally, one of my clients, a firm of insurance underwriters with the Corporation of Lloyd's, had a specialist unit trust devoted to British government fixed-interest stocks. It was agreed that I could join and launch the proposed new fund through their unit trust management company.

Meanwhile, there was uncertainty about the future of Nivison in the post-Big Bang world. Many stockbroking firms were being acquired by UK and overseas corporations. Being a family company, jealous of its reputation, this seemed an unlikely course. If it was to remain an independent company, there were significant hurdles to overcome. Foreign companies had ceased to raise money from issuing bonds on the UK stock market and the local authority yearling bonds business was likely to disappear. To make matters worse, deregulation of commission charges would cause some stockbrokers to attract business by cutting commission charges to a barely profitable level. The lucrative fund management business, and a specialist bond trading, would provide the backbone of future operations.

Included in the fund management business of Nivison was Glenfriars Unit Trust. It had been formed in 1970 and was classed as a 'master portfolio'. The term is no longer used, but in those days it referred to a broadly based fund which had the appearance of the type of portfolio a private investor would hold. The unit trust was the amalgamation of the Nivison family portfolios and was an efficient method of managing client monies. As capital gains tax was not liable on switches in the portfolio, and only one decision per stock was necessary, the advantages were considerable. I thought that this unit trust would fit in well with my new venture, and approached Lord Glendyne, who was head of the Nivison family and controlling partner. He immediately latched onto the idea, but much to my surprise suggested that Glenfriars Unit Trust Managers Ltd should be the investment management vehicle. We could not persuade the other company to bring its unit trust under our wing, but that was no great loss.

The decision was made and Glenfriars Portfolio Managers Ltd became a stand-alone company with one unit trust, which was renamed the Glenfriars Private Portfolio Fund to better reflect its objectives. I became a director and was appointed manager of the £15 million unit trust. Although it was a global fund, the portfolio was mainly invested between shares in leading UK and US companies, where the greatest potential seemed to lie. The plan was to then, as soon as practicable, launch a smaller company unit trust. Having been a stockbroker for my entire career, I had no contacts in that industry. To resolve the problem, I contacted Guy Libby to see if he would take us on as a client. At the time he was still a partner in the firm with which Norris Oakley had merged, but was also managing his own unit trust. Much to my astonishment, he expressed an interest in joining us. He was allowed to join and bring the management contract for the unit trust that he managed. We were missing an income fund and Guy volunteered to form and run the Glenfriars Higher Income Fund.

Preparations for the launch of our two new funds were underway when, on 19 October 1987, an important milestone in my career and the stock market occurred. Three days previously, in the early hours of the morning, I was driving home from London with my wife and six-year-old daughter, only to find the exit on the M25 closed. It was pretty annoying as I was three miles from home but now had to take a 20-mile detour to get back. Several other roads were shut and the police were out in force to redirect traffic. Fortunately, we arrived home in one piece and the following morning discovered that the UK had been hit by a storm, with winds of hurricane force, up to 110 miles per hour. Nearly all of the local roads and the railway lines were blocked by fallen trees and I was unable to go to work that Friday. Elsewhere, a large proportion of public transport was out of action and many people were unable to travel.

While this was happening at home, hostilities broke out between Iran and the US. On 15 October 1987 an Iranian missile hit an American super tanker and another US vessel was hit by a similar missile on the Friday. In response, on the Monday, two US warships shelled an Iranian oil platform. This may have been coincidental, but global stock markets collapsed on what became known as Black Monday. During the next two weeks, the worst-affected markets were New Zealand (down 60%), followed by Hong Kong (down 45%) and Australia (down nearly 42%). By the end of the month the UK had fallen by 26% and the US by 22%. Part of the problem might have been a reaction to the huge rises that had taken place over the last few years, but in the US it was blamed on computer trading.

The introduction of the computer brought an element of sophistication to the stock market. It has always been possible to place what is known as a stop-loss order, where – with the view to limiting a loss – a share will be sold if it falls below a certain price. This type of order could now be programmed into a computer, as could other trading strategies. To avoid settlement problems, it became popular to deal in the futures market and computer technology enabled investors to take advantage of anomalies by programming trades between the futures and conventional cash market. As a consequence, there could be a snowball effect due to the momentum of computer-programmed orders being triggered by abnormal price movements.

In the UK, computer systems were less advanced and trading was generally confined to the conventional stock market. However, there was a market in traded options. A call option gave the holder the right to buy – and a put option, the right to sell – a share at a set price on a predetermined date in the future. The investor would pay a premium over the market price for a traded option and this would fluctuate to reflect movements in the actual market price of the shares. For each traded option that was created there had to be a reverse side of the deal. Thus, in the case of a call option, somebody received payment to deliver the shares when the traded option expired. With a put option, the counter party would be required to buy the shares on the expiry date. More often than not the settlement would be in cash, with no shares changing hands.

For the institution prepared to buy or sell shares in the traded option company, the business of underwriting options for a fee seemed like money for old rope. With the sharp fall in the market, things did not turn out to be so rosy. One well-known institutional investor actually underwrote a huge number of traded option puts for the unit trusts which it managed. With the sharp fall in the stock market, there was a huge liability to purchase shares on which there were losses of at least 20%. This situation should never have occurred and the institution was forced to accept full financial responsibility for the loss.

The problem in the UK was an imbalance of orders. The Great Storm of 1987, as well as stopping me from going to work, caused havoc elsewhere. On that Friday, all London markets were closed without warning. Consequently, when the stock exchange reopened on Black Monday, there was a deluge of sell orders. To me, this was great news as it would enable me to start my new career as a fund manager with shares priced at a much more attractive level.

PART II
The Fund Management Years

8

The Start of the Journey

The transition from stockbroking into fund management is not as difficult as it might appear. In fact, in my opinion, it is an easy route. One of the reasons for this is that a stockbroker should be able to judge the potential investment merits of a company. With a reputation at stake, a poor investment recommendation will be taken badly by a client. In my role as a stockbroker, there was an extra onus as I was directly responsible for my own research and investment ideas. It was clearly in my long-term business interest to make sure that I picked likely winners. The experience of the 1973 bear market helped me develop into a contrarian investor and now was the time to put into practice what I had been preaching. There was no better place to begin this new career than after the 1987 crash. The FTSE 100 had fallen from 2301.9 to 1801.1 on Black Monday and reached a low of 1565.2 by 9 November 1987.

Up until that time, Glenfriars Unit Trust Managers was solely an in-house management company of Nivison and had never marketed the Private Portfolio Fund to outside investors. One of the marketing problems we faced was to comply with the Financial Services Act 1986 concerning polarisation. This meant that we were only allowed to recommend our unit trusts to the public if we could justify that they were better than all similar funds. Considering the large number of unit trusts in existence, this was a truly challenging task, but we were able to overcome the problem by stating that each of our unit trusts was unique. For example, in the case of the Glenfriars Private Portfolio Fund, we had a minimum investment size of £250,000 and invited clients to think of it as though it were their personal portfolio. Potential new investors would have the comfort that existing Nivison family members had already transferred the bulk of their investments into the fund, which had been in existence since 1970. It was described as a complete portfolio rather than one of several funds the investor would hold.

In much the same way, my new fund was designed to be a vehicle for investors to hold smaller companies. However, I did not want it to be another smaller company fund that would suffer when the economy deteriorated. From a selfish viewpoint, I would have been unhappy to crystallise a capital gains tax liability by having to sell my personal holding when the outlook for smaller company shares become murky. The solution was to have the flexibility to invest in recovery situations and shares in out-of-favour sectors of the stock market. As a result, I was able to switch between small and larger companies when appropriate. Effectively, this made it different from all other unit trusts and gave me a fairly wide investment mandate.

In 1988, the government ruled that advisors could either work for one insurance company or become an independent practitioner. Consequently the regime of the independent financial advisor (IFA) was born. Today polarisation is not a problem as funds are mainly marketed directly to independent financial advisors or professional firms which are then able to provide an impartial recommendation to their clients. Some investors will deal on their own behalf after setting up discretionary accounts with firms such as Hargreaves Lansdown, but it would now be unusual for fund management groups to directly target individual private client investors.

On 1 February 1988, the Glenfriars Investment Opportunities Fund (Opportunities Fund) was launched when the FTSE 100 stood at 1777.6. Save & Prosper Group Ltd was appointed as comptroller and registrar and National Westminster Bank became the trustee. For its year-end we chose 15 November; being my birthday, it was a memorable date. On a practical note it enabled us to produce a managers' interim report for the period to 15 May 1988. In the days before fact sheets were required, it was useful to have this as marketing literature.

When the first interim report was published, the Opportunities Fund had a very concentrated portfolio containing just 22 holdings, of which four were quoted on the Unlisted Securities Market (USM). The USM was launched in 1980 to cater for companies that did not qualify for a full listing. These were either too small or did not have a three-year trading record. As little as 10% of the capital needed to be floated on the stock market. In June 1995, the Alternative Investment Market (AIM) was formed and companies quoted on the USM were given 12 months to transfer to AIM or delist.

My most successful USM investment was a company called Norfolk House Group, which owned and developed petrol-filling stations and commercial property. I acquired the shares in March 1988 when they were placed on the USM at a price of 100p. It raised money through a 4-for-9 rights issue at a price of 190p per share in February 1990 and moved to the main market two months later. I was surprised that the company needed to raise funds and felt that its expansion plans were too ambitious. Having more than doubled its value I decided to take the profit, which was just as well – the company became overstretched and went bust one year later.

A similar story applies to Resort Hotels, which I acquired when the shares were also placed on the USM in March 1988 at a price of 14p. I decided to try its hotel in Brighton, but chose an unlucky weekend when it caught fire. Perhaps the weekend was not unlucky, though, as I sold the holding shortly afterwards at a decent profit. The shares were introduced to the main market in November 1989, but went into receivership in 1994, despite raising money through two rights issues.

All bar three of the other holdings in the May 1988 portfolio have subsequently been taken over. The other two USM holdings were in Creightons & Holmes and Marchant (now Huntworth) and both managed to survive.

All of the original portfolio holdings were sold many years ago, but one of the investments was in Daejan Holdings plc, a share I have subsequently bought and sold on numerous occasions. In recent years, the Opportunities Fund has contained an interest in the company; its share price has appreciated more than sixfold from 15 May 1988. Daejan was formed in 1935 to hold and manage plantations on the islands of Java and Indonesia, but by 1955 these interests had been sold. The company remained dormant until 1959 when it acquired a number of landmark buildings in London. Today its portfolio consists of commercial and residential properties in the UK and US, having a value of more than £1.6 billion.

During the next six months to 15 November 1988, interest rates were to rise sharply from 7.5% to 13%. The FTSE 100 finished marginally higher at 1802.3 and the Glenfriars Investment Opportunities Fund's offer price had increased by 26.6%. Some changes had been made to the portfolio and there were now 26 holdings. The bulk of the investments remained in smaller companies, with 70% being capitalised below £100 million. By May 1989, the unit offer price had risen by 38.9% from its launch, with the FTSE 100 up 15.2% at 2047.5. It was now time to take stock. There were some clouds on the horizon, but the stock market continued its upward spiral and the FTSE 100 reached 2426 on 5 September 1989. Interest rates approached 15% and, in October 1989, Nigel Lawson resigned as chancellor of the exchequer. By way of a precaution, I reduced the holdings in companies capitalised under £100 million to 57.4% of the portfolio value, with more than half of these being classed as asset situations.

Meanwhile the international situation looked uncertain. On 2 August 1990, Iraq invaded Kuwait with the excuse that it was owed US $14 billion from the Iraq–Iran conflict of 1988. It also voiced the opinion that Kuwait's overproduction was depressing oil prices. The occupation of Kuwait lasted for seven months until intervention by US-led forces proved successful. At the time there were fears that the situation would spread to Saudi Arabia and this, plus the loss of production, caused oil prices to rise from US $21 per barrel to US$46 per barrel by October 1990. As a result of the uncertainty, by 28 September 1990, the FTSE 100 had fallen back to 1990.3.

This period proved to be the most challenging time in the fund's history. With interest rates at 14.875% for much of the year, small companies underperformed badly and the mid-price retreated to 94p, thereby extinguishing previous gains. Against this background, and drawing on my 1973–74 experience, I was able to reposition the portfolio to take advantage of a market recovery by adopting a defensive investment strategy. Companies valued over £100 million increased to 71% of the portfolio which, unusually for me, contained 12% cash. Shares in companies such as British Aerospace, Greene King, ASDA, Burton and National Westminster Bank were held as recovery situations and only four of the original holdings were still retained. A point of interest is that 15 of the 22 holdings have subsequently been taken over.

We now move into events that were to result in what was known as Black Wednesday. Under Nigel Lawson there was a private sector credit-based boom, which caused an increase in inflation together with a large current account balance-of-payments deficit. A rise in house and oil prices added fuel to the flames. John Major was appointed chancellor of the exchequer with a brief to lower the rate of inflation while maintaining a strong exchange rate. To achieve this, in October 1990 the British government joined the European Exchange Rate Mechanism (ERM). This was a process whereby sterling would be pegged to the deutschmark and kept within a 6% variance of the benchmark rate of DM2.95 to the pound. The two methods for realising the objective would be interest rate changes and the use of foreign currency to buy sterling. Interest rates had risen from a low of 7.375% in May 1988 to 14.875% in October 1989 and were cut to 13.875% on the arrival of the new chancellor. Over that period my first house had risen from £40,000 and was approaching £70,000 in value – not bad, remembering that it had been purchased for £3,000. Mortgage payments were at a crippling level for first-time home buyers. The net effect was a recession brought about by the rapid fall in consumer confidence and spending.

By now public opinion polls were showing discontent with Mrs Thatcher as leader of the Conservative Party and, following a leadership election in November 1990, she was replaced by John Major who in turn appointed Norman Lamont as chancellor of the exchequer. With the downturn in the economy, inflation fell from 9.5% in 1990 to 3.7% in 1992. However, it had become increasingly difficult to keep sterling within the ERM stipulated range. Sensing this, speculators, led by George Soros's Quantum Fund, sold sterling with a view to buying back at a cheaper level. The situation came to a head on 15 September 1992, now known as Black Wednesday. To keep sterling in the defined ERM limits, the Bank of England entered the market, buying the pound from the speculators. At 11 am, when this did not work, interest rates were hiked from 10% to 12% and then, in a panic move, to 15%. Despite this, sterling remained below the defined floor and an announcement was made that Britain would move out of the ERM and the 15% rate hike would be cancelled.

Black Wednesday cost the Treasury £3 billion and earned a profit of £1 billion for the Quantum Fund. Within a week, interest rates were down to 8.875% and reached 5.875% in January 1993. In the month that followed Black Wednesday, sterling fell from US$2 to the pound to US$1.75 to the pound and five months later touched US$1.40 to the pound. Inflation was under control and remained below 4% until 2007. Government credibility had suffered a significant blow, but the Conservatives were to remain in power after John Major's surprising win in the April 1992 general election with an overall majority of 21 seats.

The period from 15 November 1990 to 15 November 1992 was a poor one for the fund; the mid-price had declined to 89.52p. During this time of high interest rates, smaller companies struggled financially and recovery situations were also finding life difficult. It proved to be important in my stock-picking approach as there was now a greater number of undervalued shares to choose from.

This enabled me to increase the number of holdings to 30. Large companies classed as recovery situations accounted for 43.5% of the portfolio and included AMEC, Babcock International, British Aerospace, Barclays and Royal Insurance. Only one share remained from the original 1988 portfolio. The next 12 months saw the benefit of the change in emphasis, with the mid-price of the fund showing a rise of 46.8% against 19.1% for the FTSE All-Share Index and 1.0% for the newly formed FTSE Smaller Companies Index.

By 1993, funds under management had not increased as we had anticipated. Part of the reason was that we had a high minimum investment of £250,000 for the Glenfriars Private Portfolio Fund and £10,000 for each of our smaller unit trusts. The front-end charge was low at 1% for the former and 3% for the other two funds. Although we were prepared to return most of this to intermediaries who introduced new business, other unit trust groups which charged 5% up front were happy to pass on a larger amount. Consequently, we did not benefit from our decent performance and had to rely on word-of-mouth recommendations. In hindsight we should have had a low minimum investment and a standard 5% upfront charge. Three of my fellow directors now wished to retire and it was decided to break up the management company.

Although the economic climate was improving and interest rates were falling, the property market was dire. In 1991, rents had collapsed and a large number of properties had been let at levels that were greatly in excess of going market rentals. Up until that time, we had occupied temporary London office space in Old Park Lane, within a stone's throw of the Dorchester Hotel. We decided to take advantage of the depressed letting market by acquiring a long lease on an over-rented property. It was situated in Suffolk Street, a quiet cul-de-sac just off Trafalgar Square. We received a payment of £22,000 to take on the lease, which looked to be a great deal at the time. However, rents continued to fall and, in 1993, we had to pay £150,000 to surrender the lease. Out of interest, money received to takeover a lease is known as a reverse premium. Fortunately, in the overall scheme of things, I did not lose out financially when Glenfriars Unit Mangers was broken up.

In early 1994 I joined Cavendish Asset Management Limited and my fund was renamed the Cavendish Opportunities Fund. This move reunited me with the Lewis family. Cavendish was in the process of launching a global unit trust along the same lines as the Glenfriars Private Portfolio Fund. It would be seeded by Lewis family money and have the characteristics of a private client global portfolio. In order to do this, a separate subsidiary to be known as Cavendish Unit Managers had to be formed. To obtain regulatory approval, it was useful for an established unit trust to join the stable. From my point of view, this was to be an ideal home as the company was part of the Lewis Trust Group, a financially robust private company. I joined with responsibility for the UK investments of discretionary clients, which included three pension funds. As the bulk of Cavendish client monies were invested in larger companies, the Opportunities Fund fitted in very well.

The huge amount of stock market volatility at a time of high inflation and interest rates meant that, so far, it had been a rocky ride for fund managers. The interest rate situation made life particularly difficult in that the double-digit yields on bonds made them an attractive alternative to equities. Equally banks were becoming cautious in their lending policies, leaving smaller companies to suffer from penal interest rates. Property values also underwent a sharp fall due to the decline in rents coupled with a rise in valuation yields. Investors had little appetite for smaller companies as demonstrated by the movement of the stock market indices. In the period from launch on 1 February 1988 to 15 November 1993, the FTSE 100 was up 74% and the FTSE All-Share by 67.5%. The FTSE Small Cap substantially underperformed and was up by a little over 20%. By comparison the Opportunities Fund unit price had increased by 35.2%.

It was always my view that, over the medium to long term, smaller companies would outperform larger ones – but this was not proving to be the case. When reviewing the Glenfriars days, I felt that the

Opportunities Fund portfolio was too concentrated and that the fall in interest rates and inflation would favour large companies with recovery potential. My stock-picking approach remained unchanged in that I was searching for undervalued situations. It just transpired that many of these were at the larger end of the market capitalisation range. The objective moving forwards was to achieve a return better than the FTSE 100 and FTSE All-Share, otherwise why be invested in shares quoted at the smaller end of the stock market?

9

Cavendish Opportunities Fund –
The Early Years

In 1995 there seemed to be a loss of confidence in John Major as prime minister and he took the unusual step of resigning as Conservative leader to stand against all comers in a reelection battle. This slightly unnerved the stock market, but he won the vote.

An even greater shock was the demise of Barings Bank. Barings, the world's second-oldest bank, established in 1762, was brought down by Nick Leeson, who at the time was head of derivatives, trading out of Singapore. It clearly demonstrated the dangers of futures contracts if they are not traded responsibly, with proper controls in place. Nikkei 225 futures contracts can be bought or sold to reflect the level of the Japanese stock market. They are traded on both the Osaka Securities Exchange in Japan and the Singapore Exchange. On occasions, it is possible to take advantage of a difference in price and deal simultaneously in both markets for a small profit. This method of dealing was known as *arbitrage* and was both legal and authorised by Barings Bank. However, Leeson breached the bank rules by taking a view on the Japanese stock market and dealing only on one side of the transaction with the hopes of closing the position later at a profit. To make matters worse, he was also head of settlements, which allowed him to falsify the returns being sent to the London headquarters.

The strategy might have worked had it not been for the Kobe earthquake on 17 January 1995, which sent Asian markets into turmoil. By December 1994, Leeson had already lost £200 million while reporting a profit of £102 million. In keeping his futures contracts open and betting on a recovery in the Nikkei 225, his losses continued to mount. It was not until the end of February 1995 that the fraud was discovered by bank auditors. Losses had then accumulated to £827 million and it cost a further £100 million to unwind the positions. At the time, Barings had reserves of only £350 million and was therefore insolvent. The bank was sold for £1 to the Dutch bank ING, which took on the liabilities. Fearing a jail sentence, Leeson attempted to return to Britain but was apprehended by German police at Frankfurt airport. For several months, he unsuccessfully fought extradition to Singapore but was eventually sentenced to six and a half years in a Singaporean jail. He was released in 1999 after being diagnosed with colon cancer, from which he recovered.

There were several large takeover moves during 1995, with the most significant being the £9 billion bid by Glaxo for Wellcome. This was closely followed by Lloyds Bank acquiring Cheltenham & Gloucester Building Society and then TSB, to become Lloyds TSB. However, arguably a more significant event was the launch of AIM in June 1995. As mentioned in the previous chapter, this replaced the USM and was designed to provide a means for small or less mature companies to raise capital. The regulatory rules were less onerous than for companies with a full listing and it provided an alternative to venture capital funding. AIM companies would require a nominated advisor (NOMAD) to ensure that the rules were adhered to; the annual cost would be less than in the case of a fully listed company monitored by the London Stock Exchange.

Between 15 November 1993 and 15 November 1995 the number of holdings in the Cavendish Opportunities Fund had doubled to 66. I was delighted that shares in so many companies could find their way into the portfolio as it provided some protection if one of the investments went wrong. I was to find that, in future years, several companies such as Barings could encounter unforeseen financial difficulties. The portfolio emphasis returned to smaller companies and there were only a dozen larger company holdings left in the portfolio. These included Rolls-Royce, J Sainsbury, Kingfisher, Tesco and British Telecom. The only holding size to exceed 2.3% of the portfolio value was 3.27% in a company called Alvis, originally the armoured vehicle manufacturing subsidiary of British Leyland. It was bought by United Scientific Holdings in 1981 and the Alvis name was readopted ten years later. Subsequently it acquired Hägglunds, the Swedish armoured vehicle manufacturer; the armoured vehicle business of GKN; and the Vickers defence systems subsidiary from Rolls-Royce. The Alvis holding was purchased for the Opportunities Fund at an average price of 95p and held until 2004, when the company was acquired by BAE Systems in a contested takeover battle at a price of 320p cash per share.

Looking at the 15 November 1995 portfolio in more detail, of the 66 stocks held more than half have since been taken over and one company (Martin Shelton) has gone into administration:

SECTOR	CORPORATE DEAL
Oil	Enterprise Oil – acquired by Shell in May 2002
Construction	John Laing – acquired by Henderson Infrastructure in December 2006
Building materials	Marley – acquired by EM Holdings in April 1999
	Redland – acquired by Lafarge Mineral in December 1997
Chemicals	Albright and Wilson – acquired by ISPG in May 1999
	Courtaulds – acquired by AkzoNobel in July 1998
Industrial	BTR (Invensys) – acquired by Schneider Electric in January 2014
	Berisford (Enodis) – acquired by MTW in October 2008
Electronics	Chloride – acquired by Rutherford Acquisitions in September 2010
	Graseby – acquired by Smiths Industries in October 1997
Engineering	Alvis – acquired by BAE Systems in August 2004

	BI Group – acquired by NIC in March 1996
	William Cook – acquired by Steel Castings in February 1997
	M. L. Holdings (Sedgemoor) – acquired by Acal in June 1999
	Vosper Thorneycroft (VT Group) – acquired by Babcock in July 2010
Pharmaceuticals	Wellman – acquired by Newmail in January 1998
	Medeva – acquired by Celltech in January 2000
Paper and packaging	Aspen Communications – acquired by Pensa in July 1999
	M. Y. Holdings – acquired by Malbak in February 2000
Breweries	Vaux (Swallow Group) – acquired by Whitbread in January 2000
Healthcare	Amersham – acquired by General Electric in April 2004
Motors	Perry Group – acquired by Guinness Peat in April 2002
Media	Midland Independent News – acquired by Mirror in November 1997
Food manufacture	Hazlewood Foods – acquired by Greencore in January 2001
	Sims Food – acquired by Global Group in July 1999
Food retailers	Iceland – acquired by Giant Bidco in February 2005
	Nurdin & Peacock – acquired by Booker in November 1996
General retailers	Bentalls – acquired by Fenwick in July 2001
	Etam – acquired by Etam Développement in January 1998
Support services	Lopex – acquired by Evelink in November 1999
	P&P (QA) – acquired by Interquad in June 2006
	Christian Salvesen – acquired by Norbert in December 2007
Life assurance	C. E. Heath – acquired by Erycinus in July 1997

	London & Manchester – acquired by FP Business in September 1998
Property	Bilton – acquired by Slough Estates in November 1998
	Chesterton – acquired by Phoenix Acquisitions in June 2003
	Greycoat – acquired by G2 Estates in June 1999
	PSIT – acquired by MEPC in September 1997
	Scottish Metropolitan – acquired by Haslemere in May 2000

In terms of performance, smaller companies continued to lag. Whereas the FTSE 100 had doubled and the FTSE All-Share was up by 92%, the FTSE Small Companies only advanced by 37.6%. All of the securities in the portfolio were selected on investment merits as having attractive valuations and it appears that others thought the same, judging by the number of companies taken over. It also seemed as though the background economic situation might be becoming more favourable for smaller companies; the percentage of the portfolio in large companies reduced from 56% to 30%.

At the beginning of 1997, the UK economy was recovering well, with the annual rate of inflation at 2.9%, interest rates below 6% and a sterling/US dollar exchange rate at around US$1.60 to the pound. The Conservative parliamentary majority was small and John Major delayed the election until 1 May. By now, Tony Blair was leading the Labour Party, which he decided had outdated policies in need of reform. He renamed the party New Labour and sought to reassure the public that it would take a responsible approach to public spending and taxation. Above all, their theme was to encourage business, with the idea that this would provide the basis of economic growth. His timing was ideal because the public still remembered Black Wednesday and the Conservative Party was seen to be in disarray. In the event, New Labour won a landslide victory, achieving an overall majority of 179 seats.

Gordon Brown was appointed as chancellor of the exchequer and business awaited the July 1997 budget with some trepidation. On the positive side, corporation tax was cut from 33% to 31%, but against this he abolished tax credits, whereby hitherto pension funds had been able to reclaim the tax charged on equity dividends. By way of a concession to traditional Labour Party members, he imposed a £4.8 billion windfall tax on utility companies. The most far-reaching move, which was seen positively by both international and domestic investors, was to pass control of interest rate rises from the Treasury to the Bank of England. The overall reaction was positive and by October 1997 the FTSE 100 had increased by more than 30% since the beginning of the year.

Delivery of the July 1997 budget coincided with the beginning of the 1997 Asian financial crisis. It started in Thailand, which had accumulated a huge amount of foreign debt at a time when its currency was pegged to the US dollar and its economy was growing at an unsustainable rate. In mid-May 1997 there was a huge speculative attack on the Thai baht, which the Thai government did not have the financial muscle to defend. The Thai baht was forced to float on 2 July 1997 and very quickly halved in value. Finance One, the country's largest finance company, collapsed and the Thai stock market lost 75% of its value. In August 1997, the International Monetary Fund (IMF) provided a bailout of more than US$20 billion. The economy had recovered by 2001 and the IMF loan was repaid two years ahead of schedule.

The next country to suffer was Indonesia, which appeared sound as it was blessed with a large trading surplus and reserves of US$20 billion. In August 1997, due to speculative selling, the Indonesian government was obliged to float the Indonesian rupiah and had to accept an IMF rescue package of US$23 billion. Before the currency crisis, the exchange rate was 2,600 rupiah to the US dollar. This fell to 14,000 rupiah to the US dollar by January 1998. It recovered to 8,000 rupiah by the end of that year but the country had lost 13.5% of its GDP. The South Korean won also more than halved in value and the Philippine peso was devalued. Speculators attacked the Malaysian ringgit, which fell from 2.50 to the US dollar to 4.57 by January 1998, and the Kuala Lumpur Composite Share Index halved in value.

The two strongest economies in the region were Hong Kong and Singapore. Hong Kong had sufficient reserves to defend its currency, which remained pegged to the US dollar, but in October 1997 its stock market still suffered a 23% fall. To combat the speculation, the Hong Kong Monetary Authority purchased US$15 billion of shares in a variety of companies, becoming the largest holder in many. Two years later it started to unwind its positions by launching an index tracker fund, which resulted in a US$4 billion profit. In Singapore, the Singapore dollar depreciated by 20%, but there was no government intervention in the stock market and the Straits Times Index fell by 60%.

Prior to the Asian financial crisis, world economies were showing good growth and, in anticipation of the trend continuing, oil production and inventories had increased significantly. The fallout in Southeast Asia, coupled with a slowdown in Japanese GDP, caused a drop in demand for oil. Between October 1997 and March 1998, oil prices fell by 40% to around US$10 a barrel. Depressed oil prices were a contributing factor to the 1998 Russian financial crisis, where the rouble lost two thirds of its value against the US dollar and inflation reached 84%.

Despite the global problems, the UK stock market performed relatively well. In the unit trust's year to 15 November 1997, the FTSE 100 was up 19.8%, but the FT Smaller Companies Index advanced by just 5.6%. The Opportunities Fund outperformed both and, over the 12-month period, was up 20.9%, with a middle price of 216.03p for the units. The number of holdings had increased to 76 and 9% of the value was invested in companies having a market capitalisation of over £500 million, with 60% in companies being worth less than £100 million. The five largest holdings accounted for 15% of the value and some valuable lessons can be learned by looking at these companies.

Unusually, the largest holding accounted for nearly 5% of the portfolio valuation, but the shares were held for less than six months. It was in Topps Tiles, which came to the stock market in June 1997 at a price of 100p. In the past I had held shares in Marley which, despite the Marley Tile brand, had proved a disappointing investment. Topps Tiles, being a specialist retailer rather than a manufacturer, was a completely different type of business. Even so, the shares came onto the market at a ridiculously low rating of just five time's prospective earnings and sporting an indicated yield of 8%. I was able acquire a full allocation, which amounted to 1.5% of the fund, and the share price performed very well. I sold the holding at an average price of around 380p. Had I sat tight I could have more than doubled my money again – or, as it happened, nearly lost the lot.

Topps Tiles competes against the likes of B&Q and Homebase. It was formed in 1963 and now operates from more than 340 stores averaging 5,000 square feet situated on main roads or trade parks close to DIY outlets. Over the years it has captured more than 30% of the tile market. Part of this success might have been down to pricing, but the main growth drivers have been choice and stock availability. Nearly half of its sales are made to trade buyers, but its employees have been trained to give advice to the DIY amateur.

In the company's first five years on the stock market its pre-tax profits increased from £4.1 million to £11.5 million and reached a peak of £39.2 million in the year to 1 October 2005. Then the wheels fell off. At that time, its balance sheet had net cash of £21.8 million and shareholder funds of £52.2 million, but the decision was made to "make the balance sheet more efficient" by returning £122 million to shareholders through a special dividend. After the payment, made in August 2006, the company had net borrowings of £99.5 million and negative shareholder funds of £63.6 million. Topps Tiles is a classic example of the destruction of shareholder value through financial engineering. Between 2006 and 2009, pre-tax profits before exceptional items fell from £39 million to £16.3 million. Debt had been reduced to £72 million, but shareholder funds were still negative at £53 million. Confidence was not helped when the directors passed its dividend and the share price collapsed to a low of 15p. The company has fortunately survived and shareholder funds at the September 2015 year-end had moved back into positive territory, while net borrowings stood at £30.5 million. The dividend was increased to 2.25p per share – still well below the peak payment of 10.7p paid in 2007.

The second-largest holding in the fund was now BTG, the share price of which had increased by 50% since the date of purchase. The shares proved to be a very profitable investment over the years; I bought and sold them on several occasions before finally disposing of a residual holding in 2010 at 208p. As in the case of Topps Tiles, it would have been better to have kept the holding as the share price has more than trebled since then. However, the company is now worth more than £2 billion and it would have been difficult to justify retaining the shares under the investment criteria of the Opportunities Fund – it can neither be described as a recovery situation nor as a company in an out-of-favour market sector.

BTG was formed in 1981 as the British Technology Group, containing the merged interests of the National Research Development Corporation and the National Enterprise Board. The former had been established in 1948 by the Labour government under Clement Attlee with the idea of developing products based on technological advances made in the Second World War. It would patent these and license them to companies in return for royalty payments. Its most famous innovation was the hovercraft; other BTG products were associated with the semi-conductor, carbon fibres and composite materials. The National Enterprise Board was created by the Wilson government in 1975 with a view to providing funds for the development of smaller companies. British Technology Group became a limited company in 1991 and, one year later, was sold to its management by the government. Its shares were floated on the stock market in 1995. It subsequently divested its non-medical interests to become a leading company in the healthcare market. Growth has been achieved organically and by acquisition and it has developed its own products as well as receiving substantial royalty revenue.

The third-largest holding of the Opportunities Fund at this time, at 2.7%, was in Framlington Income & Capital Trust, purchased as New Throgmorton Trust. This was a split-capital investment trust where all of the income would go to the income shares, which would be redeemed at par, and the capital growth would be attributed to the capital shares, on which there would be no dividend. Further gearing was provided by a 12% debenture stock repayable in 2008, plus a bank overdraft. The Cavendish Opportunities Fund held the capital shares, which were sold within 18 months of purchase, having doubled in price. I have to thank my Norris Oakley experience for finding this little gem.

Fourth in size was an AIM share called Sibir Energy, which accounted for 2.2% of the fund. This was to become a story of scandal, dishonesty and corruption and would tarnish the reputation of AIM. It was founded in 1996 and was floated on AIM the following year. Through corporate acquisitions and several complicated deals, Sibir became a fully integrated oil company based in Russia with production and exploration assets in Siberia, plus an interest in the Moscow refinery and retail petrol stations. Corporate governance issues arose ten years later when the company announced that it was to acquire a portfolio of hotels and land projects from its largest shareholder. These were to include the Irkutsk Tea Factory development and the ill-fated Russian Tower Moscow scheme, which was intended to become Europe's tallest building. Press reports suggested that the shareholder had pledged his Sibir shares against these property ventures and the banks were seeking margin calls following repercussions of the credit crunch. It was reported that Sibir had advanced US$115 million, but was in fact owed US$325 million. In the event, the CEO was suspended and the transaction abandoned.

When I originally purchased the holding, Sibir had been able to acquire its oil and gas assets at an attractive valuation. As we have seen, the Russian economy was in turmoil and oil prices were around US$10 per barrel. The stock market valuation of Sibir suggested that the oil reserves were in the books at a value of around two US cents a barrel. So despite the political risks, I invested 1% of the portfolio in the shares at an average price which was to double in value in a short space of time. At one stage Sibir was one of the largest companies listed on AIM, but the property scandal caused the share price to fall to 133.5p. However, fortunately for shareholders, six months later the company was acquired by Gazprom Neft at a price of 500p per share, which valued the company at £1.9 billion.

The fifth-largest holding in the fund, at just over 2% of the portfolio, was in Perry Group, which was established in 1908 as a motor distributor. It was a London-based Ford main dealer which I had followed since it obtained its stock exchange listing in 1972. A separate subsidiary was formed in 1993 to deal exclusively in accident repairs. The motor division was sold to the management team in 2001 and the company changed its name to Nationwide Accident Repair Services Ltd. It was acquired by venture capitalists the following year and came back to the market in 2006 through a listing on AIM. I had sold the bulk of the holding prior to the takeover which, being at a sizeable discount to the underlying net asset value, was made on unattractive terms. When compared to my other large holdings, Perry Group can best be described as a mediocre investment. Not quite a doggy stock, but I do remember, many years ago, being chased by an Alsatian when doing a survey of the spare land behind one of the company's workshops!

Again the portfolio was dominated by companies that were to be taken over. These included Marley, Chloride, Alvis, ML Holdings, Vosper, Wellman, Aspen Communications, Perry, Lopex and Bilton, which we have already mentioned. The others were as follows:

SECTOR	CORPORATE DEAL
Oil	Pentex Energy – acquired by Sibir in April 1998
Building and construction	McAlpine – acquired by Carillion in February 2008
	Wilson Connolly – acquired by Taylor Woodrow in October 2003
Building materials	Breedon – acquired by Ennstone in June 2000
Chemicals	Holiday Chemical – acquired by Yule Catto in February 1998
Industrial	Cookson – acquired by Vesuvius in December 2012
	Wardle Storeys – acquired by Edlaw in January 2000
Electronics	Racal – acquired by Thomson-CSF in June 2000
	TLG – acquired by Wassall in October 1998
Engineering	David Brown – acquired by Textron in February 1999
	J Dickie – acquired by Eliza Tinsley in September 1998
	Vickers – acquired by Rolls-Royce in November 1999
Paper and packaging	Porter Chadburn – acquired by Mail-Well in April 1999
	Wyndham Press – acquired by Daybreak in May 2006
Textiles	Claremont – acquired by Courtaulds Textiles in October 1998
	Courtaulds Textiles – acquired by Sara Lee in May 2000
Beverages	Matthew Clark – acquired by Canandaigua in December 1998
	Merrydown – acquired by SHS in May 2005
Food producers	Cavaghan & Grey – acquired by Convenience Foods in March 1998
	Perkins Foods – acquired by Lowcloss in February 2001
Household	Jeyes – acquired by IWP in June 1998
	Stoves – acquired by Precis in January 2001
Pharmaceuticals	ML Laboratories – acquired by Vectura in January 2007
Hotels	Queens Moat – acquired by Britannia in March 2002

Media	Adscene – acquired by Denitz Media in October 1999
	Capital Radio – acquired by Global Radio in June 2008
	Maiden – acquired by Titan Outdoor in April 2006
	Southnews – acquired by Trinity Mirror in November 2000
Food retailers	Brake Brothers – acquired by CDR in July 2002
	Budgens – acquired by Musgrave in July 2002
Retailers	Oasis – acquired by Sierra in August 2001
	Wyevale – acquired by West Coast Capital in June 2006
Breweries	Gibbs Mew – acquired by Enterprise Inns in March 1998
	Inn Business – acquired by Punch in September 1999
Support services	Sanderson – acquired by Sonarsend in January 2000
Fund managers	Edinburgh Fund Managers – acquired by Aberdeen Asset Management in October 2003
Property	Bilton – acquired by Slough Estates in November 1998
	Milner Estates – acquired by Delancey Estates in October 1999

Of the remaining holdings, ten were eventually to go into receivership. Bizarrely, none of these were 'blue-sky' loss-making companies but were in traditional industries. I lost money on just two of these, having sold the other holdings long before they experienced financial difficulties. However, a lesson to learn is that a spread of interests in a portfolio can protect against the odd mishap. A later chapter is devoted to some of the more notable blow-ups.

10

Dotcom and Millennium Bug

The National Association of Securities Dealers Automated Quotations, the world's first electronic stock market, was launched in 1971. Its name is a huge mouthful, so it is not surprising that it became known as NASDAQ. Initially it was purely a quotation system, providing information on the bid and offer spread of certain US securities. When the stock market crashed in October 1987, it was difficult to reach some market makers over the telephone. To solve the problem, the Small-Order Execution System was established. This made it possible to input orders electronically and to have an automatic update on the number of trades and volumes. It is still the largest electronic stock exchange, with shares in more than 3,000 companies traded. In terms of market size, NASDAQ is the second-largest in the world, behind the New York Stock Exchange.

Shares traded on the NASDAQ Exchange tend to be technology companies (though not exclusively so), and the NASDAQ Composite index is generally accepted as a proxy for this area of the stock market. Apple, Google, Amazon and Microsoft feature amongst the most substantial companies listed on the NASDAQ Exchange. Back in 1997 the internet was growing at a significant rate and investors were carried away with the enthusiasm of any company with a name suffixed by *.com*. The NASDAQ Composite stood at 1583.51 at the close of business on 14 November 1997 (the

Opportunities Fund's year-end) and peaked at 5048.6 on 10 March 2000. Investment fundamentals had long been forgotten by that point and investors were chasing the pot of gold at the end of the rainbow. Some companies eventually met expectations, but many more failed in a spectacular fashion.

In the United Kingdom, investors were also to experience a dotcom boom. The most spectacular movements were seen in shares quoted on AIM. The share prices of many technology and biotech companies experienced sharp rises and valuations became unrealistic. On 14 November 1997, the FTSE AIM All-Share Index had closed at 985.7. It reached an all-time high of 2924.9 on 3 March 2000. A more representative index, known as the techMARK Index, was formed in January 1996 and was designed to reflect the performance of shares in the technology sectors of the UK stock market. It increased from 1026.38 at the close of business on 14 November 1997 to a peak of 3387.37 on 10 March 2000. During this rise, the phrase "it is different this time" was widely heard. Analysts were justifying values by looking at earnings estimates two or more years into the future. If a price–earnings ratio was too high they would talk about the price–earnings growth (PEG) of a company share. All of this was pretty frothy stuff.

A major potential problem facing the technology industry was the Millennium Bug which, in theory, would cause computers to malfunction when reaching the year 2000. The fear was based on the premise that many computer programmers used only the last two digits to signify a year as a shortcut. Thus, 1997 was denoted as 97, but 00 might then be recognised as 1900 rather than 2000. The other two problems were the possibility of reverting to zero once 2000 was reached and some programmes not recognising 2000 as a leap year. Corrective action was taken by many organisations by upgrading their computer systems but, in the event, casualties were minor and there were few incidents. However, the considerable publicity did bring technology to the public and investors' attention.

As mentioned, the dotcom bubble burst on Friday 10 March 2000 and the next two years were painful for those investors who had speculated in this area of the stock market. The NASDAQ Composite fell from its 5048.6 high to a low of 1114.1 on 9 October 2002, whilst the FTSE AIM All-Share fell from its peak of 2924.9 to 588.6, reaching its low on the same day as the NASDAQ. During the period, the decline accelerated following the terrorist attack on the World Trade Center on 11 September 2001, which led to trading being suspended for four sessions on the New York Stock Exchange. It has been reported that more than half of all US dotcom companies did not survive beyond 2004. There certainly were some spectacular failures. Shares linked to the 'old' economy also saw some volatility over the dotcom period. The FTSE 100 increased from 4741.8 on 14 November 1997 to reach its high of 6930.2 on 31 December 1999, only to fall back to 4091.6 by the Opportunities Fund's 15 November 2002 year-end.

The difference between the UK and US experience in the dotcom era was that there were fewer dotcom companies in the UK stock market and these were much smaller in size. Instead, investors were driven towards technology, media and telecom companies (which became known as TMT), a section of the market fashionably referred to as the 'new' economy. Having lived through the Australian mining and UK property booms, I had decided to have little exposure to the type of company where valuations seemed stretched. In fact, Vodafone was valued at some £240 billion by the stock market and was selling at 50× earnings. In the early days, this was a growth company, but due to increased competition it quickly became more of a utility company. After selling its interest in Verizon for £84 million and distributing shares and cash, the stock market value is today a little over £50 billion.

A company called Baltimore Technologies was the UK equivalent to the Australian mining company Poseidon. It was an Irish-based internet security software company which, at its peak, had 1,400 employees. In the year to 31 December 1999, the company reported a substantial rise in revenues to £74.2 million from £23.3 million the previous year, but this was at a huge cost. During the year, the company had expanded its global presence from 22 to 38 cities and the number of employees had increased from 480 to 1,185. Consequently, a loss of £25.4 million was reported, but this was ignored by investors and the company entered the FTSE 100 with a market value of £7 billion. From then on, it was in a downward spiral. The company was forced into several restructuring moves and the share price fell from 1375p in March 2000 to 17.5p in July of the following year. By 2003, it was a cash shell, with assets of around £20 million. I might have missed out on this type of spectacular share price movement, but at least I slept well at nights and had little exposure to the bubble when it burst.

The other high-profile casualty was Bookham Technologies, which had been founded in 1988. It became the first company to manufacture optical components for integration into silicon-integrated circuits and also technology to increase the speed of computer networks and the internet. The shares came to the stock market in April 2000 at a share price of £10. Investor enthusiasm pushed the price to a high of £53 by August 2000, which valued the company at £6 billion. This led the shares to be included in the FTSE 100 for a short while, but the share price then collapsed. By the end of the year, it was below the £10 issue price. To make matters worse, by the middle of the following year the company was forecasting a 50% decline in sales and the share price fell to 210p. In 2002, Bookham acquired the optical components businesses of Marconi and Nortel Networks and in the next four years made four further significant acquisitions, one of which cost £118 million. It delisted from the London Stock Market in 2004 and changed its name to Oclaro following a merger with Avanex, a US company which had purchased the optronics business of Alcatel and the photonic business of Corning. Oclaro Inc has a NASDAQ quote which today values the company at less than US$250 million. Back in 2000, Dr Andrew Rickman, the founder of Bookham, sold 1.2 million shares (about 1% of the share capital) to raise £40 million!

By far the biggest UK casualty of the dotcom bubble was a once well-regarded company which had been in existence since 1886 and at one stage was valued at £35 billion. Like Topps Tiles, the company was a prime example value of destruction by financial engineering.

In the 12 months to September 2001 the share price was to fall from
£12.50 to less than 29p. Through a series of acquisitions the company
had built up a debt mountain of £4.4 billion and had made a loss
of approaching £100 million before goodwill write offs of nearly
£3.5 billion. In the past, it had made profits of just under £1 billion
and had £1.4 billion of cash supporting a market value of £10 billion.
By selling its defence business to BAE Systems, and acquiring a
number of telecommunication companies at inflated prices, it had
moved from being an old to a new economy company. Eventually,
the bulk of the trading assets were sold to Ericsson and the shares
were taken over in 2007 by a specialist pension fund manager that
was solely interested in the management of its £2.7 billion pension
fund. The company was renamed Marconi in December 1999 having
been known as General Electric Co or GEC. It is a classic example
of how the mighty can fall.

By the time of the Opportunities Fund's interim report on 15 May
2000, the portfolio was reduced to 62 holdings, of which only 15
were held in the 15 November 1997 portfolio. Over that time, the
mid-price of the Opportunities Fund units had increased by 65.4%
– as compared to a rise of 38.5% for the FTSE 100 which, at 6247.7,
was close to its high. The FTSE AIM All-Share had fallen from
a peak of 2924.9 on 3 March 2000 to 1750.5 by 15 May 2000 but
had still advanced by 77.6% since 15 November 1997. Despite its
outperformance, I was nervous about investing in shares listed on
AIM; the fund only held four such shares, representing 3.4% of the
portfolio. I had tended to run my winners and had three holdings
which accounted for more than 3% of the portfolio.

The largest holding, ML Laboratories, had grown to 6.6% of
the portfolio but was reduced to a little over 1.5% in the next six
months. The company was concerned with the development and
commercialisation of medical products and devices. At the time,
it had launched in the UK and had trials elsewhere for a product
called Adept, which was a solution delivered via laparoscopy to
stop adhesions after abdominal surgery. A product called Extraneal,

for use in peritoneal dialysis, was being sold in 27 countries by the American company Baxter Healthcare and had captured one third of its European dialysis patients. In addition, European approvals had been received for Clickhaler, a dry powder delivery device for respiratory drugs. Several products, covering cancer treatment and management, AIDS treatment and prevention, were under development and in clinical trials.

Unfortunately, as with many companies in the biotech/drug delivery area of the market, ML Laboratories was losing money due to the high costs associated with developing its products. Regulatory approval was a costly process that could take much longer than expected. In the dotcom boom, investors were happy to back companies with innovative ideas and many drug development companies were relying on the stock market as a source of finance. As with Baltimore Technologies, a potentially very profitable company was undone by over-optimistic and unsustainable expansion plans. Eventually, I sold the rump of my holding in 2005 at a small loss.

My second-largest holding was in the employment agency firm, Reed Executive, which represented 3.9% of the portfolio and had more than doubled in value since the shares had been acquired in 1998. The company hived off its specialist healthcare recruitment company, Read Health, to shareholders through a demerger in July 2001, but the Reed family eventually reacquired both operations through successful takeover bids. In the meantime, I had sold both of these holdings at reasonable prices.

Town Centre Securities was the third-largest holding, making up 3.2% of the portfolio. This was a property company with interests in the provinces, of which the most significant was the Merrion Shopping Centre in Leeds. It is a company which I knew from my Norris Oakley days and I was able to pick up the shares at less than half the underlying asset value. The share price had already risen substantially since my original purchase in 1998, but I sold the holding later in the year when it had appreciated in value by a further 20%.

The 15 May 2000 portfolio still contained Wilson Connelly, Alvis, Perkins Foods, Jeyes, Stoves, Merrydown, Brake Bros, ML Laboratories, Perry, Oasis and Sibir – all of which, as mentioned earlier, would one day be taken over. There were 16 newcomers to the portfolio that would meet the same fate:

SECTOR	CORPORATE DEAL
Building and construction	Prowting – acquired by Westbury in June 2002
Aerospace	McKechnie – acquired by BlueAzure in October 2000
Electronic	Dowding & Mills – acquired by Rydenor January 2006 Linx Printing – acquired by Linx Acquisitions in January 2005
Engineering	Lincat – acquired by Middleby in May 2011 Wellington – acquired by Fenner in May 2005
Automotive	Britax – acquired by Seton House in August 2001
Household	Optoplast – acquired by Optoplast plc in June 2002 Pifco – acquired by Salton in June 2001
Food producers	Hazlewood Foods – acquired by Greencore in January 2001
Health	Biocompatibles – acquired by BTG in 2011
Distributors	Action Computer Supplies – acquired by Insight in October 2001
Leisure	Clubhaus – acquired by Park Lane Acquisitions in May 2004
Media	Teamtalk – acquired by UK Betting in July 2002
Support services	Reed Executive – acquired by James Reed Partners in May 2003
Transport	ABP – acquired by Admiral Acquisition in August 2006 P&O – acquired by Thunder FZE in March 2006

Seven of the companies acquired since November 1997 were to ultimately go into liquidation.

The fall in stock markets between 2000 and 2003 can be partly attributed to a recession that started in the European Union, where the euro had been introduced on 1 January 1999. Following its inauguration, the euro fell sharply, but recovered to reach parity with the US dollar in July 2002. France and Germany entered into a recession which lasted for about six months and officially ended in May 2002. The US economy also showed signs of recession after being rocked by the Enron scandal, which came to light in October 2001 just after the US stock market had recovered its poise in the wake of the 9/11 attacks on the Twin Towers.

Enron was an energy trading company formed in 1985 through the merger of Houston Natural Gas and InterNorth. It grew to become the seventh-largest US quoted company but had achieved this by falsifying its records to show US$63.4 billion of assets; it was America's biggest audit failure at the time. The company auditor, Arthur Anderson, had its audit licence voided after being found guilty of destroying documents relevant to the US Securities and Exchange Commission (SEC) investigation. In all, 16 people pleaded guilty of crimes committed at Enron and five outsiders were found guilty. Kenneth Lay, the chairman, was found guilty of six charges of fraud, which could have resulted in a maximum of 45 years in jail, but he died before being sentenced. Jeffrey Skilling was convicted of 19 counts of fraud and faced more than 24 years imprisonment, reduced by ten years in 2013. Rick Causey, the chief accounting officer, was sentenced to seven years in prison after eventually pleading guilty and the chief financial officer, Andrew Fastow, was sentenced to ten years after pleading guilty and testifying against the others.

Essentially, the company traded oil and gas at market prices. It adopted the procedure of recognising trade sizes rather than profit as revenue. Between 1996 and 2000, in a market that was growing annually at no more than 3%, Enron reported revenues rising from

US$13.3 billion to US$100.8 billion. For the first nine months of 2001, the figure increased to US$138.7 billion which moved it into sixth position in the Fortune Global 500. Profits on long-term contracts were being estimated and recognised at the start, rather than over the life of the contract. Special purpose companies were formed with outside investors in order to disguise debt, hide losses and purchase Enron assets and shares. These were shown as investments rather than being consolidated into the Enron accounts. There were also derivative contracts where profits were recognised at an early stage and yet actual losses would eventually be made. These and other fraudulent accounting practices led to the company being declared bankrupt with US$23 billion of liabilities at the end of November 2001.

Incredibly, the Enron scandal was eclipsed by an even larger financial fraud. It involved WorldCom, America's second-largest long-distance telecoms carrier. From the year 2000 to its bankruptcy in June 2002, the company reported profits of more than US$10 billion, but had actually incurred an overall loss of US$73.7 billion after including a US$47 billion write-down of impaired assets. It had logged US$107 billion of assets with more than US$40 billion of debt, and had improperly accounted for US$3.8 billion of expenses in 27 countries. From a trading angle, the company experienced falling prices in an industry suffering from overcapacity.

The CEO, Bernie Ebbers, had built the company – which at one stage had a stock market valuation of over US$100 billion – by making a number of large acquisitions. He had borrowed more than US$480 million, secured against his shares in the company, and would have been liable to make payments to cover the margin if the share price declined. In order to disguise the losses, there were a number of accounting misstatements and Bernie Ebbers was found guilty and sentenced to 25 years in prison for US$11 billion of accounting frauds. As in the case of Enron, the chief financial officer received a lesser sentence of five years by pleading guilty and giving evidence for the prosecution. Maybe it is better to be in the engine room rather than steering the ship! It was hoped that, because of its stricter accounting standards, the UK stock market might decouple from the US stock market – but this was not to be the case.

Between 15 May 2000 and 15 November 2002, the Cavendish Opportunities Fund fell by 27.8% – albeit outperforming the FTSE 100, which fell 34.5%, and the FTSE Small Cap, which was down 42.2%. It was a period when I was able to purchase shares at attractive levels in order to position the fund for the eventual stock market recovery. The portfolio now contained 68 holdings, including six listed on AIM and 40 new holdings.

The largest holding was in MS International, now the only share to be held continuously in the portfolio since 1995. The company manufactures forklift truck arms, petrol station canopies and defence equipment such as navigation tables and gun turrets for the Royal Navy. On 15 November 2002 the holding had grown to become 4.1% of the portfolio valuation compared to 1.4% on 15 May 2000 and was the only holding greater than 3% in the portfolio. I had not added to the holding during the period.

I did not realise before writing this book how many of the companies I have bought have been taken over. More than half of the holdings purchased in the period were eventually acquired.

SECTOR	CORPORATE DEAL
Oil and gas	Dana Petroleum – acquired by Korea National Oil Corporation in September 2010
Building and construction	Baggeridge Brick – acquired by Wienerberger in June 2007

McCarthy & Stone – acquired by Mother Bidco in October 2006 |
| Electronic | Alba – acquired by Geeya Technology in December 2012 |
| Engineering | Lincat – acquired by Middleby in May 2011 |
| Healthcare | Celsis – acquired by Nastor Investments in September 2009

Ferraris – acquired by NAV Bidco in January 2008 |

	Reed Health – acquired by James Reed in December 2005
Pharmaceuticals	Axis-Shield – acquired by Alere in October 2011
	BioFocus – acquired by Galapagos in October 2005
	Cobra – acquired by Recipharm in February 2010
	Goldshield – acquired by Midas Bidco in December 2009
	PowderJect– acquired by Chiron Corporation in July 2003
Retail	Austin Reed – acquired by Darius Capital in December 2006
	Jacques Vert – acquired by Minerva Bidco in December 2011
	Monsoon – acquired by Drillgreat in December 2007
Media	Wyndham Press – acquired by Daybreak Acquisitions in May 2006
Transport	Salvesen – acquired by Norbert Dentressangle in May 2006
Software	Kewill – acquired by Kinetic Bidco in July 2012
	MMT – acquired by Microgen in November 2003
	nCipher – acquired by Thales in October 2008
	NMT – acquired by Volvere in November 2006
	Yeoman – acquired by Trafficmaster in April 2004

Inevitably there were some companies which fared less well – three of the new holdings eventually went into receivership. The market was to fall further before recovering but I felt that the portfolio was well placed to face the future. In a similar way to other bear markets, it was a great opportunity to acquire shares that looked substantially undervalued.

II

Lose Some, Win Some

Between April 2000 and autumn 2001, Boots switched its entire £2.3 billion pension fund scheme into long-dated bonds. Previously, 75% had been invested in equities and the remainder in short-dated bonds. To help guard against erosion of the capital value by inflation, 25% was invested in index-linked bonds; eventually this was raised to 50%. It was a dangerous precedent to set but occurred at a reasonably high level of the stock market. The subsequent fall in interest rates made the move palatable. There was a knock-on effect when the dotcom bubble burst. The fall in the stock market caused solvency margins to come under pressure. At the beginning of 2003, the FTSE 100 had almost halved from its 31 December 1999 peak and several pension funds were, on paper, unable to match their liabilities. Consequently, actuarial calculations forced a number of other large pension funds to reduce their equity exposure at the bottom of the market.

The stock market having declined virtually throughout the whole of 2002 was set to fall further in the early months of the new year. There was uncertainty about the situation in Iraq; the FTSE 100 reached its low of 3287.04 on 12 March 2003, just 12 days before Western forces invaded that country. In the next four years, the FTSE 100 would recover to reach 6376.49 on 19 May 2008. It would be an interesting period during which a number of major companies would disappear from the stock market. Due to their size, I did not have holdings in these firms – but I think it is worth recording such notable FTSE 100 companies dropping out of the index.

In 1820, a lecturer named Goldsworth Gurney discovered that by introducing a jet of oxygen and hydrogen into a flame and adding a small amount of limestone, a blinding white light would result. This technique was developed by others for use as theatre lighting – hence the term 'limelight'. The technology was first used in Covent Garden in 1837 and came into general use by 1860. (It was replaced by electric lighting at the end of the century.) A company was formed in 1886 to manufacture oxygen for this usage – and in 1903 a major new market in oxyacetylene welding also emerged. The two world wars created significant demand for oxygen for use in the steel-making process. The company grew through acquisition and diversification, becoming a member of the FTSE 100 and a constituent of the FT 30 (a now little-used index designed to capture the essence of British firms). It was known as British Oxygen until 1978 when it was renamed BOC Group plc. It was acquired by the German company Linde in 2006. At the time, BOC was the world's second-largest supplier of industrial gases and the cash takeover valued the company at £8.2 billion.

ICI, an original constituent of the FT 30, was arguably a more widely known company. It, too, would vanish from the stock market in this period. It was formed in 1926 through the merger of four companies that produced chemicals, explosives, fertilisers, insecticides, dyes, non-ferrous metals and paints. It later established a pharmaceutical business, which was transferred into a separate company called Zeneca Group. Eventually, this latter firm merged with Astra AB to become AstraZeneca, a FTSE 100 company. Having already divested many of its other businesses, the decision was made by ICI in 1997 to move away from commodity chemicals and in that year it acquired Unilever's speciality chemicals business for US$8 billion. This left ICI with borrowings of £4 billion. It sold most of its other businesses to eliminate the debt and was left with its main operation being Dulux paint. Its pension fund was a legacy issue: it had £9 billion of liabilities. Despite this, ICI was acquired in 2007 by AkzoNobel NV in a takeover worth £8 billion. It was a sad end to a company which at one stage had been the country's largest manufacturer and considered the bellwether for British industry. AstraZeneca was to fare much better – it now has a market value in excess of £60 billion.

Another company linked to the pharmaceutical industry was Boots. Its origin can be traced back to 1849 when John Boot, an agricultural worker, opened a store in Nottingham selling herbal products. His younger son, Jesse, was responsible for opening more stores in Nottingham and establishing branches in Lincoln and Sheffield. He also sold proprietary medicines and household goods at very competitive prices. His ambition was to create a nationwide chain. Ten stores had grown to 500 between 1890 and the start of the First World War. He was to retire in 1920 and sold the company to United Drug Company of America. In 1933, a consortium, led by Jesse's son John, bought back Boots from the American company. By that time, it had expanded the network to 1,000 branches and had acquired the Timothy Whites and Taylor chain of 622 shops in 1968. Around the same period, diversification into drug manufacture and research was taking place. The company developed the painkiller Ibuprofen and the Nurofen brand, which was sold to Reckitt Benckiser in 2006. An unusual acquisition in 1991, to be sold in 2002, was Halfords, the bicycle and car parts business. Boots merged with Alliance UniChem in 2006 and, in the following year, became the first FTSE 100 company to be acquired by private equity in a £11.1 billion takeover.

A company which has incorporated the Spanish and Portuguese colours in its flag started trading between those countries and London in 1835. It was incorporated in 1840 by Royal Charter under the name Peninsular and Oriental Steam Navigation Company and is now known as P&O. At the beginning of the 20th century it had built up a business based upon contracts for the delivery of mail and was fast becoming a commercial shipping and passenger line operator. By 1926, through corporate acquisitions and ship purchases, its fleet had hit a peak of nearly 500 ships. P&O had lost 85 vessels in the First World War and a total of 179 would be sunk in the Second World War. Activities were broadened, through further acquisitions, to cover dry cargo vessels, tankers, cruise liners and ferries. Perhaps the best-known purchase was the European Ferry Group trading as Townsend Thoresen. A diversification into property investment and development commenced in 1974 under the name Bovis, but these interests were exited in 1999. A year later, the cruise line was spun out, and became Carnival Corporation in 2003, after merging with the company of that name. In 2006, P&O was acquired for £3.5 billion by a company owned by the Dubai government. This marked the end of a constituent of the FT 30 since 1947.

Pilkington was another household name that vanished from the stock market during this period. The company was founded in 1826 and by 1860 had nine furnaces producing sheet glass. Ten years later, it started the manufacture of plate glass and, by 1903, was the sole UK producer. Increased capacity in Europe and the United States had led to significant competition from imported glass. Pilkington survived due to its wide range of products and its ability to drive manufacturing costs down through innovation. Over the 50 years it was able to establish manufacturing operations in the Americas, Australasia and Africa. By 1960, Pilkington had developed a float-glass process, whereby a ribbon of glass could be formed by floating the raw materials over a bath of molten tin – producing high-quality flat glass. It financed its operations by licensing this process, which also enabled the company to diversify into other glass-related products. Its shares were floated on the stock market in 1970. In the following years, the company produced several innovative products such as self-cleaning glass. The shares did not make the FT 30 but were included in the FTSE 100 at the time of its acquisition for £1.3 billion in 2006 by NSG Group, a smaller Japanese company.

Hanson plc was another member of the FT 30 and the FTSE 100 to be taken over in 2007. It took its name from Lord Hanson, who set up the company in 1964 with the idea of acquiring undervalued asset situations to be broken up and sold off at a profit. The concept was known as 'asset-stripping' and Hanson became the most successful exponent of this strategy. The company's acquisitions ranged from chemicals and stores to building materials. Its most successful purchase was Imperial Tobacco Group plc, which cost £2.5 billion in 1986. Subsequently, it divested Courage Brewery, Finlays, Imperial Hotels and the Ross Group for £2.3 billion. In 1996, Hanson divided itself into four separately quoted companies. Imperial Tobacco, renamed Imperial Brands, is today a FTSE 100 company with a stock market value approaching £40 billion. Millennium Inorganic Chemicals was to be taken over for US$1.3 billion and the Energy Group for £4.5 billion. Hanson was left with the building materials business and was purchased in 2008 by HeidelbergCement for £8 billion.

I have three daughters and around this time the two youngest were in their mid-teens. They had discovered make-up – to me, a horribly expensive consumer product, which dad had to pay for. An even worse expense was clothing. Spring, summer, autumn and winter seasonal necessities were intertwined with outfits for parties and holidays. Naturally they would not wear the same outfit twice and 14 bikinis were required for a two-week holiday. The latest and most expensive style of trainers, it goes without saying, was also a must. Shopping expeditions were a chore, with the girls wanting to visit as many of the most expensive clothes shops as possible. However, mean old dad had a great ploy of rationing the amount that they were allowed to spend in these upmarket outfitters – while allowing them to spend whatever they wanted in Primark, which sold decent clothing at affordable prices. At the time, they did not want their friends to know that they shopped there and consequently dad had to carry their Primark brown paper carrier bags. Due to the financial benefit, this was something that I was only too keen to do. Today, my girls are proud of the bargains they get with their own money – and happy to be seen with arms full of Primark bags.

Primark is a wholly owned subsidiary of Associated British Foods plc, the world's second-largest sugar producer. It also supplies other food ingredients, together with well-known grocery products including Mazola, Ovaltine, Ryvita and Twinings. Primark was originally based in Ireland and opened its first store in Dublin in 1969 trading under the name Penneys. Four years later, the first store was opened in the UK, but traded under the name Primark as the American company J C Penney owned the rights to the Penneys name. By the year 2000, the chain consisted of 100 stores, to which it added 40 acquired from Littlewoods in 2005. At the beginning of 2015, the chain covered 287 stores, with 164 in the UK, 40 in Spain, 37 in Ireland and the remainder elsewhere in Europe. Its range of fashionable clothing is made specifically for Primark and is sold at low-cost, affordable prices. It is of great credit that the company has created a product sought after by the younger generation. Due to the size of company, I did not invest in Associated British Foods – but used Primark as an exemplar when looking for investment opportunities in smaller companies in the retail sector.

Other companies that have been successful in transforming shopping habits have been discount retailers such as Aldi and Lidl (both family owned) – plus, more recently, the 'pound' shops. Again, taking my daughters as an example, they now deliberately use these outlets in search of bargains. Ten years ago, I was faced with such comments as: "Don't you dare embarrass me by going in those shops" or "You will only get me in there over my dead body". Today it is difficult to drag them away from these outlets.

Of course, the bargain store is not a new concept. In 1884, a Polish man named Michael Marks opened a Penny Bazaar in Leeds. Several other market stalls were subsequently added to the company in other parts of the country. Over the years, the company established a substantial chain of department stores and became the first UK retailer to breach the £1 million pre-tax profit level. In the year to 31 March 1998, pre-tax profits for Marks & Spencer peaked at £1.2 billion – then halved in the following year, as the share price declined from its high of 669p in October 1997 to below 175p in October 2000. Unlike Primark, the company has been unable to achieve strong growth and 15 years later pre-tax profits were only a little over £500 million. M&S is a constituent of both FT 30 and the FTSE 100. In May 2003, the share price was still languishing at around 280p when it received an unsolicited takeover offer at 400p per share. Had this been successful, Marks & Spencer would have been another iconic company to disappear from the stock exchange.

By 15 May 2008, the Opportunities Fund shares had reached 549.7p, which represented a rise of 122% from 15 November 2002. Over that period the FTSE 100 had advanced by 52.8% and the FTSE Smaller Company index by 74%. There were 69 holdings in the fund, of which 41 had been acquired over the five-and-a-half year period from 2002. The most noteworthy change had been in the oil and gas sector, which increased from 2.9% to just over 16% of the portfolio value. Otherwise, the MS International share price continued to perform well – the holding now represented 4.8% of the fund. There were two other significant sized holdings by virtue of their share price performance. One of these turned out to be a spectacularly good investment and the other a complete disaster. Fortunately, I reduced the latter before its share price imploded.

The successful investment can be attributed to my cat. I acquired it as a kitten in 2004 and booked an appointment, with the local vet, for it to be spayed. After enquiring when the cat should be returned to the surgery for the stitches to be removed, I was told that there was no need as the incision had been sealed by the use of superglue. Upon investigation, I discovered that a company called Advanced Medical Solutions (AMS) had launched a product in Europe called Liquiband, following regulatory approval. It consisted of a fast-setting adhesive and a liquid bandage painted over the wound to stop infection. The product could be used on large incisions such as a caesarean section or on small cuts such as a gash on an eyelid. There were a number of advantages to the product:

- the patient did not have to return to the hospital to have stitches removed

- there were no unsightly 'knitting needle' scars

- the problem of bacterial infection through the stitch holes was avoided

- it was easy to administer by a surgeon or a post-operative nurse

- it was quick to apply and inexpensive.

The core business of AMS was a product portfolio for wound care. Its key product was bandaging that included silver alginate, a wound dressing based on seaweed. AMS had a number of major companies as partners, including Johnson & Johnson, which rolled out its own-label advanced bandaging brand in the United States. At the time, the company was loss-making but the balance sheet contained net cash of £3.6 million. This was sufficient to see it through to profitability without any need of further funding. I bought a holding at an average price of just over 9p, which valued AMS at a mere £12 million. It was included in the May 2008 fund valuation at a price of 33p, representing 4.8% of the portfolio value. Today the company has reached a stock market value of more than £450 million.

The less happy experience was an investment in a company called International Ferro Metals Limited. It was founded in 2002 and raised £99 million through a listing on AIM in September 2005. Together with project finance of £79 million, it had sufficient funds to construct and operate a ferrochrome production facility capable of producing 267,000 tonnes per annum of charge chrome. Ferrochrome is an alloy of chromium and iron used in the production of stainless steel to protect against corrosion and produce a shiny appearance. The company mined chromite at Buffelsfontein, South Africa and in the next two years would construct two covered furnaces plus production facilities. Full production from the first furnace was achieved in 2007 and the company produced a respectable profit on the back of rising commodity prices the following year.

I did not subscribe for shares at the time of the original share placing at 35p, but bought a holding in 2006 at an average price of 28p after a colleague had visited the operations. At the beginning of the following year, I attended the annual Africa Mining Indaba conference in Cape Town and spent a day at the International Ferro Metals facility. The company's initial success led to it transferring from AIM to the main market in August 2007. By May 2008, its share price was close to its high at 159p and the holding accounted for 5.7% of the Opportunities Fund's portfolio value. I reduced my holding to more than cover the initial outlay – but then saw the balance quickly decline in value. The demise was partly due to a fall in the price of ferrochrome, but production problems, rising costs and competition from Chinese producers were also to blame. Unforeseen, the company failed to secure sales through what was described as a "guaranteed offtake agreement in Asia". Future management expansion plans seemed impossible to achieve. The share price fell to 2p, which valued the company at only £11 million. The shares were subsequently suspended and it is unlikely that shareholders will see any return on their investment. I had a separate holding in the Cavendish AIM Fund and felt obliged to sell when the company obtained its full listing. It was a fortunate decision as the shares had been purchased at an average price of 30p and sold at 135p.

It seems as though takeover activity is a bull market phenomena: more than 30 companies in which I had an investment were taken over between 2002 and 2008. The May 2008 portfolio contained holdings in Dana Petroleum, Chloride, Axis Shield, Goldshield and Jacques Vert – all of which were still to be acquired by predators. The following new holdings were also in companies that would suffer the same fate:

SECTOR	CORPORATE DEAL
Aerospace	Umeco – acquired by Cytec in July 2012
Telecoms	Spectrum Interactive – acquired by Arqiva Broadcast in July 2012
Media	Taylor Nelson Sofres – acquired by WPP in November 2008
Oil and gas	Nautical Petroleum – acquired by Capricorn Energy in August 2012 Venture Production – acquired by Centrica in August 2009
Software	Morse – acquired by 2e2 in June 2010
Technology	Trafficmaster – acquired by Vector Capital in July 2010

On examination, the portfolio consisted almost entirely of shares in smaller companies. It had also changed considerably over the years – only seven holdings remained since 15 May 2000 when the FTSE 100 had last been at a similar level.

Apart from the many takeovers, a major feature of this bull market was the popularity of AIM as a means for smaller companies to raise money. A large number of shares quoted on AIM appeared on my radar screen. Potentially, this posed a number of problems for me, the foremost being that I did not want the Opportunities Fund to be swamped with AIM-listed shares, nor did I wish to substantially increase the number of holdings in the fund. The solution was to start a fund dedicated to AIM shares. Thus, 5 October 2005 marked the birth of the Cavendish AIM Fund. On that day the FTSE AIM All-Share was 1086.2, but by the time of the first report on 15 November 2005 had fallen by 8.6% to 992.7. It seemed an excellent time to invest and, by the year-end, 62% of the portfolio was invested between 46 different AIM shares – with only eight already held in the Opportunities Fund portfolio. The net asset value of the AIM fund, launched at a price of 100p, had increased to 100.55p.

Between the 5 October 2005 launch date and the 15 May 2008, the FTSE AIM All-Share index fell by 5.8% – a truly poor performance when compared to rises of 2.8 % in the FTSE Smaller Company index and 15.2% in the FTSE 100. The Cavendish AIM Fund asset value had declined by 1.8% over this period and the portfolio contained 71 holdings, of which nine were also held in the Opportunities Fund. The greatest exposure was to the oil and gas sector, which accounted for nearly 7.2% of the portfolio value – mining was just 2.8%.

Several interesting stories would emerge on AIM-listed shares I held, but these will be left to a later chapter. In the meantime, I was holding shares in a large number of smaller companies at a point where the stock market was at a relatively high level – and about to crash.

12

"Whoops"

Here comes the crash which beats all bar the 73% collapse of the
FT 30 in 1973. Between May 2008 and March 2009 the FTSE
100 fell by nearly 44%, the FTSE Smaller Companies index virtually
halved and the AIM index declined by more than 63%. On 9 March
2009 the Cavendish Opportunities Fund share price was 259.3p and
the Cavendish AIM Fund shares were priced at 52.45p – both down
by nearly 50%.

Perhaps the only small consolation to shareholders in the funds
I managed was that I was in the same boat as them: the bulk of my
own personal monies were invested between the two. It was like
being the captain of the Titanic, though thankfully only a few of my
investors jumped overboard while the band kept playing.

The FTSE 100 had almost halved since its peak on 31 December
1999 and the Opportunities Fund shares were down by 23.7% over
that period. The AIM index was looking very sick at a level of 373.8.
Nevertheless, low share prices suggested a bright new beginning was
possible if you could find the right bargains.

The global financial crisis gave rise to the 2008–2012 global
recession. In the United States, the problem stemmed from
irresponsible lending in the house market boom, which peaked
in 2004. Credit was readily available and financial lenders were
advancing loans on highly competitive but less-than-commercial

terms. Often loans would be made at above-average rates of interest to those with low credit ratings, where there was a high risk of a default on repayment. To make matters worse, and to create demand, the loans often carried a low rate of interest in the early years before reverting to the market rate. These risky financial instruments were known as subprime mortgages and were secured on property assets. To create an investment which offered an above-average income return, a number of subprime loans were then bundled together to create an instrument known as a mortgage-backed security.

All was well – until house prices began to fall. In some cases borrowers defaulted on their repayments because of divorce, loss of job, illness or inability to service the loans. In others, when house prices fell, the value of the loan exceeded that of the property, leaving little incentive for some to keep up repayments. It became clear that mortgage-backed securities were no longer covered by underlying assets. They were assigned junk bond status. The problem was huge: two US quoted companies, Fannie Mae and Freddie Mac, were estimated to hold 13 million substandard loans amounting to US$2 trillion. Between 2006 and 2008, US house prices fell by about 20% and over 9% of all mortgages were in default or subject to foreclosure proceedings. Banks had taken on huge amounts of debt in order to acquire mortgage-backed securities and other complicated financial instruments that were fast losing their value.

The greatest casualty would be Lehman Brothers, which became the largest bankruptcy in American history. This investment bank had taken on a significant level of borrowing to invest in housing-related assets – so that a 5% downward movement in that market would more than knock out its asset value. Warning signs were seen as early as August 2007 when the company closed its subprime lender. However, Lehman still held large positions in subprime mortgages and, one year later, reported substantial losses. There were reports that the Korea Development Bank had sought to buy the company and that Bank of America and Barclays Bank might become involved in a rescue attempt. Nothing came of this. Lehman filed for bankruptcy on 15 September 2008. Bear Stearns, having already experienced financial difficulties, had been acquired on the cheap by J.P. Morgan earlier that year. Merrill Lynch, another well-known name, was taken over at the beginning of 2009 at a knockdown price by Goldman Sachs. Morgan Stanley required government support. Fannie Mae and Freddie Mac needed to be nursed back to health. All of these were substantial companies in US financial circles.

Another company caught up in the subprime situation was American International Group Inc., better known as AIG. It was founded in China in 1919 and listed on the New York Stock Exchange in 1984. Through acquisitions and corporate deals, the company became a multinational insurance corporation and America's largest underwriter of commercial and industrial insurance. AIG made some major mistakes. It did not reinsure its risks associated with the mortgage market and used funds to buy mortgage-backed securities. Following the collapse in the US housing market, AIG was faced with settlement of a significant number of insurance claims at a time when it suffered increasing losses on its mortgage-related investments. It had insured US$441 billion of loans, which included US$57.8 billion of subprime loans. A credit rating downgrade in September 2008 required AIG to deposit additional funds to its counter parties. AIG did not have sufficient resources and had to be bailed out by the US government, which created a US$85 billion credit facility in return for 79.9% of the company's equity. Thanks to this intervention, the company has survived, with a stock market value of around US$75 billion. The US government eventually made a profit of more than US$22 billion from its largest ever bailout operation.

Looking at the situation in the UK, the collapse of Lehman Brothers was equally significant – it had been a major force in the London stock market. The company provided finance and acted for almost 100 hedge funds. When the US parent filed for bankruptcy, the administrators in charge of the London operation immediately froze all open and unsettled trades. This had a ripple effect and caused panic selling as investors tried to protect their interests. With help from the Bank of England and the European Central Bank, a complete collapse of the financial system was avoided.

In hindsight, the problems might have been identified earlier. A year before Lehman Brothers collapsed it had become increasingly difficult to raise funds in the money market. In September 2007, Northern Rock, then a FTSE 100 company, had to ask the Bank of England for support ahead of its maturing loans. Northern Rock had been formed through the merger of two northern building societies. Traditionally, these advanced mortgages using money from depositors but, in a dash for growth, the enlarged company had started to raise funds in the money market. By 2007, some 75% of its funds came from wholesale credit markets – which seemed fine until investors became nervous of subprime loans and anything linked to mortgages. Following news of the Bank of England's support, Northern Rock's share price fell sharply and savers started to withdraw funds from branches. To stem the tide, the chancellor of the exchequer made an announcement that the government would guarantee all deposits made with Northern Rock. By February 2008, its financial position had not improved and the government acquired the bank's business, rendering the ordinary shares worthless.

The Lehman situation brought to a head various problems which lay within the rest of the UK banking system. At the beginning of October 2008, the British government announced a £500 billion package of loans and guarantees to support the banks. The Bank Recapitalisation Fund was formed, but the only recipients were Lloyds and the Royal Bank of Scotland (RBS), where the government ended up with a majority equity holding. In the case of Lloyds, the bank had taken on a commitment too far by agreeing (with Gordon Brown's encouragement) to a merger with HBOS, which, through its Halifax business, had become the country's largest mortgage bank. RBS became a problem bank after an over-aggressive acquisition programme. Of the others, HSBC was refinanced by the injection of

£750 million from its international parent and Barclays resorted to private investors for additional capital.

A challenge that all banks now faced was the need to strengthen their balance sheets in order to cope with future problems. This required them to reduce their gearing, which could be achieved in several ways. Government backing would provide a temporary solution but could not be considered a long-term answer. Raising capital by way of rights issues could also provide a quick fix. Alternatively, funds might be raised through the sale of assets or non-core businesses. As a last resort, banks could seek repayment of loans from their customers. Under these circumstances, and until such a time as balance-sheet restructuring was completed, banks were unwilling to undertake new loans to all bar customers with the best credit ratings. Hence a problem arose: the British government urged banks to lend to small and medium-sized companies while simultaneously insisting that banks improved their capital adequacy ratios. Many companies struggled through lack of capital. The deterioration in the mortgage market led to falling house prices and loss of confidence which drove the UK economy towards recession.

The UK stock market's recovery from this crash began in 2009 and coincided with the announcement that the Bank of England had commenced a programme of quantitative easing – a means of market manipulation designed to pump money into the economy and push interest rates down to an artificially low level. The process involved the central bank buying gilts and high-quality bonds from institutional investors, who could recycle sale proceeds by the purchase of further bonds or for lending purposes. Between March 2009 and the end of October 2009, £175 billion had been spent by the Bank of England in buying these assets. With a sustained period of low interest rates on the horizon and shares at incredibly low valuations, it was little wonder that the stock market turned a corner.

Between 15 May 2008 and 15 May 2009 (the period of our interim reports), the FTSE 100 had fallen by 30.5%, the FTSE Smaller Companies by 30.7% and AIM by 51.5%. By comparison, the

Cavendish Opportunities Fund shares were down 48.7% and the Cavendish AIM Fund shares by 44.5%. Both funds had lagged the sharp market recovery since the March 2009 low and were up by about 12% against rises of 23% for the FTSE 100, 38% for the FTSE Smaller Companies and 30.7% for AIM. However, the lost ground would be more than made up in the future.

At 15 May 2009, the Opportunities Fund had a portfolio of 74 holdings. Of these, there were interests in 17 new companies and, for the first time in many years, I had investments in large company recovery situations. It had been a great time for moving against the crowd by acquiring FTSE 100 shares that were on their knees and completely out of favour with investors.

Given the travails of the sector during and since the global financial crisis, the banking sector appeared on my radar. I must confess to having previously lost money – though not all of my investment – in Northern Rock. When the share price tanked in 2007, I thought that Bank of England support would only be needed temporarily and that Northern Rock would get back to health once confidence had been restored in the bond market. It seemed a good time to acquire shares – but the share price continued to fall and I ended up selling the investment at a loss.

After 2008, HSBC and Standard Chartered seemed the safest of the bunch but their share prices had not fallen by much and I was not interested in making a profit no greater than 50%. RBS looked too risky at that point of the cycle, though later on I would acquire a holding. I was left with the choice of Barclays or Lloyds, and purchased a small interest in both.

Financial companies usually perform badly in a bear market. Insurance companies can be particularly vulnerable as underlying asset values will fall sharply to reflect the fall in value of their equity portfolios. However, nothing ventured, nothing gained: I decided to buy shares in two insurance companies. The first was Aviva. At the time it was the world's fifth-largest insurance company in terms of worldwide gross premiums. It had been formed through the merger of Commercial Union and Norwich Union assurance companies in May 2000. The share price peaked at 1138p in August of that year. By May 2008 it stood at 652p and fell to 245p by October 2008. Worse was to come – the share price hit a low of 163p in March 2009. At that point, the company was boasting a historic dividend yield of 20%, clearly signalling a coming cut in the dividend. The underlying net asset value at 31 December 2008 was 486p per share, down from 763p per share a year earlier. In my view, all of this was discounted in the depressed share price.

Prudential Assurance Company was my other choice of investment in this sector. The company had a unique position in the stock market through the diversified nature of its business activities. A particularly strong area of growth for it was the life assurance business in Asia. The firm was also pursuing the annuity business in North America. In the UK, Prudential's fund management business – M&G – was still attracting new funds, while the life assurance side produced above-average returns. It was even possible for the company to send out a message of confidence to shareholders by increasing its annual dividend by 5%. However, in bear markets very few company shares can move against a general trend. Prudential shares had hit a high of 1079p in December 2000. They were priced at 726p in May 2008. By March 2009, the share price reached a low of 207p.

Both Aviva and Prudential were sound FTSE 100 companies which had suffered share price falls due to investor panic and the rush to sell in order to restrict portfolio losses. To a stock picker, this was a once-in-a-lifetime opportunity to pick up bargains. Actually that is not entirely true – the 1973 stock market crash had created a similar situation. This time, I needed no encouraging in committing monies to buying shares that had been mispriced in a falling market.

Another area that suffered from adverse investor sentiment was the aerospace and defence sector. It was feared that defence-spending programmes, from the Ministry of Defence in the UK and Department of Defense in the US, would be cut and recessionary conditions would prove harmful for the commercial aircraft industry. BAE Systems shares had fallen by 30% to a level where the dividend yield was in excess of 4% and the shares were selling at less than 10× earnings. Likewise, Rolls-Royce shares – having fallen by 23%, with a yield now of 3.8% – also looked attractive on a single-figure price–earnings ratio. Both companies had strong order books, which gave a high level of visibility. I therefore purchased a small holding in each. The fact that the share prices of both companies had outperformed gave a degree of comfort that they would gain support from investors when the market recovered.

A much more speculative purchase was in housebuilder Taylor Wimpey. The company had been formed through the merger of Taylor Woodrow and George Wimpey on 3 July 2007 to become the largest UK housebuilder, with interests in the US, Spain and Gibraltar. The pro forma balance sheet of the combined companies at the time of the merger contained net debt of £1.2 billion, but this was well covered by ordinary shareholders' funds of £3.5 billion after deducting goodwill. After spending £250 million in buying back its own shares, net assets by 31 December 2007 had fallen to £3 billion and borrowings were £1.5 billion. By 2008 the housing market was in sharp decline. That year, Taylor Wimpey sold its construction business for £74 million and incurred exceptional write-offs of nearly £1.9 billion, which reduced ordinary shareholders' funds to £1.7 billion. Borrowings were still at £1.5 billion and it was not until 2009 that the company was able to raise £500 million via a one-for-one rights issue at a knockdown price of 25p. Two years later, having refinanced its debt and sold the North America interests for US$955 million, the company came out of intensive care and subsequently the share price had breached the 200p level.

The final FTSE 100 company to be bought into the fund as a recovery situation was BT. At the stock market peak on 30 December 1999, the price of British Telecom was 1053.25p and the shares accounted for more than 7% of the FTSE 100. It was an old economy company that was about to be attacked by the up-and-coming mobile and cable operators at a time when there was a need for investment in a fibre-optic cable system. The decline came quickly. Exactly one year later the share price had fallen to 398p after the company passed the final dividend in a programme to reduce its net debt of £27.9 billion, on which the interest charge was £1.3 billion. Divestment of Yell and O2, asset disposals and a record £5.9 billion rights issue reduced debt to £13.7 billion. By 31 March 2009 net debt in the balance sheet had fallen to £10.4 billion. However, in the banking crisis, this was still too high. The fall in the stock market, plus low interest rates, caused particular uncertainty by giving rise to a significant pension fund deficit. The company's dividend was cut from 10.4p to 6.5p and the share price sank to a low of 71.4p. My average purchase price was 86.8p – I sold at a price of 142.5p later in the year. At the time this looked good, but it is not quite so clever when considering that the share price later surpassed 450p.

Thus, for the first time since 1995, I had acquired a range of FTSE 100 shares for the Opportunities Fund. That is not to say that I was concerned about the prospect for smaller companies. In fact, the portfolio contained a great many of these, which offered substantial upside. I was pleased that I had launched the AIM Fund, even though the market timing was unfortunate. Some changes had been made here and the portfolio at 15 May 2009 now contained 61 holdings, of which 19 had been held since 2005. Oil and gas shares now accounted for 14% of the fund and mining 2.4%. The majority of holdings were in profitable, dividend-paying companies.

Perhaps the greatest success story for AIM was ASOS, the online fashion retailer for younger people. The company was founded in 2000 and listed on AIM in October 2001 when shares were placed at 20p, valuing the company at £12.3 million. I was persuaded to attend a company visit in October 2005 and immediately afterwards purchased 100,000 shares at a price of 75p. It was not the sort of investment I would normally consider as the shares were selling at 62.6× earnings. However, the company had a strong infrastructure in place and was stocking 1,800 clothing lines – increasing by 150 new items per week. I remained uncomfortable with the high stock market rating for the shares and gradually reduced my holding. By May 2009, the ASOS holding was down to 35,000 shares, valued at a price of 391p. I sold my last few shares in 2013 at a price of just over £20, only to see it reach £70 in March 2014 – ascribing a market value of nearly £6 billion to the company. There was no margin for error and after profit downgrades the share price retreated to below £25, though it has subsequently shown strong recovery to reflect an improvement in trading.

The stock market revival occurred around the time that the UK minimum interest rate was reduced to 0.5%, having fallen from 5% six months earlier. My funds were on the verge of having a period of strong performance.

13

'Baggers'

Due mainly to a sharp increase in energy costs, the annual average rate of UK inflation increased from 2.2% in 2009 to 4.5% in 2011. It was then brought under control and fell to an average of 1.5% in 2014. During this period oil prices ranged between US$90 and US$100 per barrel and UK interest rates were reduced to 0.5%. From May 2010, the country had a Conservative/Liberal Democrat coalition government, which saw a need to stimulate growth while implementing a programme of austerity. An important measure enacted to achieve this was an immediate reduction in corporation tax from 28% to 26%. Further cuts were to follow; the rate fell to 20% in 2015. Although there were several uncertainties regarding other countries in the eurozone, the UK economic background created a favourable environment for companies to prosper.

With low bond yields and miserable returns from bank deposits, it is not surprising that the London stock market was to experience a rising trend. In March 2015, the FTSE 100 broke above the all-time high reached on 31 December 1999. For this chapter, I will be discussing the performance of the funds, indices and stocks from 15 May 2009 to 15 May 2015. At the end of the period, the FTSE 100 closed at 6960.5 and had therefore risen by 60% since 15 May 2009. Over that time, the FTSE Smaller Companies index was up by 111%, but the FTSE AIM All-Share had lagged and advanced by just 51%. The Opportunities Fund price had risen from 341.2p to just under £11 and the AIM Fund price from 61p to a little over 159p. In both cases, the investment strategy remained unchanged by being invested in undervalued shares and maintaining well-spread portfolios without having a concentration in a few individual stocks.

On 15 May 2009, the Cavendish Opportunities Fund held shares in 77 companies. MS International shares had continued to perform well and now represented 3.6% of the total value. There were no other holdings greater than 3% of the portfolio. Thirty holdings of the 77 were still retained in the 15 May 2015 portfolio; in the meantime, 15 of the companies were taken over and nine went into liquidation. Part III of this book will explain in further detail why the Opportunities Fund outperformed the stock market, remembering that in 15 years the prices of its shares had appreciated more than threefold at a time when the FTSE 100 had shown little change.

This chapter is devoted to 'baggers'. A share such as Advanced Medical Solutions (AMS), where the price had risen by 15 times since the date of purchase, would be termed a '15-bagger'. Had the share price risen by ten times it would be known as a ten-bagger (and so on). In the case of AMS, the growth in earnings fully justified the share price performance – and there still looks to be further potential moving forward. I had, on occasions, trimmed the holding but am content to retain an average size interest. I will give brief details of some other baggers to show where part of the growth in the value of the funds occurred.

A company formed in 1886 and floated on the London Stock Exchange in 1933 with a product recognised worldwide might be expected to have become a constituent of the FTSE 100. Sadly, it was to stay a small company – and almost became a casualty of the banking crisis. The company is Avon Rubber, best known for its automobile components and ranked alongside Dunlop in the manufacture of motor car tyres. One of the company's areas of expertise is gas masks, which it had been producing since the 1920s. A major decision was made to develop a new respirator for use by American Armed Forces in challenging conditions such as nuclear, germ or chemical warfare. The new US Joint Services General Purpose Mask programme took Avon ten years to complete at great expense.

I first purchased a holding in 2002 at a price of 130p. The shares offered a dividend yield of 5.8% and were selling at 7× earnings. The stock market value of the company at this price was £35 million and the balance sheet showed ordinary shareholder funds to be £77 million. Debt was high at £41 million but this was counterbalanced by an operational cash flow of £23 million. In 2006, the company sold its main automotive business to virtually eliminate balance-sheet debt. By 2008, Avon had run into losses and, with borrowings escalating to £15.9 million, a new management team thought it appropriate to pass the dividend. However, much had been achieved and the company received an initial five-year US$112 million contract for the new respirator from the US Department of Defense. In December 2008, the share price had reached a low of 25p but recovered to 67p by 15 May 2009. Thankfully, I used the weakness to add to my holding as strong profit growth and good earnings visibility looked to be achievable. By 15 May 2015, the share price had risen to 805p – the holding had become a 12-bagger.

The next bagger, also founded in 1886, was floated on the stock market in 1919 to raise £300,000 and become the first quoted housebuilder. By the outbreak of the Second World War, it was thought to be the country's largest, but then retrenched – and in 2003 finally sold its housebuilding subsidiary for £48 million. The company is named Henry Boot after the family founder and is now mainly a land development company. It owns land on its own account or under option. Planning permission is sought and when successful the land is either sold or developed by the company. Other interests include construction, plant hire and the recent formation of a small housebuilding subsidiary. One of the main attractions was and is its strong asset-backing, which provides a substantial source of growth. From May 2009 to May 2015 the share price had risen nearly threefold, but it had become almost a five-bagger from my original investment in 1996.

Daejan Samoedra Estates Ltd was incorporated in 1935 to acquire rubber and coffee plantations on the island of Java and elsewhere in Indonesia. These interests were sold by 1955 and it became a dormant company with a listing on the London Stock Exchange. In 1959, the Freshwater family injected its property assets into the company and changed the name to Daejan Holdings. It subsequently acquired portfolios of residential and latterly commercial properties, but remained under family control. I have bought and sold shares in this company on several occasions in the past and purchased a holding at a share price of £20 in late 2009, to see it rise to £56.40 by the time of the May 2015 valuation. Daejan was one of my original holdings in the Opportunities Fund after I purchased an interest in 1988 at a share price of £10, which makes it a five-bagger over that 27-year period.

The chemical sector contained shares in a couple of companies which were to become baggers. In 1844, two entrepreneurs formed Harrisons and Crosfield, a company named after them. It was to become one of the largest UK traders in tea and owned rubber plantations in Indonesia and Malaya. After diversifying into chemicals and divesting the non-chemicals businesses, in 1998 it changed its name to Elementis. Between May 2009 and May 2015 the shares became a 12-bagger, with the share price increasing from 26.25p to 315p. A similar story was seen with Synthomer, but this was merely a five-bagger. The company, formerly known as Yule Catto, has a history which traces back to 1863. It owned rubber and palm oil plantations in Malaysia and later acquired several chemical companies. Following a number of divestments, the company became a specialist producer of lattices and speciality emulsion polymers. Both Elementis and Synthomer had exploited specialist knowledge within their companies to move into growth industries and build on their expertise in Asian markets.

XP Power became a six-bagger during the period under review. The company is a world leader in power conversion equipment, specifically for converting AC into DC current and vice versa. Originally the company supplied products from the United

Kingdom, but decided at an early stage to move its manufacturing base to Southeast Asia. It also developed its own products for its blue-chip customers and gained wide recognition across a broad range of industries. A similar six-bagger is a company called Porvair, which specialises in an extensive range of filtration products used in a large number of fields from mining to nuclear and aerospace. Both XP Power and Porvair have seen the need for – and benefited from – innovative product development programmes.

An even more spectacular performer was Senior, which was not quite a ten-bagger, but between May 2009 and May 2015, the share price increased from 34.5p to 318p. The company is a manufacturer and supplier of components for the aerospace and automotive industries. It was formed in 1933 and has grown organically and through acquisition. As with shares of other companies in this chapter, the share price fell sharply during the banking crisis and reached a ludicrously low level. Bearing in mind that the company supplied Boeing and Airbus, where there was a long-term highly visible order book, the shares looked a snip. I acquired my holding at an average price of 37p, when the shares were selling at 3.8× earnings and yielding 7%. Borrowings looked high at £174.5 million, but the company was generating £74.6 million of net cash flow from its operations.

A surprising bagger was TT Electronics, a company involved in supplying sensors, controls and other components to automotive manufacturers. As with the other manufacturing companies already mentioned, TT Electronics has been at the forefront of product design for its customers. It suffered from a global downturn in trade at a time when its gearing was high. Consequently, pre-tax profits fell from £21.1 million in 2008 to £0.8 million in 2009 and the dividend was passed. As a result, the share price at 15 May 2009 stood at 27p, which seemed much too low when considering that the net cash flow was approaching £84 million. Following a major reorganisation, prospects improved and earnings in 2014 had recovered to 12.9p with a dividend of 5.5p being paid. The share price on 15 May 2015 was 154p, to make it in excess of a five-bagger.

A successful investment quoted on AIM was M&C Saatchi, the advertising agency which came to the stock market in 2004. The management was very astute and decided to take advantage of the global recession to expand the firm's offices in an orderly fashion. Today the network is complete and consists of 25 offices situated in 18 countries. This has enabled it to attract a number of prestigious international companies as clients. As well as traditional markets, the company is taking advantage of the growth in mobile communications. My initial holding in the Opportunities Fund was acquired at a price of 76p in March 2010 and had risen to 339p by the time of the 15 May 2015 valuation.

The most unusual bagger was another AIM company called Eckoh, a survivor from the dotcom era. In 2009, the company was the largest UK provider of speech recognition services and has subsequently diversified through an acquisition into providing a secure payments system. In the UK, the company has been successful in obtaining a number of significant-sized contracts from Capita Customer Management, while the US provides an even greater opportunity. The chip-and-pin style of card payment is a relatively new concept in America and Eckoh is able to provide a user-friendly, secure payment system. Due to well-documented credit card identity theft and the prospect of eye-watering fines, the US market is ideal for the Eckoh product. In May 2009, the share price was 6p and had risen to 38p to become a six-bagger by May 2015.

It is gratifying to see companies becoming baggers on their own accord by acquisitive or organic growth, but during this bull market numerous companies became baggers after being subject to takeover bids. The Opportunities Fund holdings were not left out of this; the following holdings were swallowed up between May 2009 and May 2015:

SECTOR	COMPANY	15 MAY 2009 SHARE PRICE	TAKEOVER SHARE PRICE
Aerospace	Umeco	167p	550p
Electronics	Chloride	160.5p	375p
Retail	Jacques Vert	7p	21p
Oil and gas	Dana Petroleum	129p	£18
	Nautical Petroleum	50.25p	450p
	Venture Production	81p	845p
Pharmaceuticals	Axis Shield	288p	470p
	Goldshield	305p	485p
Technology	CSR (Cambridge Silicon Radio)	328p	900p

Although the collapse in the stock market after the banking crisis created the opportunity to invest in a large number of shares at depressed prices, it gave me one major problem. As well as smaller companies, there were a substantial number of large company shares which were significantly undervalued. At this stage in the stock market cycle, I did not feel it appropriate to load the Opportunities Fund portfolio with larger company shares. In any case, the choice of company was restricted: the fund was and is only allowed to purchase recovery situations or shares in out-of-favour sectors of the stock market. There were many other securities outside these definitions that looked ideal to buy. A further problem was that the fund was obliged to sell once recovery had been achieved or if the sector returned to favour. I wished to buy what I wanted and to hold shares in a company until its full potential had been realised. Having had a similar problem when I wished to buy a large number of shares quoted on AIM, I arrived at the same solution: in May 2010 the Cavendish Select Fund, holding shares in large and medium-sized companies, was launched.

The investment process for the Select Fund was similar to the Opportunities and AIM Funds; to own a spread of interest in shares that appeared undervalued and attractively priced. Highly rated growth stocks were generally ruled out, but could still be held if there were compelling reasons. One difference was that the fund would own slightly fewer holdings – 60 turned out to be an ideal number. As with the other funds, there would be no deliberately large holdings and it would therefore not replicate the FTSE 100 or FTSE All-Share indices. A disadvantage would be that the fund would underperform when substantial amounts of monies flowed into large FTSE 100 companies, but it was hoped that the stock selection would provide outperformance.

Several share prices performed well, but there are four that appreciated by at least threefold. Top of the pack was Taylor Wimpey. I acquired a holding at an average price of 30p. In the case of the shares held in the Opportunities Fund, I sold when the price reached 100p as it was no longer a recovery situation and the housebuilding sector had returned to favour. The Select Fund had no such restraints and the holding was retained. The share price at 15 May 2015 was 183p, making it a six-bagger.

The second-best performer was also a housebuilder. It was formed in 1972, floated on the London Stock Exchange in 1985 and, through organic growth and several acquisitions, had become a FTSE 100 company with a valuation in excess of £6 billion. The company is Persimmon and the shares were acquired at an average price of 375p; they were valued at 1870p in the May 2015 valuation, by which point they had become a five-bagger.

The next company was St. Modwen, a specialist property regeneration developer of brownfield sites often on former industrial locations where specialist decontamination work was required. On the back of 25 years' experience the company had been able to acquire land at very attractive prices. About half of its 6,000-acre portfolio comprises residential land, with 10% commercial land and the remainder completed properties held for investment. It has 100 in hand but three developments – the 50% joint-venture New Covent Garden in London; the 468-acre former motor car site at Longbridge, Birmingham; and the 65-acre Swansea University campus – overshadow the rest. The shares were valued at 152p on 15 May 2010 and became a three-bagger when moving through the 450p level in 2015. However, more recently the company has experienced growing pains.

Restaurant Group shares were the final ones to rise by threefold over the period. The company was formed in 1979 to run Garfunkel's; the following year it acquired Chiquito, the Mexican food restaurant chain. However, its most successful restaurant is Frankie and Benny's; the first branch was opened in 1995. By 2015, the group operated 470 restaurants, of which half were Frankie and Benny's and one third Chiquito. One reason for their success is that the sites are well chosen, in prominent positions including airports and near cinemas. In some ways I was surprised that the share price performed as well as it did, but moving forward the directors felt that there was potential for further organic growth. More recently growth has faltered and there has been fears that the Frankie and Benny's concept has reached maturity. The share price overreacted and gave me a chance to have a second bite at the cherry.

Turning to the AIM Fund, there were also several holdings which had increased by more than threefold. Here was the area where acorns had the potential to grow into oak trees. Three healthy saplings, Advanced Medical Solutions, Eckoh and M&C Saatchi were also held in the Opportunities Fund and have already been mentioned. Nautical Petroleum was also a potential oak tree, but was taken over after the share price had increased by nine times. Others became baggers through organic growth, sometimes helped by acquisitions, and covered several sectors of the stock market.

Michelmersh Brick was purchased as an asset situation with recovery potential. The downturn in the housebuilding market coincided with an overcapacity in brick manufacture which led to a high level of brick stocks. Even though Michelmersh is a specialist manufacturer, it was not immune from the problems which beset the industry. Apart from a fall in the price of bricks, the huge rise of energy costs created pressure on margins. Consequently, the company turned in a small loss and passed the ordinary share dividend. All was not doom and gloom: the share price of 23p was well below the net asset value, which included valuable property assets, and I felt confident that someday the housing market cycle would recover. The company was able to dispose of surplus land after obtaining planning permission or could use it for landfill purposes. When the property market recovered, surplus brick stocks were soon used up and the uplift in prices returned Michelmersh to profitability. By 15 May 2015, the share price had improved to 82p.

It is unusual for an AIM-listed company in the construction sector to become an eight-bagger, but this occurred with Renew Holdings plc. Its origin can be traced back to 1786 when a surveyor, Y. J. Lovell, acquired a century-old building firm and named the company after himself. The company was acquired by Walter Lilly in 1955 and went public in 1968 as a diversified group with interests ranging from building to plant hire and property development. In 2004, the company reported a loss of £7.4 million but maintained the dividend. A new management came on board and established Renew Holdings as a broad-based engineering company specialising in road, rail and environmental markets. The share price reflected the successful transition and moved up from 34p in May 2009 to just under 300p in May 2015.

Solid State attained bagger status for me over a much shorter period. It was established in 1971 and admitted to AIM in June 1996. Operations cover design and specialist manufacturer of industrial/ rugged computing products, battery power solutions, secure communications systems and electronic components for use in harsh environments. Due to its expertise, in July 2014 the company obtained a major contract from the UK Ministry of Justice (MOJ) for the supply and maintenance of offender-tagging devices. A growing order book elsewhere underwrote growth prospects and I acquired a holding in December 2013 when the company raised funds at a share price of 242p to finance a small acquisition. By May 2015, the shares had become a three-bagger with a share price of 814.5p. Unfortunately, the MOJ decided not to proceed with the tagging contract and the share price gave up much of the gain.

Another share price to advance by more than threefold over a relatively short period was in a company called Clinigen Group. It operates in the healthcare market but has developed a niche position by acting as a supplier of commercial medicines to companies in the process of undertaking clinical trials. Customers are situated in more than 130 countries and it is important that the medicines supplied are suitable for various regulatory environments and are constant in both format and temperature. Clinigen has also acquired four drug licences from large pharmaceutical companies and sees ownership and sale of approved drugs as a growth activity. There are the additional benefits of removing the risk and huge costs associated with the research and development programmes for new drugs. I acquired shares at a price of 164p when the shares were floated on AIM in September 2012; the share price had advanced to 637.5p by May 2015.

A further company which, since 1998, has specialised in acquiring drugs is Alliance Pharma. It differs from Clinigen in that it acquires and licenses mature pharmaceutical products that have been in the marketplace for several years. Its product portfolio covers rights for more than 50 established and speciality substances. Often the products are in relatively small markets and do not attract much competition from generic drug manufacturers. No money is spent on new drug development and marketing budgets are fairly low. Most therapy areas are covered by the business, which is also building brands in the dermatology, oncology and nutrition areas. Between May 2009 and May 2015, the shares became a four-bagger when the share price increased from 10p to 43.5p.

Healthcare is an area of growth and another company that listed on AIM during the period was EMIS Group. In 1987 the company commenced development of software for use in doctors' surgeries and rolled out its first commercial product in 1990. It was the first system to enable patients to book appointments online and order repeat prescriptions. An additional pioneering move was to develop a system whereby patients could access their own medical and clinical records, which could also be used by hospital pharmacies. Today the company has more than half of the General Practitioner market while 36% of high street pharmacies use its systems. Expansion is taking place into other areas of the National Health Service. Fortunately, I was able to participate in the IPO when the shares first listed on AIM in March 2010 at a price of 300p, which compares to a May 2015 price of 931.5p.

As technology evolves, businesses are relying more and more on the internet, Wi-Fi, emails, online banking and cloud computing. There is now a need for hosting services and reliability, particularly in mission-critical applications. Iomart was formed in 1998 and has evolved into one of Europe's largest providers of managed hosting, cloud computing and business reliance services. The group owns its own data centre and network infrastructure. It also has eight UK and six global data centre locations. Already more than 100,000 customers use its services and IT infrastructure outsourcing is forecast to grow significantly in line with a greater use of the web. In May 2009, the share price was just 35p – it increased to 232.8p by the time of the May 2015 valuation, becoming a six-bagger.

The final bagger was a German software company which listed on AIM in September 2005, but had been in existence since 1982. SQS Quality Systems AG is one of the largest independent providers of software testing and quality managed services. Historically, companies have undertaken such work in-house, but outsourcing can provide a truly independent review of software systems at a lower cost. This is important when regulation is becoming more onerous. The company covers a wide range of industries, including finance, logistics, telecommunications, IT services, civil service and energy. Its customers include the likes of Barclays, BP, Credit

Suisse, Deutsche Post, Dresdner Bank, T-Mobile and Zurich Group. Growth has been achieved both organically and through acquisition. The shares were included in the May 2009 valuation at a price of 145p and had reached 610p when the May 2015 valuation was struck.

PART III
Putting it Together

14

Processes

Part I covered the stockbroking years and some of the factors which influenced my career as a stock picker whilst part II traced the fund management days. I now want to delve a little deeper with a view to describing my investment process.

There are several approaches to equity investment but the primary methods comprise either quantitative or fundamental analysis. The former is a pure mathematical process while the latter is based upon knowledge of the rudimental factors that affect the valuation of company shares.

Today, the boffin sitting in the office using a slide-rule to make calculations has been superseded by the superfast computer, which can be programmed to automatically place trades in the stock market. This is an extreme example of how the quantitative approach using mathematical formulae can be employed to generate short-term capital gains. Construction of a share portfolio with a longer-term horizon might also use quantitative methodology, but in a different way. Taking a global portfolio, the geographical distribution between stock markets might be calculated mathematically by making an allocation based on historical fiscal data. Similarly, the percentage invested in each stock market sector could be computed in a similar manner. Finally, share apportionment might then be done using mathematical criteria. Quantitative analysis can be used to compare the merits of different companies and to produce portfolios which try to outperform a share index by producing a portfolio that closely replicates that index.

Fundamental analysis is the process of valuing a company using historical data on companies, markets and businesses. The idea is to discover either mispriced company shares or companies that offer strong growth potential. For those investors interested in income, fundamental analysis is required to determine the sustainability of, and potential to increase, dividends. Many factors have to be taken into account such as balance-sheet strength, borrowing limits, trading prospects as well as industrial and economic factors. The fundamental analyst can then be in a position to reach a conclusion on whether a particular share is cheap or expensive. Stockbrokers will usually arrive at a buy, sell or hold recommendation according to their findings.

I invest purely in UK shares and therefore do not have to worry about the allocation of funds between global stock markets. When I managed the Glenfriars Private Portfolio Fund from 1988 to 1994, I discovered pitfalls in running a global fund. Fortunately, this was a fund where a few wealthy clients had injected their share portfolios – as such, the idea was to select the stock markets that offered the greatest potential rather than trying to obtain a balanced global weighting. At the time, Japanese and European stock markets appeared expensive and, because of our conservative fund management approach, emerging markets were ruled out. This left the UK and US as the principal areas for investment.

The American stock market looked expensive compared to the UK, but there were many more leading companies in which to invest. About 40% of the portfolio consisted of US companies and comprised holdings in such well-known names as Heinz, Kellogg's and McDonald's as well as four large healthcare companies. One important lesson I have learned from investing in international stock markets is that currency translation can materially affect share valuations. It is very frustrating to see a share price improve, but then to experience the gain being wiped out by an adverse movement in the exchange rate. The other problems I found were the difficulty in obtaining stockbroker research and, because of time zones, access to company result presentations. Another snag was being out of contact with overseas stock markets when they did not coincide with UK time. Nowadays, with technological advances such as mobile phones, the internet and sophisticated currency hedging programmes, this has become less of a problem. Nevertheless, there are a sufficient number of attractive UK-listed companies so as not to worry about such time-consuming distractions.

My stock-picking approach is known as a bottom-up strategy. In other words, I invest in individual shares that appear undervalued on fundamental grounds without particular regard to market sectors. The alternative, a top-down approach, is first to allocate holdings between market sectors and then to select shares in those sectors. There are merits in both methods, but I feel that the top-down style is best suited for substantial-sized funds where there is less choice and manoeuvrability. The fund manager of a £1 billion portfolio containing 100 holdings would find it difficult to acquire or dispose of an interest in shares of a company with a market value of less than £100 million. In such a case it is crucial to select large company shares in stock market sectors best suited to domestic and global economic conditions. Due to the size of the funds that I manage, there is no such problem – I can freely invest in relatively small companies.

One of the dangers of the bottom-up method, though, is that a share portfolio can be less-diversified. As I am looking to buy undervalued shares, I will often be invested in areas of the stock market that are out of favour with investors. This, in turn, may lead to a concentration of interests in some market areas. From the early days of managing my parents' modest portfolio, I have learned to mitigate such risks by not investing large sums in individual companies. It is a contra-cyclical approach and sector weightings will therefore change as economic conditions vary (more on that in the next chapter).

A question I am often asked is: 'How do you identify attractively priced shares?' Quite often the answer is: purely by accident. I have already mentioned the story of how my cat led to the purchase of shares in Advanced Medical Solutions. On another occasion, I bought shares on the back of a stockbroker's *sell* recommendation. It happened when I received an email from a stockbroker advising me to sell shares in Taylor Wimpey at a price of 24p. At the time the company was on the verge of selling its North American housebuilding interests, the proceeds of which would be used to virtually eliminate borrowings. The UK housing market was depressed and Taylor Wimpey shares were quoted at a significant discount to its underlying net asset value of 60p per share. The stockbroker clearly saw some doomsday scenario on the horizon. I didn't – and my 1973 stock market experiences taught me that then was the time to invest. I felt that at some stage, even if not for several years, house prices would recover – and in the meantime the company would survive. I bought shares for both the Opportunities and Select Funds at around 30p. When the share price had recovered to 107p it could no longer be considered as a large company recovery situation and I felt obliged to take a profit on the Opportunities Fund's holding. The Select Fund had no such restraints and I maintained the interest in order to take full advantage of the recovery in the housing market – though I slightly reduced the interest when the share price broke through the 200p level.

Unfortunately, this sort of situation rarely occurs – but a search for new ideas is seldom far from my mind. Sometimes stockbroker research will throw up an original idea, but more often it will refer to current results where an upgrade or downgrade has already been reflected in a share price. I prefer to consider an investment idea that does not have blanket coverage. Having said that, I feel that stockbroker research is a useful tool when judging the investment merits of a company.

The most useful way of identifying an attractive investment is from company results. These are published from seven o'clock each morning in the form of regulatory announcements. I make a point of being at my desk by 6 am in order to trawl through press comment, company figures and trading updates. These will often feature companies I am familiar with or have followed for years. Occasionally a new idea will emerge; STV and Lok'nStore are two situations where Regulated News Service (RNS) announcements triggered a purchase of shares.

STV is the company that owns the independent television licence for Scotland. Originally there were 16 television franchises in the UK, including one for the Channel Islands, two in Scotland and one in Northern Ireland. After a series of mergers and takeovers the English licences are now held by ITV, leaving STV owning the rights over Scotland. Further consolidation was seen when UTV Media sold the TV rights over Northern Ireland to ITV. In February 2012, STV announced its preliminary results, which showed pre-tax profits of £14 million for the year to 31 December 2011 against £12.5 million in the previous year. Earnings per share were up from 34.3p to 38p and the net cash flow was £16.2 million. The company had a stock market value of £40 million and the shares looked cheap as chips. However, there were three main problems:

1. Debt was high at £54.5 million.

2. The company had a pension fund deficit of £23 million.

3. A major institutional shareholder was seen to be offloading its holding.

I have followed media companies for several years and felt that STV was a sound business in which I was prepared to take an interest. Due to the availability of shares from the selling institution, I was able to acquire 4.6% of the company at an average share price of 106p for the Opportunities Fund and various other discretionary clients of Cavendish. My reasoning was that the shares were being acquired at 2.8× earnings and its sizeable net cash flow would be sufficient to strengthen the balance sheet. Fast forward four years and the shares have become a dividend-paying three-bagger in a company which is quoted at a discount to ITV.

Lok'nStore is a similar example of an undervalued company. I arrived in the office one bright sunny morning in November 2012 to find that this company had produced stunning results. Its pre-tax profit was up 35% at £1.9 million and the dividend had been increased from 3p to 5p per share. Funds generated from operations were 13p per share and its net asset value was 228p per share. The share price was 120p and, much to my surprise, did not change on the back of these results. It was the first time that I had come across the company and the share price action suggested that there might be a problem. On enquiry, I discovered that an active fund owning an equity interest approaching 29.9% was trying to sell its holding. A stockbroker was in charge of placing these shares and I indicated that I would buy a holding for my AIM and Opportunities Funds on the provision that the balance of the holding was placed with other investors. Nothing happened for a couple of days and, remembering STV, I decided to take the plunge. With the share price hovering around the 120p level, I was fortunate enough to acquire 1.64 million shares at a price of 108.5p, which included the entitlement to the dividend of 5p. Shortly afterwards, the balance of the holding was placed with institutions and the shares have subsequently become a three-bagger.

There were good fundamental reasons for buying shares in Lok'nStore. The company operates self-storage depots in the UK. From a trading point of view, the upturn in the housebuilding market would boost the demand for self storage, which translates into both higher occupancy levels and rental rates charged to customers. Since costs are fixed, the extra revenue would be of direct benefit to profits. As we have seen from an earlier chapter, the value of a commercial property is related to the income it produces. Consequently, by 2015 the net asset value of Lok'nStore had increased to 286p per share. Today the company owns a portfolio of 28 self-storage and two document-storage stores with four more planned. The extra space will contribute to future earnings growth.

It is not difficult to pick shares in a company which is trading well, but this is only half the battle. The timing of an investment is just as – if not more – important. In an ideal world, it is clearly best to buy when the stock market is at a low level and sell after a rise. However, in between there are many opportunities for taking advantage of individual share price movements.

Strategies can change depending on whether the stock market is rising or falling. In the case of a bull market, it is usually correct to run with profits as many investors follow the upward share price momentum. Rather bizarrely, a share can be recommended as a 'chart buy' when the price breaches a previous high. This philosophy can work well, as seen in the case of ASOS, but it can be a dangerous journey – as investors saw with the likes of Poseidon or Tasminex in 1970. From personal experience, it can be frustrating to sell too early – but once a share looks overvalued it is worth taking a profit. Of course, there comes a stage when most stocks appear expensive – in which case the stock market is probably too high. It is my view that an example of this type of overvaluation can be found in the bond market when yields on short-dated bonds are less than the long-term rate of inflation.

On the buying tack, a bull market can create an opportunity to acquire shares on the back of downgraded expectations or profit warnings. A company can undershoot a profit forecast for a number of reasons. The most serious problem can be financial irregularity within a company; I have found that type of situation is best avoided. An announcement concerning deteriorating sales can lead to a chance for picking up shares cheaply. In that case, extra-special attention needs to be made to make sure that there is not an insurmountable problem. Occasionally, a market, as in CDs and DVDs, can disappear as new technology takes its place. More often, there is a delay in the ordering cycle, giving rise to an unexpected decline of profits in one financial period and leading to an increase in the next. A fall in raw material prices will be reflected in a reduction in profits for shares in the natural resources sectors of the stock market. Poor results and the sale of shares by company directors can also harm sentiment. Finally, a sell recommendation in a newspaper tip sheet or from a stockbroking firm can also cause a share price to fall.

To take advantage of a falling share price, one has to be sure of the investment case and that the event triggering the movement is not a terminal one. Due to the workings of the stock market, a share price will often overreact to bad news. Most regulatory announcements are produced on company news channels each day, shortly after 7 am. The London stock market opens at 7.50 am and goes live at 8 am, which gives time for the opening share prices to be determined. In the case of FTSE 100 shares and the majority of other equities, the opening price is based upon an auction process where buyers and sellers enter orders into the stock exchange computer system. The initial deal, known as the uncrossing, is fixed at a price where buyers and sellers are matched by volume. In the case of shares where there is no system for inputting orders, the market makers will fix the opening share price level. When a company produces disappointing news, there is a natural reluctance for investors to buy – the opening price can therefore overreact and be well down on the previous-day closing level. Investors can be unnerved by a sharp downward share price movement and be prompted into panic selling. I have found that it is usually best to wait for a couple of days before placing a buy order.

In the case of a bear market, one's approach must be different. It is usually correct to take a profit when a share price spikes higher after positive news. The potential buyers on the back of momentum have usually vanished and, inevitably, the share price will drift lower to lose most of the gain. If the share price continues to rise, other share prices are in a downward spiral giving rise to a number of alternative investment propositions. A company which produces poor news will no longer attract value investors. Instead, a hedge fund manager may well establish a short position by selling shares with a view to buying back in future at a lower price. The term 'like catching a falling knife' is an apt description of the attempt to buy shares in a falling market.

One quirk of a bear market is that it throws up tremendous anomalies, particularly in smaller company shares. An important fact to remember is that stock market movements can be governed by greed in a rising market and fear in a falling one. There will always be sellers of shares, whether from a deceased account or the need to raise funds to obtain finance. On the other hand a buyer of shares is under no obligation to deal and is able to select the timing of a purchase. Consequently, in a bear market, a smaller company fund manager needing to raise funds will sell what *can*, rather than what *should*, be sold. One of the reasons that I love bear markets is that it allows me to find steals. As I experienced in the 1973 and subsequent bear markets: on occasion, stock market valuations of companies can bear little resemblance to their underlying worth.

Investment timing can be helped by technical analysis – a posh way of saying 'to look at share price charts'. The most common form of technical analysis is the line chart tracing a share price movement. Today computers are able to record a share price passage as it occurs and a graph can be produced to show the actual change in real time. This can be useful for day traders who actively buy and sell shares throughout the day in order to profit from stock market movements. To the longer-term investor, a chart of the closing middle price of a share is useful when making decisions on the phasing of an investment. There are also investors who completely ignore fundamental analysis and trade purely on chart interpretation: apart from line charts there are bar, candlestick, point and figure charts and many other variants to analyse. Each requires a different interpretation, but the ultimate objective is to predict the future direction of a share price.

I find that a simple line chart can be useful in deciding when to buy or sell a share. It will show whether the share price is in an upwards, downwards or sideways trend and also where there has been past selling or buying interest. In simple terms, if one can imagine a series of upright and inverted triangles joined together, the upward and downward apexes are the points of resistance and support. Ideally shares should be sold near the resistance and bought close to the support levels. However, life is not that simple and other factors such as news flow and stock market conditions can come into play. More complicated formations, such as flags or head-and-shoulder patterns, I leave to others. Nevertheless, I find that charts are helpful in showing historic trends, which can act as a guide when arriving at an investment timing decision.

A question worth asking is: does one invest for the best possible return or the best return possible? When seeking the best return possible, the portfolio manager will hold shares in a small number of companies which have been selected to provide the maximum level of capital appreciation. Investment authorities have identified the dangers in this approach and have imposed some strict investment limits for quoted funds. The most important of these are that no individual holding must account for more than 10% of a portfolio and that holdings in excess of 5% must not, in aggregate, total in excess of 40% of the value. There are several funds which come close to these parameters and risk poor performance if one of the large holdings goes wrong. On the other hand, successful stock selection from having large positions can bring stellar returns. It has been seen already that I prefer to hold a large number of stocks. A risk I face is having a concentration of stocks in a poor-performing sector of the stock market.

The stock-picking approach involves acquiring attractively priced shares rather than picking shares purely based on the size of company, often going against the trend. As mentioned earlier, some would define it as a contra-cyclical approach; I would not disagree. However, there is no point in buying shares at depressed prices unless there is strong recovery potential. Being a contrarian investor, I have found that stock market sectors can move in and out of favour depending on the economic background. By the same token, investment themes can also change. I favour the value approach and there are many ways to identify undervalued investments. It may be that value is seen in an asset situation, recovery prospects or potential from the re-rating of a company.

Asset situations are generally thought to mostly occur in the property sector, but this is not always the case. I have mentioned Lok'nStore, a quasi-property company where the value of its self-storage stores will fluctuate in line with their earnings. It is equivalent to owning a property portfolio with daily rent reviews. Pub companies, motor distributors, retailers, housebuilders and industrial companies such as brick manufacturers can also own undervalued assets. An even better example is shares of oil and gas companies, which can stand at significant discounts to underlying asset values. An important fact to remember, though, is that values can fall as well as rise – and there is little point in holding shares in loss-making companies with high levels of borrowing.

In the case of a recovery situation there are several questions to ask. The principal things to determine are the quality of the business and its financial strength. Sometimes a share price can reflect that a company is in a declining market. Here, the demise of the CD and DVD is a classic example of markets that virtually disappeared overnight. With other areas, such as housing, demand and values can fall quite sharply – but will ultimately recover. Financial strength is of paramount importance and I would prefer to give up some of the growth potential by investing in a company with a robust balance sheet. It is difficult to predict recovery and I want to be invested in companies that can survive difficult times.

When considering companies due for a re-rating, it is often those with good earning visibility not fully recognised in the stock market valuation. Typically these companies will provide reliable profit growth and their shares can be quoted at a discount to the average price–earnings ratio for the stock market. My theory is that at some stage in the future equity shares will be favoured over bonds and the FTSE 100 could sell at 20× earnings. This represents an earnings yield of 5% – far better than the current return from bonds or bank deposits. Equities might be more risky, but in my opinion they offer much better long-term returns. In fact, at the height of past bull markets, the stock market price–earnings ratio has been in excess of 30×. In those days, equities appeared as overvalued as bonds look today. If I am right in my reasoning, shares selling at 16× earnings today could, in the future, achieve a rating of 25× earnings. Companies of this nature can appear in several, but not all, sectors of the stock market.

Some businesses such as housebuilding, travel, plant-hire, retail, property and mining can be cyclical depending on economic conditions. Other areas like insurance, banking and financial services can be subject to a change in fortunes depending on stock market levels and interest rates. Having my contrarian approach, I tend to buy shares in sectors when they are completely out of favour with investors. Though not intentional, sector weightings in the Opportunities Fund portfolio can alter substantially over a period and the next two chapters are devoted to analysing these changes as seen from my stock-picking perspective.

15

Horses for Courses

As one would expect, the idea of creating a passive fund which tracked an index first originated in America. The first fund of this type was formed in 1970 to track the Dow Jones Industrial Average, but the most significant launch occurred five years later. The First Index Investment Trust was formed with the object of tracking the more broadly based Standard & Poor's 500 index. It later changed its name to the Vanguard 500 Index Fund. From modest beginnings, with assets of US$11 million, the fund is now worth in excess of US$200 billion.

The advent of the computer age has also allowed for greater sophistication in the form of exchange-traded funds (ETF). These are freely traded on the stock exchange and can cover many asset classes, including gold, oil futures, bonds, foreign currencies as well as stock market indices and specific sectors. ETFs are created or cancelled by large institutions, known as authorised participants, who manage a basket of underlying securities to replicate the benchmark. The basket of assets will be increased or reduced in line with the net investment or redemption in the ETF. Through the use of derivatives, it has also become possible to gear up the potential return.

The most widely known ETF is nicknamed the 'spider' – the S&P 500 Depository Receipt (SPDR). It has an average value of US$130 billion and a daily volume of more than US$25 million shares. There are numerous other ETFs available to investors and it is reported that over 20% of US equity mutual fund assets are invested in index funds. The advantages are: low running costs, specific areas of investment are clearly identified and represented, and it is possible to short sell (to sell an ETF which is not owned on the hope of buying it back more cheaply at a lower price). To a multi-billion dollar mutual fund wishing to replicate an index, an ETF can be a much more logical investment than buying an interest in the underlying securities.

For a UK investor, there are a wide range of ETFs and index-tracking funds available. Some of these are a good way of investing in certain market areas but, in the past 15 years, a fund which tracked the FTSE 100 would have been a poor long-term investment. Since its high on 31 December 1999, the FTSE 100 has struggled to breach, and stay above, that level. There is good reason for this. It is an index weighted by size of company, with five companies accounting for about one third of the value. Currently these stocks are BP, Royal Dutch Shell, GlaxoSmithKline, HSBC and Vodafone. Back in December 1999, BT (British Telecom) accounted for just over 7%, but has fallen back to less than 2.5% of the FTSE 100. The influence of the poor performance from shares of Britain's largest quoted companies demonstrates the dangers of investing in an unbalanced index. It also provides a lesson that I have already learned. The Cavendish Opportunities Fund holds around 70 stocks and has seen its value increase by more than threefold over the period from December 1999. In the meantime the FTSE 100 has made little progress.

For a number of years BP was considered by several fund managers to be a core portfolio holding. Back in 1999, it accounted for almost 9% of the FTSE 100 and provided a decent and growing dividend yield. As such, the shares were held by a large number of income funds and were a requisite holding for those wishing to track or replicate the FTSE 100. However, the company had always been accident-prone. The Texas City Refinery explosion, which killed 15 and injured 170 workers, occurred in 2005. This was followed by the near-sinking of the US$1 billion Thunder Horse oil platform, the repair of which kept it out of commission for a further three years. The following year saw another record set when a leak in the Trans-Alaska pipeline caused the Prudhoe Bay spillage, which was and remains the largest in Alaska.

The Deepwater Horizon oil spill in April 2010 became the largest accidental release of oil into maritime waters in history. It resulted in substantial fines and caused BP to sell a number of its prize assets. Prior to the news, the share price was around 650p, providing a dividend yield of 5.6%. Within a few weeks, it had more than halved to reach a low of 302p, wiping more than 4% off the FTSE 100 Index in June 2010. The dividend was cut and investors relying on the income also suffered a savage decline in capital value. It became a large company recovery situation which might have proved an ideal holding for the Opportunities Fund, but I much preferred to be invested in smaller companies in the oil and gas sector of the stock market. A major problem that I had with BP was its need to replenish its reserves. With production running at 3.2 million boed (barrels of oil equivalent a day) significant deals or exploration success is required to solve this dilemma.

An advantage to holding smaller companies in the oil and gas sector (involving, say, an investment of 1.5% of the fund), is that a BP-type mishap with one cannot be too damaging to the fund's value. It is a volatile sector of the stock market. My first venture into the area was in mid-1988 when I bought and, shortly afterwards, sold shares in a small company called British-Borneo Petroleum. During the next few years the company grew by acquisition and I repurchased a holding in 1999, by which time the company had 40,000 boed of production and reserves of 2,602 million barrels. Like BP, this looked to be a sound investment, with income from production used to help subsidise its deep-water-drilling exploration programme in the Gulf of Mexico. British-Borneo shares were acquired as a recovery situation because the share price reflected a number of problems at a time of low oil prices. As before, the shares were not held for long as the company was taken over by the Italian company Agip in May 2000. My second venture into the sector, for a brief period in 1993, was a company called Lasmo – also acquired by Agip.

British-Borneo Petroleum and Lasmo were both medium-sized companies; my third purchase was a smaller company called Goal Petroleum, which had several production interests and 50 licences in the North Sea. The shares were purchased in 1993 at a price of 55p and the company was acquired two years later by Talisman Energy in a cash offer worth 97.5p per share. In 1995, Lasmo and Goal were replaced by Enterprise Oil and Premier Oil. The former was taken over by Shell in 2002 at a price of 725p, which compared favourably to my purchase price of 340p. Premier Oil has retained its independence and has shown significant growth over the years. Interests in several other oil companies were subsequently purchased, but up until 2006 the sector accounted for less than 5% of the Opportunities Fund portfolio.

In May 1997, I bought a holding in a small company called SOCO International, which came to the stock market via a placing of shares at a price of 260p – raised to fund its operations in Southeast Asia, the Middle East and West Africa. Despite positive news flow, the share price performed poorly, which allowed me to add to the holding. Over the next three years, additional purchases enabled me to reduce the average cost price to 77p. Drilling success prompted the share price to improve to 189p, which prompted me to sell at a decent profit. However, the story does not stop there. On the back of a major Vietnamese oil discovery in 2004, I bought back a holding at a price of 260.5p. In the wake of a number of profitable asset sales, and becoming a major producer in Vietnam, the share price reached £23.60 by November 2007 – thereby becoming a nine-bagger.

An even greater bagger is Dana Petroleum, a company formed in 1994 to exploit prospects in the North Sea. I acquired a holding in 2003 at an average price of about 160p. A year later, the price breached the 200p level. The company was acquired in July 2010 by the Korean National Oil Company in a cash offer of £18 per share, which valued Dana at £1.8 billion. At the time, the management argued that the shares were worthy of a £23 price tag. As it was, both Dana and SOCO had become examples of how acorns can grow into oak trees.

One constantly reoccurring theme is my dislike of having a significant percentage of a portfolio in one or more holdings. Rather reluctantly, as their share prices moved higher, I reduced my holdings in Dana and SOCO. Fortunately, this was not too much of a problem as shares in a number of other oil and gas companies were just as appealing. In November 2005, the oil and gas interests in the Opportunities Fund consisted of just Dana and SOCO, which together accounted for 3.7% of the portfolio. By 2007, I held shares in seven companies in the sector, which comprised 14.8% of the portfolio; Dana and SOCO were 3.8%. Until 2012, more than 10% of the Opportunities Fund portfolio was represented by shares in the oil and gas sector, but the weighting then dropped to 6.3%. In the intervening period, the sector holdings changed quite considerably since several of the companies were taken over.

I have mentioned Dana already; several other holdings that I lost through takeovers featured companies involved in North Sea activities. The following demonstrate the potential that can be achieved from shares in this area of the stock market. Venture Production came to the stock market through a placing of shares in 2002 at a price of 170p. The holding was purchased for Opportunities Fund at an average price of 674p in 2007. It was acquired in 2009 by Centrica in a cash offer of 845p per share. Nautical Petroleum shares were placed with investors on AIM in 2002 at an equivalent price of 2p after adjusting for a subsequent consolidation of 20 old shares for one new share. The holding was first purchased for the Opportunities Fund at an average price of 21p in 2007. It was acquired in 2012 by Capricorn Energy in a cash offer of 450p per share.

The timing of a purchase is an important factor and I barely broke even on the next two holdings. EnCore Oil came to the stock market through a placing on AIM in 2001 at an equivalent price of 1p after adjusting for a subsequent consolidation of five old shares for one new share. The holding was purchased for the Opportunities Fund at an average price of 85p in 2011. It was acquired in 2012 in a share offer from Premier Oil at a level equivalent to a price of 87p. Valiant Petroleum shares were placed on AIM in 2008 at a price of 750p. The holding was purchased for the Opportunities Fund at an average price of 460p in 2011. It was acquired by Ithaca Energy in 2012 in a partial share offer which valued the shares at a price of 448p.

One of the advantages of investing in an exploration and production (E&P) company at the smaller end of the spectrum is that even a relatively small discovery can prove transformational. Once a company has been successful in obtaining a drilling licence, it owns a valuable and negotiable asset. It is then possible to 'farm down' (sell a proportion of the interest to a partner) in order to reduce both the drilling cost and the risk of not making a commercial find. Today, there is considerable sophistication behind drilling decisions, such as commissioning a 3D seismic programme to establish an area where oil is likely to be trapped in a reservoir.

In the case of a pure exploration well, the risks are considerable. Even if oil is found, it might not be moveable or of sufficient size to make it a commercial find, and even with a reasonable-size discovery the costs of putting infrastructure in place might prove uneconomic. However, to a smaller oil company the rewards can be considerable. An appraisal well is less risky as it is made to establish the extent of an existing find, to provide information on the size of a field, quality of oil and the flow rate. As each stage of the move towards successful production is achieved, the value of the reserves increases. This can allow exploration companies to dispose of an interest rather than being subject to the large amounts of capital expenditure involved in bringing the discovery into production.

Over 2014–2015, oil prices more than halved and understandably many investors avoided buying shares in the oil and gas sector. The supply of oil simply outstripped demand, leaving a global surplus.

In the past, OPEC members have cut production with a view to maintaining high oil prices, but on this occasion they did not reduce quotas. This provided an opportunity for me to acquire interests in a number of companies at a fraction of what I believe is their true worth. I predominantly invested in companies that operate in the North Sea, preferring those with production. The idea was to have about half a dozen holdings in the Opportunities and AIM portfolios where the original cost per holding would be 1.5% of the overall fund's value. In the Select Fund, I wanted to hold interests in four medium-sized oil companies – but am prepared to take up to a 2% interest per holding.

It is my view that smaller companies in the oil and gas sector will produce the future ten-baggers. However, these can be risky investments – there can be donkeys in the stable. I have owned a couple of such donkeys, as you will see in a later chapter dedicated to Mumford's greatest disasters. One of the problems often facing these firms is a high level of balance-sheet debt. In several instances, junior oil companies have needed to renegotiate their banking covenants, which were set when oil prices were much higher. To date, banks have been accommodating – but this may not always be the case, and a huge rise in interest rates would alter the equation. Equally, a further sharp collapse in oil prices would have a disastrous effect on finances. Despite this, I prefer to own an interest in a number of potential ten-baggers rather than safer shares, such as BP or Royal Dutch Shell, where a 50% rise in value is less probable.

Where companies in the oil and gas sector have to make significant discoveries to replenish reserves, large pharmaceutical companies face a similar problem by having to replace drugs when patents expire. The cost of gaining approval and bringing a new drug to market can be enormous and it is estimated that the success rate is only 10%. It is necessary to obtain patents in order to encourage research into new drugs and to protect drugs from being copied by companies that have not incurred the development expenditure. The monopoly situation created by a patent allows a price structure whereby the pharmaceutical company can recoup its costs and produce a profit. However, it is important that a company does not abuse this pricing power.

It has been estimated that, on average, it can cost many hundred million dollars to develop a new drug and bring it to market. The most important market is America. In 2014, the US Food and Drug Administration (FDA) approved 41 new products against 27 in the previous year. A series of clinical trials are necessary in order to prove that a drug is safe and effective. The first clinical trial occurred in 1747 when a physician, James Lind, conducted an experiment to examine the consumption of citrus fruit as a cure for scurvy – a killer disease for seafarers on long voyages. He selected 12 scurvy-ridden sailors, who were paired into six groups and given identical diets. This was supplemented by either a glass of sea water, a quart of cider, drops of vitriol, six spoonfuls of vinegar, barley water or two oranges and one lemon. The two sailors given citrus fruit showed a full recovery within a week and a small improvement was seen in the group taking cider. This trial would be termed an 'observational' one as opposed to an interventional study, where investigators measure and actively manage a drug's progress.

The purpose of trials can be to prevent a disease occurring, to treat a disease with a new drug or combination of drugs, to improve the quality of life where the illness is likely to be terminal or to test unapproved drugs on those patients who have no other options. There are five phases in the drug testing process. Phase 0 is undertaken on a small number of people to test what effect the drug has on the body and that it acts as expected. Phase 1 is undertaken on a larger group and tests for safety and dosage evaluation. Phase 2 tests for effectiveness on a greater number of individuals and can identify less-common side effects. Phase 3 will determine the final approval based on effectiveness and safety of the drug using a large group of people. Phase 4 is an ongoing process which monitors a drug through its lifecycle. In phases 2 and 3, a drug is measured against a placebo (innocuous substitute) where the subjects can be unaware of whether they are taking the real or imitation medication. A blind study is where the participant is unaware of which treatment is being taken and a double-blind one is where the researcher is in the dark until the tests are completed. Rather bizarrely, placebos have been known on occasion to have the more positive reaction on participants.

Due to the complexity of trials, it can take years to get a drug on to the market. Often new drugs are either reformations of existing ones or replacements of treatments already in existence. The challenge for a larger pharmaceutical company is to discover a blockbuster product which is novel and has potential for significant sales. In the case of GlaxoSmithKline, group sales have been stable since 2008 and its new drugs have produced insufficient revenue to replace that which has been lost to generic completion on patent expiry. In 2015, the company had sales of £24 billion and spent £3.1 billion on its core research and development programme involving 13,000 persons. Like the major oil companies, it is difficult to make progress when you must run in order to stand still.

At the 31 December 1999 peak for the FTSE 100, GlaxoSmithKline accounted for 4.6% of its value and in 2015 it was just over 4% which is hardly inspiring. One redeeming feature is that the shares have offered an attractive dividend yield, and unlike BP, payments have been progressive. Due to its size, GlaxoSmithKline is unlikely to become a ten-bagger, but it could conceivably double over a long period. By comparison, smaller companies, such as Alliance Pharma and Clinigen, without having to invest in research and development, have already shown good growth. I would prefer to hold these or shares in companies situated elsewhere in the healthcare sectors. Strangely, my first foray into the pharmaceutical sector was through Wellcome Trust in 1993. Two years later I doubled my money on the shares when the company was acquired by GlaxoSmithKline.

An area which I now avoid is biotech, where even the prospects of mega returns do not compensate for the considerable risks. Some of the stories seem quite plausible. I remember attending a lunch where the managing director of a biotech company was demonstrating technology using a salt and pepper pot. He was talking about the body's immune system, claiming that people were too hygienic – which caused weakness in the body's immune system. To compensate, the company had produced an injectable product using an extract from rhinoceros droppings. Preliminary results looked impressive, but when it came to testing on cancer patients the placebo worked just as well.

Another interesting product that looked to have a good chance of success was being developed by Phytopharm, an AIM-listed company. In 1995 the company acquired the patent to an anti-obesity drug derived from a South African plant, *Hoodia gordonii*. Scientists produced a powder form of the molecule termed P57, which was isolated as producing an appetite-suppressing effect. A promising partnership was entered into with Pfizer, the major US pharmaceutical company, but this ceased when Pfizer closed the division dealing in that area. In 2004, a fresh agreement was signed with Unilever to develop a Slimfast shake incorporating P57. The relationship lasted for four years and was then aborted for safety and efficacy reasons. A cooperation agreement was then reached with the Council for Scientific and Industrial Research in South Africa to fund its development, but the patent was dropped in 2010. Originally, P57 was thought to be a potential blockbuster drug, then a lower-valued food supplement – but neither application came close to gaining regulatory approval.

A risk that smaller drug development companies face is running out of money. During the process of obtaining regulatory approval, a company will incur a number of costs, some of which can be calculated but very few of which are avoidable. Business plans are usually made on conservative assumptions, but often foiled by timing delays. The regulation process is slow in itself, but sometimes the regulator will require additional data which can put back a decision for many months. A danger is that a company burns through its cash resources and is forced to raise funds on unfavourable terms. Apart from a decent dividend yield, one of the attractions of

GlaxoSmithKline is that it boasts a strong cash flow and is unlikely to experience financial problems.

My preference in other areas associated with healthcare would be in medical devices and software. A good example of the former is Consort Medical, which manufactures drug-delivery products. When facing a drug patent expiry or a different revenue stream, a pharmaceutical company will often consider a novel method of drug delivery. This will often involve a drug being reformulated in a powder form to be administered with an inhaler similar to an asthma pump. Consort manufactures these inhalers, including ones that give a measured dosage and incorporate a dial to show a count of the number of times it has been used. The benefits are avoiding an overdose through administering the wrong amount or taking the dose twice by mistake. A drug reformulation still has to go through rigorous regulation hurdles before achieving marketing approval and this can be a time-consuming process. Two benefits are creating a barrier of entry to competitors and providing earnings visibility to Consort Medical. Where its device is incorporated in regulatory tests, it would be expected to be used when the product comes to market. Consort Medical has a strong pipeline of new product launches and has also acquired an outsourcing manufacturer of drugs for pharmaceutical companies.

The National Healthcare software programme goes back to October 2002 when a plan was formulated to connect 30,000 general practitioners to 300 hospitals in a central record programme to cover patient records in a secure manner. An organisation called NHS Connecting for Health was formed on 1 April 2005 to deliver and maintain a nationwide IT structure. The programme was originally budgeted to cost £2.3 billion over a three-year period but this was wide of the mark and, in June 2006, the National Audit Office priced the cost at £12.4 billion over ten years. There were overruns and the project was aborted in 2010 when the cost had already exceeded £10 billion. This presented an opportunity for individual software companies to provide IT systems for separate areas within the health service. As mentioned in a previous chapter, I hold an interest in EMIS which services 46% of GP surgeries and the Opportunities Fund also has a holding in Servelec, which provides patient records and administration services for the mental health, community health and social care sectors. Both companies have good recurring revenue streams and are benefiting from modernisation of the National Health Service.

So far my comments on the oil and gas and pharmaceutical sectors have applied to the Opportunities Fund. In the case of the Select Fund, I would hold shares in four medium-sized oil companies which do not have the reserve replacement problems of Royal Dutch Shell and BP. Equally I would hold BTG in preference to GlaxoSmithKline or AstraZeneca. As mentioned in an earlier chapter, BTG was formed through the merger of the National Research Development Corporation (a government entity formed in 1948) and the National Enterprise Board in 1981. It was privatised in 1992 and listed on the London Stock Exchange three years later. Having divested its industrial interests, it has become a broadly based medical company growing both organically and by acquisition. With a stock market value of a little over £2 billion, the company is of the size that successful projects can have a material impact on results.

In the case of the AIM Fund, there is a far greater choice in both stock market sectors. There are more than 100 oil and gas companies listed on AIM, covering most areas of the world. I have tended to confine my investment to those companies operating in the North Sea and, at any one time, would have around half a dozen holdings. The choice is even wider in the healthcare sector. Here, I have up to double the number of stocks in the portfolio, covering mainly profitable companies in diagnostics, pharmaceuticals, and consumer products used in hospitals. Unsurprisingly, I avoid unprofitable biotech companies as it would be like backing rank outsiders in the Grand National. Maybe I would miss a Foinavon, the 1967 Grand National outsider who won when all the other horses fell at the 23rd fence, but why take the gamble?

Although smaller companies may be perceived to carry more risk, I would prefer to own a basket of potential ten-baggers than have 14% of a portfolio in BP, Royal Dutch Shell and GlaxoSmithKline. The next chapter continues with the theme of how tracking the FTSE 100 has been disappointing.

16

Big is Beautiful?

In 1846, the United States of America declared war on Mexico. In the same year, California proclaimed its independence and was annexed to the US, and Iowa became the 29th state of the Union. In Britain, a racehorse called Pioneer, ridden by William Taylor, won the eighth running of the Grand National, and the first commercial telegraph service was established by the Electric Telegraph Company. Thirty-two years later, Alexander Graham Bell demonstrated his invention of the telephone to Queen Victoria, and the following year the first telephone exchange was opened. Telephone and telegraph services were owned by private sector companies, but, in 1912, most were acquired by the General Post Office, then a government department. Under the Harold Wilson government, it was decided to nationalise the undertaking. The Post Office Act of 1969 established a public corporation which separated the businesses into postal and telecommunications.

The British Telecommunications Act 1981 was designed to take the telecommunications business away from the Post Office with a view to liberalising and bringing competition into the industry. British Telecom (BT) became an independent company and, shortly afterwards, a licence to run a national network was granted to Mercury Communications, a fully owned subsidiary of Cable & Wireless plc. In 1984, the Thatcher government sold 52.4% of British

Telecom to the public in what at the time was the world's largest issue of shares. The remaining government holding in the company, now renamed as BT Group plc (BT), was sold in two tranches during 1991 and 1993.

In the year to 31 March 1992, BT made a pre-tax profit of just over £3 million on turnover of £13.3 billion. For the 12 months to 31 March 2015, the company produced a fractionally higher profit on turnover of £17.8 billion. There were good reasons for this lacklustre performance. Perhaps the two most important factors were the emergence of mobile phones and competition from new telecom operators, which were now allowed access to BT's fixed-line network. This occurred at a time when fibre optic cables were required to replace the traditional copper wiring. At the time of the dotcom bubble, BT's balance sheet had become overstretched and, as touched on earlier, it was forced to raise funds through a record-sized rights issue of £5.9 billion. In addition, it sold its international directories business Yell for £2.14 billion and demerged the wireless interests of O2.

All was not lost: BT has moved with the times. It now provides a significant broadband service as well as sports TV channels, in particular having acquired broadcasting rights for certain football matches. However, it still has to contend with a pension fund deficit of £7 billion and borrowings of £5 billion. In 2015, the share price was less than half the 1053.2p reached on 31 December 1999 – but it is worth remembering that it has seen worse times, having fallen to 71.4p in March 2009. Lucky holders who bought at this low now have a six-bagger whilst those who purchased at the high have seen their investment halve in value. Who said that risks and share price volatility is lower with large companies? It was painfully clear that BT shares were unlikely to double from their peak – and conversely, unless the company went bust, that it could easily experience a significant rise from the share-price low. Those investors who bought a FTSE 100 tracker fund in December 1999 were effectively investing 7% of their money in BT at its all-time high. With the index little changed, BT today represents less than 2% of its value. I would rather take the risk of holding an interest in four smaller companies which at least have the capability of becoming ten-baggers.

Up until 1985, BT was the only mobile communications service available to the public. The government then issued national licences to Cellnet (a BT subsidiary) and Racal-Vodafone, a subsidiary of Racal Electronics. Racal Telecom was floated on the London Stock Exchange in 1988 when 20% of the equity was issued to the public. In 1991, the company was renamed Vodafone after Racal Electronics had placed its holding with shareholders. The name was an abbreviation of 'voice data phone' (I remain unsure of where the 'f' is in phone). For the year to 31 March 2015, Vodafone revenues reached US$42 million from 446 million subscribers, making the firm the second-largest mobile telecommunications company behind China Mobile. This was achieved by organic growth and through acquisitions. Unlike BT, the company was in a new and growing market. This was reflected in the share price, which increased by 35× from flotation to a peak of more than 400p in March 2000. By then other companies had moved into the mobile market – and, filled with global aspirations Vodafone had expanded too quickly.

The share price fell back to a low of 82p in July 2002. By 2015 it was only a little over 200p – still well below the March 2000 peak. When the FTSE 100 reached its December 1999 high, Vodafone had a weighting of 6.8%, but this is now down to around 3.4%. To be fair, I can see why, at the time, these shares appealed to investors seeking capital growth – but I would not be comfortable having 6.8% of a portfolio invested in one company. Vodafone started as an acorn, grew into an oak tree, but then reached maturity. I would prefer to have been invested in three or four saplings. Having said that, I *have* held BT and Vodafone in the Opportunities Fund for short spells – though only when share prices had fallen to ridiculously low levels.

In 1866, Jesse James held up a US bank for the first time and the Reno Brothers committed the first US train robbery. Twenty-seven years earlier saw the start of the first Opium War. At the time, Britain wanted to buy porcelain and tea from China but was required to settle in silver. The British were unprepared to do this and overcame the problem by illegally importing opium from India to China and then insisting on payment in silver. To crack down on the trade, China seized large quantities of opium from British merchants in the port of Canton. In retaliation, a British Naval fleet attacked and inflicted defeat on several Chinese strategic positions along the coast. As part of the surrender settlement, China granted Britain a 99-year lease on the island of Hong Kong.

The second Opium War occurred in 1856 after Chinese officers searched a ship and upset Britain by lowering the British flag. Peace was achieved in 1860 after British and French military forces stormed Peking. As a result, the opium trade was legalised. Sir Thomas Sutherland, a director of P&O, foresaw a boom in trade between Europe and the Asian Pacific region and in 1865 raised HK$5 million to establish the Hong Kong and Shanghai Banking Corporation plc, which was incorporated one year later.

A century later the Hong Kong and Shanghai Banking Corporation had growth aspirations, and in 1980 it made an unsolicited takeover bid for the Royal Bank of Scotland. This was blocked by the British government and it had to wait another 12 years to gain its first foothold in Europe. This came when it acquired Midland Bank, which had a history dating back to 1836 and was a constituent of the FTSE 100. The group is now known as HSBC Holdings plc and, due to its international presence, was less affected than others by the global banking crises. Its market weighting actually increased from 5.2% to 6.2% from 31 December 1999 to 2015.

Another company to benefit from the opium trade was the Chartered Bank of India, Australia and China (commonly known as the Chartered Bank). It was incorporated in London by the grant of a Royal Charter from Queen Victoria and, in 1858, opened branches in Calcutta, Bombay and Shanghai, and, later, branches in Hong Kong and Singapore. The firm's original business was in the discounting and re-discounting of opium and cotton bills – an extremely profitable enterprise as a result of boom conditions in those commodity markets. Since 1862, it has been authorised to issue bank notes in Hong Kong and its business developed into providing finance for the tea, rice, sugar, hemp and silk trades. About the same time, the Standard Bank was founded and a short while later financed development of the Kimberley diamond fields, and, from 1885, the Johannesburg gold fields. The banks merged in 1969, adopting the name Standard Chartered Bank. In 1986, Lloyds Bank made an unsuccessful takeover approach. In 2000, Standard Chartered acquired Grindlays Bank to extend its interests in India and Pakistan. Today the company is based in London and operates 1,200 branches worldwide.

Both HSBC and Standard Chartered Bank weathered the 2008 banking crisis well, but encountered problems seven years later when Southeast Asian economies suffered from the effects of the slowdown in Chinese economic growth. In the case of HSBC, it had represented 5.2% of the FTSE 100 in December 1999 – by 2015, it stood at a little over 6%. Not a great performance, but better than the other five large constituents of the FTSE 100. Standard Chartered had been a shooting star; more recently it became a fallen one. On 30 December 1999 the share price was 810.4p. It reached 1652.9p in December 2007, but fell to a low of 565.5p in March 2009. This was followed by a spectacular recovery to a peak of 1950p in November 2010. Five years later the share price had again fallen below 600p after the announcement of a quarterly loss and a restructuring programme which involved a rights issue to raise £3 billion.

Since my experience of the 1973 stock market crash, I have always been a little wary about buying shares in the banking sector – though I have seen it as an area where opportunities for making money can at times occur. In the case of the Opportunities Fund, I could only buy when the sector was out of favour or when bank share prices had crashed to a level where they could be classed as recovery situations. I held HSBC, Standard Chartered Bank and National Westminster Bank for a brief time in 1993–94 when they accounted for nearly 4%

of the Opportunities Fund portfolio. The sector rallied sharply and within months all of these holdings were sold at good profits.

I did not revisit bank shares until 2009 when the credit crisis caused the banking sector to crash. By November 2011, I had invested 3% of the Opportunities portfolio between Barclays, Lloyds and Royal Bank of Scotland. Underlying profits were showing improvement, but banks were continuing to suffer substantial asset write-downs and fines due to a number of regulatory breaches, such as the mis-selling of payment protection insurance (PPI). In the past, shares in UK banks were considered to be reliable, high-yielding income stocks, but following the 2008 banking crisis this was no longer the case. Consequently many income funds were forced to sell and, with a lack of buying interest, share prices became unduly depressed. In the 15 November 2011 Opportunities Fund valuation, the price of Barclays was 171.25p, Lloyds 27.3p and Royal Bank of Scotland 212p. I sold the holding in Barclays at a price of 264p a year later and in July 2014 sold Lloyds at 74p and Royal Bank of Scotland at 346p.

In the case of the Cavendish Select Fund, I could take a longer-term view and therefore retained interests in Barclays and Royal Bank of Scotland. However, with Lloyds it seemed sensible to take a profit as a proposed reduction in the British government's holding would put a cap on the share price. Equally problems were beginning to emerge from Standard Chartered, meaning the latter seemed to be a better long-term opportunity to make a profit. I made the switch, but would have achieved better terms had I left it until Standard Chartered announced its restructuring and rights issue.

At the 31 December 1999 market high BP, BT, Vodafone, HSBC and GlaxoSmithKline accounted for 32.3% of the FTSE 100. The top five constituents are now HSBC, British American Tobacco, BP, GlaxoSmithKline and Royal Dutch Shell – which comprise about 29% of the value of the index. Sector concentration is even more striking than it used to be, with seven sectors accounting for around 60% of the value. Top of the list are the banking and oil and gas sectors, which each represent a weighting of 13%. These are followed by pharmaceuticals at 9% and approximately 6% in basic resources, tobacco, telecommunications and insurance.

Basic resources covers seven companies and is dominated by Rio Tinto and BHP Billiton, which together make up half the sector. It can be an extremely volatile area of the stock market depending on the level of commodity prices. An example of this is Glencore plc, which describes itself as "one of the world's largest global natural resource companies and a major producer and trader of more than 90 commodities". Its history stems from a 1994 management buyout of the commodity trader Marc Rich & Company AG, which had commenced commodity trading in 1974 and was reported to have lost US$172 million in the zinc market. Glencore gained a listing on the London stock market in 2011 through an IPO which raised US$11 billion at a price of 530p. Despite the offer being four times oversubscribed, the shares did not close at a premium and three institutions behind the issue had to support the share price to avoid it falling to a discount. Two years later the company completed a merger with Xstrata, a FTSE 100 mining company specialising in copper. At one stage in 2015, following investor concerns about gearing, coupled with a sharp fall in the copper price, the shares fell below 70p.

My interest in the basic resources sector has recently been confined to the Cavendish Select Fund, where my principal holdings have been Antofagasta, BHP Billiton, Randgold and Rio Tinto. These might not have the same recovery potential as a Glencore-type situation, where there is greater operational gearing, but should nevertheless benefit from any recovery in commodity prices. In the case of the Opportunities Fund, I have purchased a holding in Antofagasta as a recovery play but otherwise confined my interest to smaller specialist situations. Similarly, a limited number of smaller mining company shares have been held in the Cavendish AIM Fund. It is fair to say this has not proved to be a great area of investment (more of that in the next chapter featuring my greatest disasters).

The UK tobacco sector contains just two companies and has been one of the big stock market success stories of the last two decades

– but one in which I have not been involved. Since the FTSE 100 peak on 31 December 1999, British American Tobacco has become a ten-bagger and Imperial Tobacco a nine-bagger. My blind spot when it comes to these stocks was caused by wariness about litigation. To date, the tobacco companies have successfully fended off the problem (though they have spent substantial funds defending themselves). Investors in the sector have done extraordinarily well. By avoiding the potential risk, I missed out on what turned out to be an outstanding area of growth.

When considering the big beasts in the insurance sector, performances range from impressive to mediocre and all the way down to dismal. Today there are six insurance companies in the FTSE 100 and the most successful is Admiral – a start-up in 1993, which launched on the stock market nine years later with a value of £711 million. It started by writing high-premium car insurance for younger drivers and has branched out to other customers, in particular families that own more than one car. Since flotation the shares have become a five-bagger.

Most other insurance companies have a longer heritage. RSA Insurance Group was formed through the 1996 merger between Royal Insurance, founded in 1845, and Sun Alliance, with origins going back to 1710. The group undertakes general insurance, including a large motor business, but has struggled in a competitive marketplace. This is reflected in its share price performance. The market value of the company has declined in value by 75% since 31 December 1999.

Fires were responsible for the formation of two insurance companies. One of the oldest insurance companies in the world was the Hand in Hand Fire & Life Insurance Society. It was formed in 1696, 30 years after the Great Fire of London, and until 1831 operated its own fire brigade. The company was acquired in 1905 by the Commercial Union Group, which had been formed by a group of merchants who objected to the rise in fire insurance rates after the Great Tooley Street Fire of 1861. Following the acquisition of General Accident in 1998 and a merger with Norwich Union two years later, the group changed its name to Aviva. The company went through a difficult period but recovered better than RSA Insurance Group and produced a superior trading record in a very competitive market. Even so, the 2015 share price was half of what it was on December 1999.

Another insurance company was established in 1848 by a group of gentlemen in a room in London's Hatton Garden. It sold insurance using door-to-door salesmen and was to pay out on one third of the total fatalities in the First World War. The company has occupied its signature red-brick building in Holborn Bars, London, since 1879. It acquired Jackson National Life insurance company in 1986 to expand into America and from 1994 made a major expansion into Southeast Asia. Five years later it acquired M&G, the fund management company, which in 1931 had launched the first unit trust in Britain. The founder members when naming the company decided on one that reflected a cautious and responsible approach to business: by now readers will have guessed that I am talking about the Prudential. Between 31 December 1999 and 2015 the Pru's share price advanced by more than 25%, reflecting the good growth seen from its Southeast Asia operations.

The two star performers in the insurance sector are specialist providers of life assurance. New Law Life Assurance Society was formed in Chancery Lane, London, by six lawyers in 1836. It originally sold policies to the legal profession but then opened up business to the general public and changed its name to Legal and General Life Assurance Society. The company listed on the London Stock Exchange as Legal & General Group plc in July 1979 and branched out into investment management, pensions, estate agency and mortgage provision. In 2015, the group was one of the top 15 UK fund managers with £746 billion under management and also arranged £46 billion of mortgages. On 31 December 1999 the share price was 155p – by 2015 holders would have seen an appreciation of more than 70%. However, it was a rocky journey. Its high level of mortgage business caused concerns at the time of the Lehman scandal and banking crisis. At one stage in 2009 the share price reached a low of 23p, giving investors the potential of a ten-bagger over the next six years.

Standard Life was the other star in the sector. It was formed in 1825 and was reincorporated as a mutual assurance company, owned by the policy holders, 100 years later. It demutualised in 2006 when shares were given to shareholders and the company was listed on the London Stock Exchange at a price of 230p. The shares have had a less bumpy ride than others in the sector – the share price has more than doubled since launch.

When I formed the Opportunities Fund in 1988, Commercial Union (now Aviva) was one of the first shares that I bought for the portfolio. Following the Thatcher government's Big Bang, the share price was depressed – but it recovered well within 12 months and I sold for a decent profit. On occasions between 1992 and 1996 I held Royal Insurance and three insurance companies which were subsequently taken over: London and Manchester (acquired by Friends Provident in 1998), Guardian Royal Exchange (taken over by AXA in 1999) and Refuge Assurance (merged with United Friendly in 1996). I did not return to the sector until 2009. At that time, just like the banks, the sector was on its knees. I bought interests in Aviva, Legal & General and the Prudential – all of which looked to be survivors and were quoted at large discounts to their underlying assets. Share prices recovered sharply and I was out of the sector by 2013. In the Select Fund, I had similar holdings – plus Standard Life – which all performed well.

The problem with tracking an index weighted by size of company is that a growth company may begin as a small percentage of the total and therefore not have a meaningful impact. In 1864, a tailor called Joseph Hepworth founded a company in Leeds named after himself. By 1917, Hepworths Ltd had become the largest clothing manufacturer in the UK, specialising in men's three-piece suits sold through its own retail outlets. A transformational change occurred in 1981 when the company acquired the Kendall & Son's rainwear and ladieswear shops from Combined English Stores. All of the Kendall shops were converted to a new format of mini department stores selling womenswear, men's clothing, footwear and a home interior range – rebranded under the name Next. Another important move, which came in 1987, was the acquisition of the Grattan catalogue company; this eventually became the successful online Next Directory business. Expansion came at a cost and, to strengthen the balance sheet the company sold 433 jewellery stores to the Ratners Group for US$232 million. In February 1982 Next's share price was 34p. By September 1987 it had become a ten-bagger, peaking at 355p. The wheels now seemed to fall off – and by 1990 it had reached a low of 15p. Thereafter the shares did not look back; they closed at 562p on 31 December 1999 and breached £80 in 2015. £10,000 invested in my Opportunities Fund at launch in 1988 would be worth around £110,000 today – the same sum invested in Next shares over the same period would be worth more than £2 million.

From a stock-picking point of view, it makes sense to hold investments in firms like British American Tobacco and Next rather than being forced to take a large holding in a mature company in order to match an index weighting. We have seen from BT, Vodafone, BP, several bank shares and mining companies that things do not always work out as expected – even top blue-chip companies can go off the rails and halve (or worse) in value. Companies can suffer from mishaps, be exposed to cyclical areas of the market, mature and cease to grow – or simply expanded too quickly. We have observed the last with Royal Bank of Scotland and Glencore. Old-fashioned industrial conglomerates can also be prone to this.

I was told that RADAR was invented in 2007 but I needed to be convinced. In 1895 a company named British Electric Traction (BET) was formed to operate tramways in the British Isles. At the peak, its services ran in more than 40 locations – but trams were replaced by buses and the last BET tram ran from Gateshead in 1951. BET itself operated a bus business in the UK between 1949 and 1967, as well as expanding into television (Rediffusion, Thames), plant hire, laundry and linen rental, shipping, printing and publishing and waste management (Biffa). Separately, in 1903 an American entrepreneur formed a company selling towels with personalised logos. He named the company Initial Services and it subsequently became a leader in a range of washroom services, employing 70,000 people in 40 countries. By 1983, BET had built up a 42% holding in Initial and acquired the company two years later.

Three years after Initial Services was formed in 1903, a Danish pharmacist opened a London office selling Ratin, a new pest-control product incorporating a form of bacteria lethal to rats and mice. In 1920, a professor of entomology produced a product to kill deathwatch beetles. He established a small factory in Hatton Garden, London, to manufacture and sell bottles of woodworm fluid. Sadly, the inventor died in 1925 from an experiment gone wrong involving poisonous fumes, but in that year his company, Rentokil, was incorporated. British Ratin acquired Rentokil in 1957, but retained the Rentokil name and, in 1969, listed on the London Stock Exchange. From 1983, the company achieved spectacular growth. The chief executive became known as 'Mr Twenty Per Cent', a growth rate which was impossible to maintain. Rentokil acquired the much larger and lower-growth BET in March 1996 and renamed itself Rentokil Initial. At the time the share price was 175p and the company continued to be an investors' darling. The share price peaked at 473p in January 1999. By December 2008, the shares had fallen to a low of 31.5p. Fortunes have recovered since, but the shares have lost their previous growth status, despite the 2007 invention of the world's smartest mouse trap – known as RADAR (Rodent Activated Detection And Riddance).

17

Ten Years of Train Crashes

Agambler will usually tell colleagues about winning bets but seldom mention the losers (often more numerous). Fund managers and marketing departments have a similar tendency. I suppose it is natural to wish to attract potential investors by dwelling on success stories, but I think that investment disasters are far more interesting. They demonstrate that investment outperformance can be achieved despite casualties along the way. They also often provide valuable lessons and can help you to avoid problem areas in future. Fortunately, in my career investment mishaps have not occurred that often – and are far fewer than the average gambler's losing wagers.

This is the first of several chapters on investments that went wrong – some with happy endings despite the companies' fates, some with unhappy endings. I have deliberately omitted chapters on my successes for a number of reasons but principally because there are too many of them and the reader might be bored by chapter after chapter of what could be seen as trumpet blowing. I also wanted to cover areas which might help the investor to identify various investment pitfalls in his or her own investing. However, who knows – at some stage I might be convinced to write a textbook on successful investment through the eyes of a stock picker.

Rather than examining problem stocks by market sector, I have decided to cover investment failures in chronological order. Looking back to the original Opportunities Fund portfolio as at 15 May 1988, there were holdings in two companies that later became train crashes.

Most notable was a company mentioned earlier, and which I always think of as the pyjama company (more on that in a minute): Resort Hotels, where I acquired shares at 14p in March 1988 when it was first listed on the USM (Unlisted Securities Market, the forerunner to AIM). Thankfully, within six months I had sold at a decent profit. The company raised a total of about £50 million through rights issues in December 1988, March 1991 and May 1992 – and went bust one year later with debts totalling £140 million. At the time, the company owned 50 properties, but Robert Feld, the managing director, had a lavish lifestyle and was reported to own properties in Knightsbridge, Sussex and France. The Serious Fraud Office (SFO) investigated the situation following the last £20 million fund raise and discovered that Feld had painted a false picture of the company's financial position. He was jailed for eight years after being convicted of making three false statements; he had nine forgery indictments. Four further fraud offences remained on file and he was disqualified from being a company director for ten years. Why is this the pyjama company to me? I sold the shares after being evacuated, in my pyjamas, from the Resort Hotel Brighton following a fire.

Norfolk House was the other casualty of this period. It was also a holding that I acquired following a placing on the USM in March 1988. It specialised in the development of petrol stations and was run by a passionate CEO who would identify strategic greenfield sites, obtain planning consent, develop a petrol-filling station area and then either sell or retain it as an investment. When I visited the company, the CEO had stacks of video recordings of each of the sites showing traffic flows, approach roads and surrounding countryside. The problem was not dishonesty but overexpansion and a high level of gearing. Coupons, by way of stamps, were issued with petrol purchases – but there was no provision to cover their redemption by customers. I doubled my money on my investment but decided to sell after the company announced a four-for-nine rights issue in February 1990. Norfolk House overextended itself further by acquiring Frost Group in a partial share offer in August 1990. By March 1991 HMRC accepted that the firm had negligible value.

Lightning strikes twice. Frost Group was a quoted company which had built up a chain of petrol-filling stations. It was run by James Frost, who managed to extract those operations from Norfolk House after it went into administration and reintroduced the company to the stock market through a placing and share offering in October 1991. Further capital was raised from rights issues in 1993 and 1995. The latter was used to partly finance the acquisition of a chain of service stations from Burmah Castrol to make it the country's largest independent operator with 400 outlets. Unfortunately, Save, as the company was now known, had taken out a £105 million loan to finance the acquisition and financial difficulties occurred when the major oil companies, which owned larger chains, started a price war. An attempted sale and leaseback of the properties failed to progress and the consortium of banks were unwilling to refinance a £57 million facility on reasonable terms. The shares were deemed valueless when the listing was cancelled in 2001. At one stage, investors would have done well from their holdings, but I did not like the fact that Norfolk House shareholders had lost all their money and, as a matter of principle, avoided the shares.

A share I think of as my 'drain' holding was a company called Gabicci, formed in 1973 and listed on the USM in November 1983. In those days, holders were issued with numbered share certificates and I had the distinction of owning share certificate number two. The company had developed a range of coordinated menswear designed to appeal to a younger age group. It had particularly unique knitwear incorporating leather strips. Trading went well for the first few years, but then the product looked tired and appealed more to the profile of a middle-aged golfer. Profits slipped and, after running into financial problems, the company was taken over by Helene plc which, in 1997, was itself placed into creditors' voluntary liquidation with an estimated deficiency of £29 million. The chairman of Helene was accused of having systematically looted the company and was disqualified by the Department of Trade and Industry (DTI) for 13 years from acting as a director of a company.

I purchased a holding for the Opportunities Fund in 1988 and disposed of the shares in 1993 at a small loss. When I was a stockbroker, I was happy to recommend Gabicci shares to smaller company fund managers. One of these was happy to build up a holding and, when I bumped into him on the way home, I would update him on the progress of his order. Our conversations would often occur on the Waterloo and City Line Underground train. When he was buying he would ask me to speak in a hushed voice but when he had built up his holding he would shout down the carriage: "Hi Paul, great stock Gabicci, how is the share price doing?" The Underground service in question runs between Waterloo and the City and is commonly known as 'the drain'. I have consequently always thought of Gabicci as my drain stock. Of course, down the drain is where the shares ended too – though, as a footnote, the brand was acquired by the owner of the Joe Bloggs label and has since been successfully relaunched into the younger fashion market.

"Mumford, get your hair cut", was a frequently heard refrain from the headmaster of Dorking Grammar School. Hair does not grow as quickly as grass but both need cutting. In those days, a visit to the barber for a quick trim was a tedious experience. Today, youngsters pay more attention to their appearance and vast sums can be spent on styling and regular visits to the hairdresser. Celebrities set the trend by spending thousands on colouring, grooming and hair extensions. Even 27 years ago this seemed a lucrative and low-risk type of business so I purchased a holding in Alan Paul plc when it was floated on the USM in June 1989. The company operated a hairdressing franchise business and, a year after flotation, doubled its size by acquiring Essanelle for £8.45 million. The deal was financed from a large rights issue on the back of a forecast for a 62% increase in profits for the year that had just ended. Unfortunately, the firm's directors, Alan Moss and Michael Rowlands, used Alan Paul to fund their lifestyles; in 1991 the firm crashed and in 1996 both pleaded guilty to fraudulently obtaining £11 million from banks and lending institutions. Moss was sentenced to three years' imprisonment and Rowland to 27 months'. I suffered a loss when the company was wound up in February 1992. Rather unfairly, I cursed my headmaster.

We now move forward to 1996. This investment was, at first, a little gem which I held for two years without losing money – but all along it was a train crash destined to happen. It was a company called Queens Moat Houses. Before I bought its shares, it had in fact already run into the buffers. The company was incorporated in 1961 and, by 1972, had established a chain of 16 hotels. In that year, John Bairstow was appointed chairman after injecting his private company hotel interests for £1.1 million of shares and purchasing a further 8% of the equity. He was the driving force behind Queens Moat's expansion via acquisitions financed by numerous rights issues. By 1993, the company had become the third-largest hotel company in Great Britain and owned 190 hotels in the UK and continental Europe. However, despite announcing half-year profits to 30 June 1992 of £38 million, borrowings were increasing and something looked amiss. As this would give rise to a breach of covenants, an investigation of the company's finances was ordered by the banks.

It transpired that the company had made a trading loss of £100 million for the year to 31 December 1992. Jones Lang Wooton valued the firm's properties at £861 million. A professional valuation made one year earlier, by another firm of estate agents, had come up with a value of £2 billion. To make matters worse, the balance sheet had net liabilities of £389 million and the prior year profit of £90 million was restated as a loss of £56 million. Three directors were found guilty of dishonesty and disqualified for seven to ten years. Bairstow obtained a six-year disqualification for negligence.

Following a restructuring, Queens Moat returned to the stock market in 1995 with a value of £24 million attributed to the equity and a share price that was down 97%. Two years later, I felt that there was good value in the shares and I acquired a modest holding which I held for a short while before selling at a small profit. After I had disposed of my interest, the company soldiered on, but the debt was still weighing heavily. Eventually, Goldman Sachs's property arm acquired Queens Moat for £544 million – but equity holders received a price of only one penny per share, which valued the company at a mere £6 million. Even worse, the holders of the £98 million convertible loan stock were obliged to convert their holdings into ordinary shares for which they received the one penny share offer, thereby losing the bulk of their investment. In August 2014, Goldman Sachs sold 11 of the 15 provincial hotels, trading under the names Crowne Plaza and Holiday Inns, for a reported £135 million.

Another hotel company that ended up appointing administrators was the Real Hotel Company, which operated 59 hotels in the UK and Europe as well as the New Connaught Rooms in London's Covent Garden. It also managed, under franchise, the Choice Hotels' brands of Quality, Comfort and Clarion hotels and owned Purple Hotels. It had a history stretching back to 1877, in the form of a company called Arden and Cobden Group, and I acquired a holding in 1995 when it was named Friendly Hotels. The shares were purchased as an asset situation: it had been awarded the master franchise from the American company Choice Hotels International (CHI) for its brands in the UK and Ireland. However, trading conditions were difficult and Friendly Hotels was restructured in 2001, which gave CHI a controlling interest in return for improved franchise terms. I sold my holding when the company returned to profitability in 2004. In January 2009, the company announced a sharp deterioration in trading and entered administration. Unlike Resort Hotels and Queens Moat, the downfall was purely due to market conditions rather than dishonesty.

An unlikely failure was a company called SEP Industrial Holdings, a manufacturer of nuts and bolts and industrial fastenings. It had been around since 1965, listed on the USM in 1987 and moved to the main market in 1993. I purchased a holding in 1996 when the company looked to be in a growth phase. At first, the share price performed well, but in 1999 the accounts were delayed and the shares suspended due to possible accounting irregularities. This led to the departure of the chairman and finance director. The suspension only lasted for two months, after which I sold the holding. I did not suffer a large loss but other long-term shareholders were less fortunate. In 2001, SEP did a reverse takeover of a software company called iRevolution at a time when IT spending was slowing. The original industrial fastenings business was sold for a paltry sum and in 2003 iRevolution became a casualty of the dotcom bubble, which left the shares valueless.

The trouble with buying shares when they appear cheap is that sometimes they are priced like that for a reason. As has been seen with Queens Moat, sometimes asset values cannot be relied on; in other cases, profits might have been overstated. Equally, overexpansion can lead to a company's downfall. One of the old darlings of the stock market was Albert Fisher. The company was incorporated in 1920. Unusually, the shares were first floated on the Liverpool Stock Exchange in 1964, before gaining a listing on the London Stock Exchange in 1973.

Until 1982, Albert Fisher was a small company distributing fruit and vegetables, running at a small loss. A change in management heralded a period of acquisitive expansion financed partly by a succession of rights issues. From a turnover of less than £10 million, sales exceeded £1 billion by 1991 and the company entered the FTSE 100 with a market value of just under £800 million. At the time of its peak, it was a supplier of fresh fruit, vegetables and seafood to major supermarket groups as well as Marks & Spencer. Sales peaked in 1995, but the company, having made about 50 acquisitions, was laden with debt – whilst also having to finance performance-related payments on past acquisitions. The following few years saw a programme of disposals and by 1998 the value of the company had plummeted to under £40 million. Despite a continuing restructuring, the level of debt remained high and receivers were appointed in 2002. Thankfully, I only held the shares for a short period in 1996.

It feels bad to lose money. As a fund manager, it is even worse to make a loss with other people's money. A small consolation is that investors should appreciate that any investment in equity shares involves some degree of risk; little sympathy is given to those losing money at the tables of a casino. The real tragedy is when money is lost through fraud or circumstances where there is no apparent risk. The next train crash did not involve fraud, but 21,000 individuals lost a total of up to £10.9 million in deposits.

The company was Uno plc. I acquired a holding in its share placing when it came to the stock market in 1996. It was a furniture retailer operating from 19 stores. During its first year as a listed company, on the back of a strong advertising programme, Uno produced like-for-like sales growth of 19%. Earnings were to treble. Disaster struck when, shortly afterwards, it acquired World of Leather, which operated 39 stores across the UK. The management had problems running the enlarged group and relied on customer deposits for working capital. Sales fell sharply. In March 2000 Uno went into administration carrying debts of £20.6 million. The insolvency agency of the DTI sought to disqualify five directors for allowing the group to trade to the detriment of customers and not protecting their deposits, with larger down payments often offered against a greater price discount. In the event, the court decided that their conduct did not warrant disqualification as they had reasonable grounds that liquidation could be avoided. I was never comfortable with the World of Leather acquisition and sold in early 1997.

My schoolboy job delivering morning papers was for the newsagent WH Smith. The company had a fleet of bright-red cast-iron bicycles. Over the back wheel was a frame constructed to support two canvas bags for carrying newspapers. Due to the weight of the bicycle, it supported just one very low gear, which enabled me to pedal up the steepest of hills on my daily four-mile journey. The bike would last forever and was manufactured by a company called Elswick Hopper, which also produced other trade bikes such as those seen in the famous Hovis advert. To me, Mary Poppins looks to have been riding an Elswick bicycle in the film of the same name.

Mr Frederick Hopper had started his bicycle repair trade in 1880 and built up a business selling bikes in the UK and abroad. The bankrupt Elswick Cycle Company was bought by the firm in 1910. Between 1905 and 1912, the workforce doubled to 800 employees. The Falcon Company, acquired in 1978, gave the group a range of racing models. By now, the Hopper name had been dropped from the brand and Elswick had developed a printing and packaging business. Competition from cheap imports from the Far East led to the original bicycle business being sold and Elswick plc was bought by Ferguson International plc. I held these shares for a short length of time in 1997. Ferguson International experienced financial difficulties and went into liquidation in January 2000. Today, Elswick sells a range of more than 300,000 bicycles annually and is part of the AIM-listed Tandem Group plc.

In 1997, I purchased a holding in a company called M.A.I.D. plc, which stood for Market Analysis and Information Database. It was formed in 1984 and ten years later listed on the London Stock Exchange with a flotation value of £89 million. The valuation looked high considering that the pre-tax profits were only £603,000, but stockbrokers were forecasting pre-tax profits of £5 million in 1995 and £12 million for the following year. A big move came in 1995 when the company raised £25 million from US investors after obtaining a NASDAQ quotation, having entered into a collaboration to supply its business information service to Microsoft for integration into Windows 95. In 1997, M.A.I.D became the world's largest supplier of online information when it acquired and changed its name to Dialog, a subsidiary of Knight-Ridder Inc, for £269 million, financed by shares to the value of £120 million and loans. Results did not live up to expectations and, with the company saddled with too much debt, the share price fell from a peak of 300p to 30p.

During 2000, the Dialog business information services were sold to Thomson for £275 million and the company changed its name to Bright Station. It then decided to concentrate on its knowledge-management software division and entered into an alliance with IBM. To reflect its new emphasis, the company yet again changed its name, becoming Smartlogik. Unfortunately, funds were being burnt through at an alarming rate. Cash balances fell from £16.3 million in December 2000, to £7.4 million by March 2001 and £2 million by May 2001. This necessitated a sale of shares at a price of 5p to raise £12 million, forecast as being sufficient to see the company through to profitability. Sadly, this was not the case. The company went into liquidation in April 2002, with the trading assets sold for a mere £2.7 million. Fortunately, I did not go through this torturous journey and had sold within a few months of purchase.

One of the earliest reported instances of insider trading occurred in 1812 when Charles Barker ignored instructions to bring news of Napoleon's retreat from Moscow to King George III. Instead, he delivered the message to Nathan Mayer Rothschild, who used the information to make a killing on the stock exchange. As a reward, Barker was helped to set up a business that sold space in *The Times* newspaper. Thus one of the oldest advertising agencies in the City of London was formed. Charles Barker plc came to the stock market in 1986 and changed its name to BNB Resources, later becoming BNB Recruitment Solutions. It ran into financial difficulties when recruitment activity dried up during the banking crisis. Administrators were appointed in 2009. I made a decent profit on my holding after purchasing shares in 1997 and holding them for less than a year.

Companies are forced out of business when they have insufficient funds to continue trading. This can be caused by overexpansion, as in the case of M.A.I.D. or a deterioration in market conditions, as with BNB Recruitment. However, a profitable company can also be allowed to fail by its banks. One such company was Alexandra plc, which I thought would have been well worth rescuing – but there were not enough other investors to support this view. Alexandra was named after Princess Alexandra, wife of the future King Edward VII, and formed in 1850 as a company selling linen and fabrics from its

Bristol headquarters. A major change occurred in the First World War when 1.5 million women went to work for the first time and demanded protective clothing for military, nursing, manufacturing and other roles. Activity increased during the Second World War when 7.5 million worked to support the war effort.

The company listed on the main market of the stock exchange in January 1985 and by the end of the 1990s had become the UK's largest supplier of workwear, corporate uniforms and nursing wear. The trend for uniforms continued to grow and Alexandra was soon supplying companies such as McDonald's, BP and Abbey National with uniforms. All was well, but when the company needed to refinance its activities it came to light that the balance sheet contained old stock and materials which were obsolete and of very little value. Business volumes and profits had fallen during the banking crisis and, when the company broke its borrowing covenants, the banks pulled the plug. Administrators were appointed in 2010 and the business was sold to a competitor at a fraction of its true worth. One consolation was that 400 jobs were saved and the company is still trading. Regrettably, investors, including myself, lost our capital.

Train crashes can happen in many areas; I had the distinction of owning the first UK biotech company to go bust. The company, Scotia Holdings, had a leading drug called Foscan, which was to be used in the treatment of head and neck cancer. It successfully moved into phase-III trials in Europe and America but failed to win approval. The directors put Scotia up for sale but did not find any takers. It entered administration in 2001. Foscan looked to have stood a good chance of success and must have had some merit, as it was sold to Singapore Technologies in a deal reported to be worth up to £65 million. Bondholders were owed £50 million and there may have been something left for shareholders – I am unsure because my holding had been sold before the company folded.

The National Minimum Age Act hit the statue books in 1998, with an hourly rate of £3.60 for those over the age of 22. Prior to this, the Trade Boards Act of 1909 had provided for boards to be set up to negotiate a minimum wage – usually for 'sweated' industries where there were low wages, long hours and often poor sanitary conditions. One of the first beneficiaries was the chain-making industry at Cradley Heath: in 1910, around 1,000 female workers doubled their wages after winning a nine-week strike. The history of chain-making in Chadley Heath goes back to 1851, when Eliza Tinsley inherited a nail-making business from her husband. At one stage, in 1871, the company had 4,000 employees producing nails, chains, rivets and anchors.

Eliza Tinsley Group plc shares were placed on AIM in 1984 and introduced to the main market in 1996. There followed a period of expansion into components for the off-highway market, with manufacturing facilities in the UK, Italy and the United States. Unfortunately, despite a range of blue-chip customers, the company was exposed to cyclical industries. By 31 March 2005, debt was £16.7 million, on which the company paid £1.64 million in interest charges. A refinancing exercise was completed in September 2005 but the company had moved into loss. November 2005 heralded a profit warning due to the effects of destocking and a downturn in UK consumer markets. Nothing came from a takeover approach and administrators were appointed in January 2006. It was a sound business, in which I had held shares since 1998. Fortunately, a buyer was found for the original Eliza Tinsley business, which is now trading successfully.

So ends the story of some notable accidents in shares that I had purchased in the first ten years of running the Cavendish Opportunities Fund. On several of these shares, I lost money – but in most I was able to sell and limit any damage. Elsewhere, as we have seen, there were many more companies that were subject to takeover bids during the period. The next chapter looks at train crashes on shares bought during the following seven years – including the dotcom era – and brings us up to October 2005, when the Cavendish AIM Fund was launched.

18

Hitting the Buffers

The UK Atomic Energy Authority (UKAEA) was established in 1954 to look after the country's nuclear requirements; the Atomic Energy Authority Act 1995 made AEA Technology Group (AEA) – a new offshoot of the UKAEA – the last privatisation issue under John Major's government. Shares were placed on the stock market in September 1996. At the time the company operated a variety of businesses stretching from nuclear safety and engineering to environmental protection and battery technology. The next few years saw further diversification through acquisitions, but results disappointed and the decision was made to concentrate on rail and environmental activities. A number of divestments were made and, in 2000, the company exited its original nuclear consultancy business. By 2006, all businesses apart from energy and environmental consultancy had been sold. I acquired a holding in AEA in 1999 and felt that there was considerable potential in the shares.

Unfortunately, as part of the privatisation plan, AEA inherited a final-salary pension scheme. Employees who transferred to AEA had the option of staying with the UKAEA scheme, but were encouraged to move to a new AEA scheme. In years to come, the AEA scheme was to present a millstone round the neck of AEA and was one of the reasons why the company eventually went into administration.

Many pensioners transferred across and lost out when a pre-pack insolvency event occurred in 2012. The level of debt incurred to finance two American acquisitions also caused instability.

Project Performance Corporation Inc. (PPC) was acquired by AEA in 2008 and Eastern Research Group Inc. (ERG) in 2010. Both acted as consultancy businesses and undertook work on climate control for the US Federal and other government departments. A reduction in US government spending and some lost orders gave rise to poor results in 2011. AEA generated £3 million of cash, but borrowings were £36.4 million and the pension fund deficit had increased from £121.8 million to £168.5 million. Administrators were appointed and AEA Europe was sold to Ricardo for £18 million and PPC to Global Analytical Information Technology Services for an undisclosed sum. Both transactions were classed as asset sales and were made without defined pension liabilities or debt.

I associate Elvis Presley, James Dean, Tina Turner and a picnic bench with the next company. When I first started buying records, I owned a mechanical gramophone which had to be wound up using a handle at the side. It played 78rpm records and had a needle known as a stylus which needed to be replaced after a certain number of plays. Thankfully, the electric record player was invented, together with 45rpm and 33 1/3rpm records containing more than one track. Technology advanced quickly: stereophonic sound was invented. In its earliest days, this involved four tracks for each recording and the need for two separate loud speakers. Four of the best-known speaker brands – Wharfedale, Mission, Quad and Cyrus – were owned by a company called Verity.

Another device designed to attract the teenage record-buying public in the past was the jukebox, which in those days consisted of a large horizontal or vertical cabinet containing up to 100 records. I had always fancied owning one of these and later in life would drive past a jukebox retailer on my way home which had two black and white pictures in the window, one of Elvis Presley and the other of James Dean. The shop sold original refurbished jukeboxes or modern ones featuring a radio and CD player. It also sold a variety of loud speakers – and, much to my surprise, I was told that the pictures of Presley and Dean were actually flat speakers that could be mounted on the wall to give a surround sound effect.

I duly made my purchase of a modern jukebox and speakers. I found that the latter were made using technology developed by a company called NXT. On further investigation, I discovered that Verity had changed its name to NXT. The technology was developed by DERA, a UK military research department, for noise cancellation problems in helicopters. NXT patented the product and entered into licence deals with multinational companies such as 3M, Toyota, Logitech, Phillips, NEC, LG and Toshiba. Applications were vast, stretching from car panels to television screens, wall tiles and computers. In fact, a company called Kensington developed a docking system using this technology for the Apple iPod. Unfortunately, NXT licensed the technology too cheaply and it did not generate as significant a stream of recurring royalty income as it ought to have done. A contract with Hallmark enabled the technology to be used in greeting cards, such as one I once received which blared out Tina Turner's 'Simply the Best'. Unfortunately, the deal did not bring in substantial revenues.

At one stage NXT had a significant number of employees based in the UK and Hong Kong but to develop its new technology it had had to sell off its original speaker brands. Salvation might have come from a new haptic technology they had developed, which gave a different vibration when various parts of a glass panel were touched. The technology was demonstrated to me on a picnicking bench in the grounds of the Cavendish head office when a practice fire alarm went off during the company's visit. NXT had changed its name to HiWave Audio by then. Shortly afterwards it ran out of money. I had purchased shares in 1999 and held them until 2013 when administrators were appointed. The flat Elvis and James Dean speakers still produce an excellent sound, but are a haunting reminder of a disappointing investment. One good thing did emerge: it made me very wary about investing in loss-making technology companies.

Over the years this has saved me more money than that which I lost from investing in NXT.

Only the British could use the term 'housey-housey' to describe a game of bingo, but did the early African explorers know that Lake Nyasa translates into Lake Lake? Nevertheless, naming the landlocked country in southeast Africa Nyasaland was more logical. Malawi, as the country is now known, was a British colony until it gained independence in 1964. Lake Nyasa was discovered by a Portuguese explorer in 1616 and visited by David Livingstone in 1859. It forms the border between Malawi, Tanzania and Mozambique. In 1877, a Scottish company, the directors of which had connections with the Foreign Missions Committee of the Free Church of Scotland, was incorporated under the name Livingstone Central Africa Company. The aim was to set up a profitable trading business with a view to eliminating the slave trade.

The company was renamed African Lakes Corporation in 1978 and then set up a number of trading posts along the shores of Lake Nyasa. Early trade had been in ivory but it had then established rubber, cotton, tea and coffee plantations, opened a number of village stores and acquired a fleet of steamships for transporting products between various ports. After disposing of the steamers in 1923, the company started an automotive business, importing Ford, Nissan and Austin Morris cars from the UK, which eventually expanded into 11 African countries. Further diversification into hotels, building companies and insurance agents occurred, followed by the 1980 acquisition of several UK motor distributors. It then established a business selling computer products – before making the mistake of setting up an internet venture.

In 1994, three Kenyan students started an African news service which, one year later, was converted to an internet business called Africa Online. African Lakes Corporation acquired an interest in 1998 and this became its internet vehicle. Several similar acquisitions followed and by 2003 it was providing internet services to over 21 countries stretching from Cairo to Cape Town. However, expansion was costly. In 2003, the company reported a pre-tax loss of £5.4 million together with a £21.8 million charge for goodwill write-offs and impairment of fixed assets. Three equity fundraisings had taken place and the plantation and motor businesses had been sold for a derisory sum.

The shares had been placed on the Nairobi Stock Exchange in 2000 at a price of 80.4p, making it the second-largest quoted company on the Kenyan stock market. When the company delisted in March 2003, the share price had fallen to 1p. It was intended to transfer to AIM, but this did not materialise and receivers were appointed in 2007, with Africa Online being sold to Telkom South Africa for a fraction of its original gross investment. I had purchased a holding in 1999 as an asset situation with an interesting technology arm, but sold in 2002 when it became apparent that things were going wrong.

The mobile phone revolution has brought several successes and some failures. Carphone Warehouse, following its merger with Dixons Retail, is now a subsidiary of Dixons Carphone plc. It was formed in 1989 with just £6,000 capital and came to the stock market in 2000. The company now has more than 2,400 stores across Europe and is the second-largest broadband supplier behind BT. In 1999, Carphone Warehouse formed a joint venture to market products provided by Personal Numbers Company (shortly to change its name to PNC Telecom). This covered the supply of 0800 and 0870 numbers, memorable mobile telephone numbers and a text-to-speech service for Carphone Warehouse customers.

PNC Telecom (PNC) now embarked on a series of acquisitions, with the most important being KJC Mobile Phones Limited (KJC), which was financed through a placing of £17.6 million of new shares and a move from AIM to a full listing. At the time, KJC was described as one of the UK's largest independent cellular mobile phone dealerships, with approximately 300,000 customers and 30 retail outlets in the south of England. Unfortunately, the mobile phone market was becoming increasingly cutthroat and a large proportion of the KJC business was with Vodafone, meaning other companies with a wider offering had a competitive edge. By 2002, there was negligible growth in the mobile telecommunications market and an overcapacity in fixed line, causing a heavy downward pressure on prices and margins. At one stage, the company was valued by the stock market at £130 million, but, in 2003 the KJC business – having incurred a £25 million impairment of goodwill charge – was sold for £2 million. This left PNC as a cash shell with no ongoing business, but a contingent liability on a number of shop leases.

In order to protect the assets of PNC and deal with outstanding lease obligations, an administration order was granted by the High Court in June 2003 and share dealings were suspended. By January 2004, the solvency position had improved, the administration order had been discharged and trading of the shares on AIM resumed. It then came to light that £900,000 of the company's funds had been drawn by previous directors for alleged compensation for loss of office. The share quotation was suspended between September 2004 and February 2005 in order for investigations to take place. There had been boardroom rows and resignations and, by 2007, the company successfully recovered around £572,000 after suing former directors for breach of fiduciary duty.

More problems emerged in 2006 when Vanguard plc, which had acquired KJC, went into administration, thereby creating a liability on a number of shop leases. PNC was now trading as an importer and exporter of electronic products and had a dispute with HMRC over a VAT claim for recovery of £1.8 million input tax. In November 2009, PNC changed its name to Tricor plc and became an investment company specialising in the natural resources industries, with the emphasis on exploration, mining and extraction resources in the UK and Southeast Asia. Without a successful outcome of the VAT dispute, the company would have been unable to survive unless a deal was agreed with creditors. Consequently, a debt-for-equity swap through a Company Voluntary Agreement (CVA) was reached, but holders of the ordinary shares found their holdings had been reduced to just 3% of the enlarged equity. I did not have to suffer through this sorry story. I acquired a holding in 2000 on the back of the KJC placing, which valued the shares at a substantial discount to Carphone Warehouse. The holding was sold in 2002 when the company issued the first profit warning.

The emergence of broadband and the internet produced great opportunities for many companies and just as many problems when the market matured more quickly than expected. Dataflex Holdings plc is a good example of the speed at which conditions can deteriorate. The company, once part of Sir Alan Sugar's Amstrad empire, came to the stock market in March 2000 via a placing of shares at a price of 195p, which valued the company at £130 million. Dataflex developed and supplied telecommunications equipment, such as single-line and multi-line routers, to alternative telecom operators. The year to 30 June 2001 started strongly but there was a significant downturn in the second six months. Poor conditions continued into the following year, but despite a recovery in the second half of 2002 it reported an annual loss of £7 million compared to a pre-tax profit of £3.2 million. Group turnover fell to less than £1 million in the six months to June 2003 and to salvage some shareholder value the trading assets were sold in a management buyout for £40,000. Throughout these troubled times, the company had maintained a healthy cash balance – and eventually just over 20p per share was distributed to shareholders. I lost money on my holding, but sold about a year before the Members' Voluntary Liquidation became effective.

A company called First Telecom was set up in 1995 by two individuals who, between them, invested an initial sum of £250,000. Growth was rapid and by April 2000 the company was providing telephony and internet services for 11,000 small and medium-sized enterprises and more than 290,000 residential customers in the UK, Germany and France. It was on the verge of being one of the first companies to launch a broadband service in Germany when it looked to float on the stock market. Instead of listing, the company agreed to an offer from Atlantic Telecom Group plc (Atlantic), which valued the company at £520 million and the founder members' stakes at £100 million.

Atlantic launched its first service in October 1996 and operated facilities in Glasgow, Edinburgh, Aberdeen and Dundee with licences in northern and southern England. At the time, Atlantic's share price was 795p, which valued the company at more than £1.7 billion. By June 2001, Atlantic had established businesses in ten German, two Dutch and four Scottish cities, but the expansion came at a huge cost. In the 12 months to 31 March 2001, the company reported a negative cash flow of £188 million and it became clear that it would be unable to service its debt mountain of £700 million. Agreement could not be reached with bondholders and administrators were appointed in October 2001. I held Atlantic shares for a short time in 2001, but sold before the company folded up. Other investors were less fortunate, including Marconi group plc – which owned 18.9% of the equity share capital.

Sir Godfrey Hounsfield invented the Computer Assisted Tomography (CAT) scanner in 1971. The first whole-body scanner was introduced in 1975. In both cases the technology incorporated a number of X-ray images taken at different angles interconnected by a computer to produce a three-dimensional image. It was developed by a division of EMI, a successful recording company famed for having produced the records of the Beatles. Its technology division, named Scipher plc, was subject to a management buyout (MBO) in 1996 and floated on the stock market in February 2000 when £30 million of new money was raised. By that stage, it held an intellectual property portfolio of 818 patents and patent applications covering 3D sound, displays, broadcast monitoring, communications, gas sensors and secure identification, with a focus on electronics, optics and magnetics. Revenue was derived from new business started since the MBO, mature business which had been in the portfolio for ten years and third-party research and development funding.

Scipher described itself as "the largest technology development and licensing company of its type in Europe". By 31 March 2003, the company had net debt of £11.8 million and raised £7 million through a placing of equity shares. This was supposed to be sufficient to cover working capital but a changed management decided upon a programme of disposals as it felt that Scipher had spread its cash across too many activities without sufficient attention to anticipated returns. Several businesses were sold, but administrators were appointed in September 2004 when negotiations with creditors failed. I acquired a holding in 2001 and felt that there was significant potential within the company. Unfortunately, this was not the case: it became a casualty of the enthusiasm generated in the dotcom era.

A sailmaking business was started in 1861 by Thomas Black, who had picked up the trade as a sailor and accumulated capital by spending two years mining gold during the Australian gold rush. He died in 1905 and Thomas Black junior acquired the business, which was then in decline due to the advent of the steamship. Like his father, Black was an adventurer, and having spent time in California had developed an interest in a growing new pastime: camping. He started to manufacture marquees and bell tents, supplying the British military with hospital and other tents during the First World War. After the war, the company switched to the production of lightweight tents to meet the demands of the increasingly popular leisure industry.

The first Blacks shop in London opened in 1928. By 1999 it had 42 retail outlets and in the same year added those of Millets, acquired through a purchase of the Outdoor Group for £51 million. By 2009, Blacks owned 256 Millets, 116 Blacks and 32 Free Spirit outlets but was making significant losses. In order to survive, it entered into a CVA scheme with its creditors, which involved varying the terms on 291 store leases. Losses continued and administrators were appointed in January 2012, thus allowing the trading assets to be sold debt-free to JD Sports for £20 million. Sports Direct plc had a significant holding and was thought to have had to write off £50 million on the interest. I also lost money on my interest, which had been first acquired in 2002, but salvaged something from the wreckage by selling at a price of 55p in January 2010.

For those people familiar with London roads, the junction of the North Circular A1 and Finchley Road is known as Henlys Corner.

Similarly, the roundabout at the start of the A30 at Hounslow is known as Henlys Roundabout. Both derive their named from Henlys, a Jaguar/Rover motor dealership formed in 1947. Henlys owned valuable real estate in London and, with a value of £11 million, was one of the companies featured in my 1971 publication on asset situations. It was acquired by Hawley Goodall in 1985 and sold to the Plaxton group four years later. There followed a management buyout in 1992, at which stage the company specialised in the manufacture and sale of coaches and buses under the Plaxton brand. Ambitions were high and the company raised £111 million from a rights issue to partly finance its £267 million acquisition of Blue Bird Corporation, an American school bus manufacturer. Conditions in the UK were difficult and the company merged its Plaxton business with Walter Alexander and Dennis, which were owned by Mayflower plc. The brands were sold under the label TransBus International, but this company went into administration after Mayflower went bust. Blue Bird had a decent order book, but Henlys was saddled with too much debt and forced into liquidation by its creditor banks in 2004. I had seen the writing on the wall and did not hold the shares for any great length of time.

Many companies have benefited from the growth in social housing and the outsourcing of repair and maintenance work by local authorities over the years. One company in this area which once experienced impressive growth was Connaught plc, which started life in 1982 as a concrete-repair specialist. Its first major social housing contract was secured in 1986. The company expanded activities into insulation, wall cladding, roofing, windows and doors. A MBO occurred in 1996 and the shares obtained an AIM listing two years later. By 2004, revenues were running at £300 million and the company had no debt. It obtained a full listing in 2006 and made several acquisitions to become a specialist in social housing, compliance and environmental services. All looked well when Connaught reported a 20% rise in pre-tax profits to £20.7 million before exceptional items for the six months to 28 February 2010.

The dividend was increased by 20% and the directors were looking forward to the future with "excitement and confidence" on the back of a £2.9 billion order book and a pipeline valued at £4.9 billion.

After the results, directors purchased shares in May 2010 at prices in excess of 300p. An unexpected announcement, one month later, stated that 31 social housing contracts had been deferred, leading to a £13 million reduction in full-year profits. There would be a further impact in 2011, but the medium-term outlook remained strong and in July 2010 directors added to their holdings at about 111p. Soon afterwards it was disclosed that banking covenants had been breached when borrowings reached £220 million against the previously advised level of £120 million. Administrators were appointed in the first week of September 2010. I had a relatively small holding in the shares and sold at about 35p in August 2010. Curiously this was the price of my initial purchase in 2003. It later came to light that there were 50,000 unprocessed social housing contracts and in October 2015 a disciplinary complaint was lodged against the company auditors and financial directors.

The medical industry has strived to increase efficiency and cut costs. One company that developed a solution to reduce the workload of hospital staff and thereby improve patient care was called Patientline. Formed in 1994, it became the leader in communication and entertainment services to the NHS. Its idea was to provide bedside TV, radio, internet, email and telephone services to eight million patients across 100 UK hospitals. Eventually the service could be upgraded to provide a means of recording patient progress and even access to medical records. The installation of fibre-optic cabling and visual monitors was a costly process and Patientline provided a novel, but controversial, solution to the problem. Under an agreement with the Department of Health it would finance the project and recuperate the cost by charging 10p per minute for outgoing calls, 49p for incoming ones and £3.50 per day for television access.

In the days when mobile phones were banned from hospitals due to possible interference with electronic equipment, Patientline had a captive audience for its fixed-line service. Criticism of its incoming call rate prompted Ofcom to instigate a review of the firm's charging structure. Ofcom exonerated Patientline from wrongdoing, but suggested that the problem lay in the licence agreement with the Department of Health. Relaxation of the rules regarding the use of mobile phones in hospitals marked the death knell for the service. With call-cost revenue declining and no alternative financing agreement, in 2008 Patientline was forced into administration after its assets were acquired by the banking creditors. I purchased a holding in 2004 after the directors gave an impressive shareholder presentation, but sold making a small loss the following year.

Northampton Town FC is nicknamed 'The Cobblers' after the town's main industry since the 17th century. By the end of the 1800s, about half of the town's male population was employed in shoemaking. A well-known shoe brand established in Northampton in 1903 was Barratts. By 1964, it had grown to 150 outlets and was then acquired by Stylo plc, a family-run business that had been established in 1935. The business prospered, but then succumbed to competition from inexpensive foreign-imported shoes. Rents were too high and the company, after losing £12.5 million in 2008, attempted to enter into a CVA with its landlords. Agreement could not be reached. In February 2009, administrators were appointed. One hundred and six stores and 165 concessions were then sold to the management but it was not a great success: in December 2011, this new business also went into administration. I can only assume that the family truly loved shoe retailing, as it went on to form another new company to acquire 89 of the Barratts stores. Needless to say, this venture also failed and administrators were appointed in November 2013. I purchased Stylo as an asset situation and was on board when the ship sank for the first time.

Check trading originated in the 19th century. It was a business where trading vouchers were issued in small amounts to customers for use in local shops. The issuing party would send representatives on a weekly basis to customers' homes in order to obtain repayment plus interest which, when annualised, could be as high as 70%. It was a highly profitable trade. In 1927, Joseph R. Cattle created a check-trading business from his drapery shop in Hull. The company, Cattles plc, floated on the London Stock Exchange in 1963 and subsequently became a diversified consumer credit company. It operated in a competitive market and had significant exposure to subprime customers. By 2009 something was amiss and the company announced that losses were such that the equity shares were valueless. The finance director, chief operating officer and compliance and risk directors were all dismissed without compensation pending an investigation into accounting irregularities and the chairman and CEO chose to resign. I held shares briefly in 2005, but otherwise was not involved.

The next chapter includes shares held in the Cavendish AIM Fund, where further scandals and mishaps were to unfold.

19

AIM Moves into the Picture

January 2016 marked the 20th anniversary of the FTSE AIM All-Share Index, which was modified in May 2005 to include all AIM-listed companies meeting liquidity and free-float requirements. It now covers 817 companies, with a total market value of more than £40 billion, and provides a dividend yield of around 1.5%. ASOS plc is its largest constituent, accounting for more than 8% of the value; the ten largest holdings represent a 20% weighting.

Due to its diversification, one would not expect the AIM All-Share to diverge greatly from the main market indices – but this has not been borne out. Over its first 20 years, the AIM All-Share declined by more than 27%, compared to a rise of a little over 85% in the FTSE Actuaries All-Share Index. The following table, showing the percentage change between peaks and troughs of both indices, demonstrates the huge volatility that has occurred in the period:

DATE	FTSE AIM ALL-SHARE INDEX	% CHANGE	FTSE ACTUARIES ALL-SHARE INDEX	% CHANGE
03-01-1996	1017.3	N/A	1816.5	N/A
15-19-1998	762.3	-25	2328.4	+28
03-03-2000	2924.9	+284	3116.3	+34
21-09-2001	804.4	-72	2128.1	-32
01-04-2003	542.4	-33	1765.7	-17
07-03-2005	1166.8	+115	2522.9	+43
09-03-2009	373.8	-78	1791.7	-19
07-02-2011	968.3	+159	3139.6	+75
04-10-2011	657.8	-32	2557.8	-19
04-01-2016	735.7	+12	3367.42	+32

Part of the reason why the AIM All-Share has performed so badly is because of the many mishaps which have befallen AIM-listed companies over the years. The Cavendish AIM Fund was formed in October 2005 and by May 2006 I had built a portfolio with 76 holdings. This chapter is devoted to the stories of some of the companies I invested in that went wrong. In some instances, fraud and dishonesty at the companies was involved. Often mismanagement or poor business plans were to blame. In other cases, banks cruelly withdrew their support or the taxman took extreme measures to obtain payment of overdue taxes.

Hibbert & Richards, a company named after its two founders, started life in 1917, specialising in clockmaking. A change of focus occurred in 1950 when the company started to supply fasteners to aircraft manufacturers. A further change occurred in 1994 when the company was taken over and concentrated on the supply of consumable and expendable parts to aerospace companies. The company changed its name to Aero Inventory in 2000 when £3 million was raised at a price of 123p through an AIM listing. At the time, the company was operating at breakeven from a turnover of £3.2 million. Growth was rapid and, in 2006, £92 million was raised through a rights issue so that the company could become a nominated supplier of components for Airbus as well as Boeing. Aero Inventory thus became a global supplier of parts, with 50 million items in stock and supply contracts in place with a number of international airlines. Pre-tax profits for the year to June 2008 had increased by 60% to US$73 million and interim results to December 2008 disclosed a further 47% advance in profits and earnings per share.

The problem that the company faced was the increased debt needed to finance inventory and infrastructure to support new contracts. By December 2008, borrowings had escalated to US$467.1 million, having been US$110 million 18 months previously. A rights issue in February 2009 to raise £11.9 million, accompanied by a US$100 million sale of parts to Air Canada, might have solved the problem – but it later came to light that stocks had been overvalued. Consequently, the auditors felt unable to sign off the June 2009 accounts, which were being prepared ahead of a proposed transfer of the share listing from AIM to the main market. Certified accounts were required by the lenders in order to renew bank facilities and the shares were suspended due to a non-financial breach of covenants. The issues turned out to be more serious than expected, whereupon stock valuations and accuracy of financial reports were questioned. The banks felt unprepared to provide additional short-term funding. In November 2009, administrators were appointed alongside the termination of the contracts of employment of the chief executive, finance director and the chief operating officer. A disciplinary case against the finance director concluded that his behaviour was not dishonest but he was excluded from the profession for three years and fined £170,000 as a contribution to court costs.

It was a tragic situation. In June the company had rejected a preliminary, but unsolicited, takeover – rumoured to be in the region of 900p per share. Trading was reported to be in line with expectations in a buoyant market and the directors felt very positive about future expansion on the back of the level of enquiries from world-class aerospace companies. As with Alexandra plc, I was disappointed that the banks pulled the plug on a decent business. KPMG, the administrators, shared this view and supported a restructuring plan. In April 2013, it was announced that the business and assets had been sold for an undisclosed sum to an American company, Diversified Aero Services Inc. At the time it was a difficult story to fathom out. I was frightened by the increase in borrowings and reduced my holding in preference to subscribing for the rights issue. My fingers were still singed as I had 0.5% of the AIM Fund invested in the holding when the shares were suspended.

Romag Holdings plc raised £7.2 million after expenses when it listed on AIM in November 2003. It is a specialist manufacturer of bulletproof and high-impact glass products with a customer list covering aerospace, security, rail and the banking industries. The funds were used to set up a production facility to manufacture photovoltaic glass for use in the renewable energy industry. All was well until October 2010 when the company announced it had to write-down the value of its stock by £3.5 million. In December 2010 Romag announced the impairment of £2.4 million of intangible assets. Effectively this was a deposit paid to a supplier of photovoltaic cells that was no longer able to supply the product.

The company was on the verge of agreeing banking facilities when it came to light that the chairman had made an unauthorised payment of £4 million into the company in order to avoid a write-down of outstanding trade receivables. At the request of the nominated advisor (Nomad), the shares were immediately suspended and administrators were appointed in April 2011. As with Aero Inventory and Alexandra, this was essentially a sound business and it came as a surprise that, when the bank withdrew its support, the goodwill and assets were sold for an undisclosed sum to Gentoo, a construction company. Romag has remained a fully owned subsidiary and continues to trade profitably under its own name. At the time of suspension my investment represented 0.7% of the AIM Fund and would have been worth far more today had its finances been on a sounder footing.

A cycling record of 3.18 minutes was once recorded on the Langbar climb in Yorkshire, a 1 km stretch of road which rises 106 metres, the steepest gradient being 20%. Langbar is also the name of something else pain-inducing: AIM's most notorious company.

Langbar was called Crown Corporation (Crown) when it listed as an investment company on AIM in October 2003. It was formed by Mariusz Rybak, who became chairman, and Wolfgang Menzel, its CEO. A company called Lambert Financial Services (Lambert), whose main investor was Abraham Avi Arad, won a contract for Crown that was worth US$633 million. It was for the construction of 14,000 dwellings, nine industrial parks, two commercial centres, three municipal buildings, a hospital, three waste treatment plants and 40 water purification systems in Argentina. Shortly afterwards, a major security contract was also apparently awarded to the company. It later transpired that these contracts did not actually exist.

Crown stated that its intention was to take a stake in the companies selected for carrying out the construction work on both projects. A subsidiary was then formed to acquire operating businesses in the oil and gas sector. It planned to purchase International Hydrocarbon Trading Ltd, a company owning the right to a 49-year lease over 100 hectares in Russia, for €235 million.

Menzel stepped down through ill-health in November 2003 and Rybak became CEO of Crown. One month after listing, Crown entered into an agreement to sell the (non-existent) Argentinian and security contracts to Lambert for US$350 million. This was to be financed by a Lambert promissory note due for payment in May 2005. The stated intention was to reinvest this profit into Russian oil and gas opportunities. Rybak remained at the helm of Crown until June 2005, when he stepped down and Stuart Pearson was appointed CEO and acting chairman – after Crown bought Langbar, his corporate finance advisory company. At the time, Pearson stated that the Lambert promissory note – a worthless piece of paper – plus interest, had been repaid ahead of maturity, and that term deposits of US$661 million were placed with the Banco do Brasil at a 7.5% rate of interest.

Brazilian exchange control regulations did not allow the funds to be freely remitted, but the company was examining a process whereby they could either be swapped for European assets or invested in a variety of Brazilian industries. Nevertheless, it was stated, in an announcement on 4 September, that US$294 million had been transferred to the Langbar head office account of Dutch bank ABN Amro in Holland. The remaining amount of around US$370 million was on deposit in Brazil, pending investment in Brazilian real estate. The July 2005 AGM made interesting reading. Stuart Pearson bemoaned the fact that, though the company had assets of £350 million worth 225p per share, and deposits were earning £25 million per annum, the share price of 62.5p valued the company at £95 million. He stated that two weeks previously he had visited Brazil and verified the cash deposits. When the company changed its name from Crown to Langbar in August 2005 it raised £4.2 million of new money while simultaneously placing 9.1 million shares held by Lambert.

All seemed above-board – but was, in fact, a deliberate scam. In the beginning, Lambert had acquired its 59% holding in Langbar for US$570 million to be satisfied by a US$275 million certificate of deposit from Banco do Brasil and US$295 million to be paid at a later date. The certificate was fraudulent and the shares were never paid for. In the meantime, Lambert Financial and Rybak had been selling Langbar shares in the stock market at prices up to £10 per share. It was an elaborate con: Pearson had been taken to a branch in Brazil which did not exist, but was a temporary office site kitted out for the occasion. While there he was presented with fraudulent documents masquerading as lucrative Brazilian contracts. On 12 October 2005, the shares were suspended pending verification of company assets. Kroll Associates, experts in this area, established that there were not, and never had been, any funds in Banco do Brasil or ABN Amro.

It turned out that Langbar had cash of just £3 million. After three years, six men aged between 56 and 76 were arrested in Spain but none were prosecuted. The SFO formally closed the file when Abraham Avi Arad – the main shareholder in Lambert, thought by some to be the principal architect of the fraud – died of a heart attack. Rybak protested his innocence, but paid back £30 million. Stuart Pearson, who had been duped and eventually pulled the plug on it all, was the one person convicted. He received a 12-month jail sentence and was barred from being a director for five years for being, at least, criminally reckless in issuing misleading statements to investors. Unfortunately as shareholders we eventually received less than 10p per share.

There are a variety of reasons why a company can go to the wall. Sometimes a compelling business idea can come unstuck by a poor business plan, lack of working capital, reliance on too few customers, insufficient working capital, lack of support by banks, execution problems, unfortunate financial planning or over-ambitious goals. Cartucho Group plc is a prime example of a company suffering from several of these maladies. The company was named after the Spanish word for cartridge sometimes associated with the ammunition belts worn by Mexican Soldiers. In this particular case, the reference was to ink cartridges used in computer printers. These are still expensive products, but in 2005 the cost was around £30 per cartridge. Cartucho raised £10 million when it listed on AIM in December 2005. It had designed and was selling a refill kiosk for ink cartridges. The device allowed an employee of a retailer to quickly and efficiently refill customer cartridges on-site. The customer would benefit from the lower cost of refilling his printer cartridge and the retailer would make an attractive margin and increase footfall through its stores. Cartucho planned to sell or rent the machines and would have recurring revenue from service costs and consumable items such as ink.

Not much could go wrong, but it did. The plan was to supply the machines and share revenue with the retailer. A contract was signed with OfficeMax, the third-largest office supply retailer in the United

States, owning nearly 1,000 stores. At the time of its AIM listing, the firm's installed base was 60 machines and the manufacturing facilities were being ramped up to produce 50 kiosks per month. By July 2006, the installed base had increased to 284 kiosks, but refill rates lagged behind expectations. It was agreed to increase the installed base to 540 kiosks by mid-September so that its major customer could increase its marketing efforts. Ten kiosks were on trial with two other major retail chains and one had been sold to a US supermarket group. However, Cartucho was experiencing growing pains and was unable to provide enough service support.

Its biggest customer forced suspension of the rollout programme until satisfactory maintenance levels could be achieved and approved. Deliveries recommenced in November 2006, and by April 2007, 592 kiosks had been manufactured and were income-producing. Unfortunately, refill rates remained below expectations and margins were under pressure. A loan facility of US$4.5 million was agreed in May 2007, but two months later, after drawing US$1.5 million, the company stated that, due to a sudden deterioration in trading, it would not be allowed to draw further funds. This was something that I had not anticipated and I still held an interest in the shares when its main trading subsidiary was placed in creditors' voluntary liquidation in September 2007. Looking back, the main problem might have been that the level of kiosk sales was too small to support the manufacturing base. Lower sales per machine also destroyed the business plan in what was a potentially lucrative market.

I sometimes wonder whether the tax inspector has toothache (perhaps he was simply provided with a poor set of dentures). It is fairly usual to see football clubs forced into administration by the taxman, but they are not the only type of business to suffer this fate. In the case of 1st Dental Laboratories plc, pressure from HMRC and other creditors, forced the company into an insolvent situation. The firm raised £2 million when it listed on AIM in 2002 with the idea of acquiring dental laboratory businesses. In 1999, there were 20,000 UK dentists in general practice in a £2 billion industry served by 2,600 dental laboratories, employing 5,500 technicians. It was a true cottage industry: over 90% of firms employed no more than two technicians at any one time. Due to legislation requirements and safety standards, the industry seemed ripe for rationalisation.

1st Dental set out to provide a high-quality national service. Acquisitions would provide cost savings, an improved product range in prosthetics, orthodontics and crown and bridge categories whilst giving greater purchasing power. Several practices were purchased, but problems arose when technicians left or retired. Also dentists preferred 'mom and pop' relationships with smaller laboratories meaning that a ten-person sales team found it difficult to find new business. By 2010 the company was working from 14 accredited sites within the UK, employing 220 staff and 97 registered technicians. For the six months to 31 May 2010, it announced a small profit and that borrowings had been reduced from £1.6 million to less than £1.4 million. However, market conditions then deteriorated and the directors felt that they could neither fulfil creditor obligations nor raise additional funds. The shares were suspended. Administrators were duly appointed and the business was sold to private equity for an undisclosed sum. Ordinary shareholders, of which I was one, did not receive any payment – a pity since, two years previously, the directors rejected a takeover approach worth up to 8.5p per share.

Before the Lehman banking crisis, it did not seem to matter which bank a customer had relationships with. After the crisis, things changed very quickly. Irish banks, having been favourites of the stock market, started to collapse. Included among these was Allied Irish Banks, one of the big four Irish commercial banks. It had grown very quickly but relied upon international financial markets to provide liquidity. When this dried up, the company required access to capital and eventually had to be bailed out by the Irish government, which injected €3.7 billion from its National Pensions Reserve Fund. The bank had a large exposure to the inflated Irish property market and needed to call in loans and rein in new borrowings. In January 2011, the company was nationalised and the shares deemed valueless.

One company which suffered at the start of Allied Irish Banks' demise was International Medical Devices plc (IDM). The company was admitted to AIM in November 2004 with the objective of acquiring companies that marketed devices to the healthcare market. It made a number of acquisitions and became a supplier of a range of disposable items in the health service. One novel product with huge potential was a retractable syringe. After a successful trial with the South Western Ambulance Service, the syringe gained NHS approval for sale into its 280 trusts. The device, claimed to be the first of its type, was needed to combat 'needle stick' (injuries from needles used in medical procedures). Apparently NHS trusts were paying out around £600,000 per annum because of staff accidentally injuring themselves in this way (including the tragic case of eight nurses who contracted HIV). The new syringe was disposable, the needle retracting into a protective housing after use.

A launch was scheduled for the second quarter of 2008, but IDM required additional working capital to finance its operations. Interim results to 29 February 2008 were announced in May 2008 and showed an operating profit of £0.3 million before exceptional costs of £1.3 million. The company had refinanced its borrowings in 2004 with Allied Irish Banks and had outstanding bank loans of £3.3 million. The chairman concluded his interim statement by reaffirming confidence in the future and a second half starting in line with expectations. Rather surprisingly, one month later the share quotation was suspended and administrators were appointed when IMD was unable to raise funds from Allied Irish to support its working capital requirements. Sadly the retractable needle device proved uneconomic, being too expensive to produce, and died with the company. I had faith in the company and thought that extra capital might have saved me losing out on the investment. Fortunately it was not a large holding in the AIM portfolio.

I have always been aware of the risks associated with shares quoted on AIM. I am keen to buy shares in companies that seem relatively safe and where little might go wrong. With this in mind, in 2006 I acquired a holding in a company called Asfare Group plc. It was a manufacturer and supplier of ladders for the fire service and had purchased a company that manufactured and sold X-ray equipment used for examining suspicious packages received in the post. Other small-scale acquisitions had also been made – but there was nothing small about what happened next. In March 2007 the company completed an £80.2 million takeover of a much larger company called AssetCo. Effectively, it was what is known as a reverse takeover; it was concluded for a share exchange accompanied by a £20 million cash raise. The enlarged group took the name of AssetCo and its chief executive, John Shannon, and finance officer, Frank Flynn, were appointed to run the group.

AssetCo was originally a leasing and asset management business of British Gas. In 2001, it won a contract from the London Fire Brigade worth £400 million of revenues over its 20-year life. Among other things, this involved owning, leasing and maintaining fire engines and equipment used by the 111 London fire stations. In the year prior to the reverse takeover, AssetCo had won a £60 million 20-year total managed services contract from the Lincolnshire Fire and Rescue service. The pro-forma offer document forecast that earnings before interest, tax, depreciation and amortisation (EBITDA) for the enlarged group would be £103.2 million, producing a pre-tax profit of £17.9 million, with debt amounting to £52.7 million. A seven-year contract to provide a 700-strong firefighter reserve capacity was signed in 2009, and in 2010 the company secured a three-year £40 million contract to provide outsourced firefighting services to the United Arab Emirates (UAE). All looked well, but in December 2010 it emerged that the company had working capital troubles. HMRC issued a winding-up petition. Upon investigation it transpired that there had been serious management and internal controls problems, leading to an operating profit of £17.4 million for the year to 31 March 2010 becoming a loss of £11.4 million. Revenue had been overstated by £23.2 million in 2010 and £6.6 million in 2009.

Three of the leading institutional shareholders recognised that there was value in the UAE contract, but while interest on the outstanding loans on the UK business could be financed from cash flow, there was no way of repaying, on schedule, the capital value from existing resources. The shareholder group was prepared to invest £10 million provided the UK business was ring-fenced. Other institutional shareholders, including Cavendish, were invited to participate in the placing. As part of the reorganisation, it was required that every 1,000 shares held be consolidated into one new share. The proposal needed shareholders' approval, but a major problem was that John Shannon reneged on his irrevocable undertaking to vote in favour of the resolution. The company successfully sought an injunction, making sure that the irrevocable undertaking stood. A total of £16 million was raised, but Shannon, who held a 29.7% stake in the company, was forced to resign and was not allowed to participate in the fund raise.

HMRC was paid in full, but an Irish bank, supported by Shannon and Flynn, took its place on the winding-up petition. Shannon claimed to be a creditor for the sum of £875,575 and Flynn for £358,216, but the company had identified counterclaims of £4.6 million and £3.5 million respectively and eventually the winding-up order was withdrawn. The ring-fenced UK fire business was sold for just £2 after the banks had agreed to write their loans down from £79 million to £43 million, leaving it with net liabilities of £49.5 million. No action was taken against the previous board of directors, but £2.5 million was written off against obligations from Shannon and court proceedings for negligence commenced against the previous auditors, with a claim totalling £42.3 million. AssetCo survives as a successful trading company managing contracts in the Middle East, but, due to a deteriorating service, the London Fire Brigade contract was handed over to Babcock International Group. I still have a holding which has done me well in its present form.

Adamind Ltd was another interesting situation. The company was formed through the merger of the media-adaptation business units of

Philips and the Israeli company Emblaze. It had developed software for use in video messaging and separately for communicating photographic images between one mobile phone and another. A total of £15 million was raised on AIM in February 2005 at a share price of 132p, giving a stock market value of £46 million. Results to 31 December were pretty much in line with expectations and the company was able to maintain cash balances of US$28.2 million despite making a loss of US$2.7 million.

Emblaze raised £15 million when it sold its entire holding at a price of 110p in March 2006. One month later, Adamind announced a profit warning caused through a delay in customer upgrades. In the event, an operating loss of US$4 million was reported and net cash had fallen to US$22 million. Takeover talks commenced, but were terminated on the news that the Financial Service Authority (FSA) was examining the circumstances behind the Emblaze share sale. When the FSA enquiry was dropped in 2007, the business assets of Adamind were sold to Mobixell Inc., a US company, for US$5.5 million and surplus funds of just over 60p per share were returned to shareholders. It was a sad end to a company which, at the time of flotation, had the goal of becoming the world leader in its mobile technology functions. For me the story had a happy ending as I was able to add to my holding at 40p on the 60p return to shareholders.

Tight financial controls are required in any business. It is surprising how sometimes a company can experience problems soon after an AIM listing, even though experts like lawyers, stockbrokers and auditors have just crawled all over the placing documents. Inova Holdings plc was a global leader in rugged computer systems used on trains, trams and buses. It was established in Germany in 1997 and had a worldwide customer list in the military, aerospace, manufacturing, energy, telecommunications, medical and transport industries. A real-time passenger information service was developed to provide trains with updates on stations, connections and train times. CCTV and infotainment services for news, weather, sport and entertainment were also on offer.

Following its £10 million fund raise on AIM in May 2006, Inova won a US$14.7 million passenger infotainment contract for the train service connecting New York and New Jersey, which carried 60 million passengers per year. This included 1,360 double video screens and equipment for 340 new trains, plus screens and interfaces for 12 stations. However, results were not going to plan. Due to implementation delays, revenues for the year to 31 December 2006 did not show the anticipated growth. Further contracts were won, but the company was running short of working capital. A takeover approach failed to materialise and Inova was placed into administration in December 2007. The finance director had been replaced in November 2006 and it was a great shame that shareholders could not benefit from the undoubted potential. My loss on this investment emphasises the need to own a wide spread of investments and to sometimes expect the unexpected!

It is estimated that six million men served in the First World War and 725,000 never returned. Of those who survived, 1.75 million suffered some kind of disability and half of these were permanently disabled. Economic conditions were tough and many ex-servicemen struggled to find employment, leading to great hardships. Lance Bombardier Tom Lister became concerned about the situation and, in 1921, formed the British Legion; its first Poppy Appeal was held in November of that year. A number of branches of the Legion were formed throughout the country, with parking services offered in their small car parks. These parking businesses were combined and, in 1928, were incorporated into the Royal British Legion Attendants Company Trust (RBLACT). In recent times, a subsidiary, known as Legion Group plc (Legion), had expanded into the provision of security, CCTV monitoring and offering services to a wide range of corporate customers, employing 1,400 trained staff, many of whom were ex-servicemen and women. In March 2009, Legion was acquired by an AIM-listed company called SectorGuard plc.

SectorGuard floated on AIM in March 2002. Its goal was to provide security, mobile-patrol and rapid-response services to industrial and residential clients. It acquired Legion for £1 and agreed to pay RBLACT £100,000 per annum for the next ten years. For working capital, it raised £2 million from a sale of shares and obtained a £1 million loan from its CEO. Legion's £1 price-tag reflected the fact that, though the firm had declared a gross profit of £4.5 million, its overheads were £5.5 million. SectorGuard changed its own name to Legion Group and, in the six months to 30 September 2009, declared a pre-tax profit of £964,000. A share-placing in November 2009 raised £1 million. In April 2010 its CCTV business was sold for £0.9 million. A further positive move occurred in July 2010, when Lloyds TSB agreed to provide Legion with a £7.5 million invoice-discounting facility. This allowed the company to repay £1.5 million of liabilities owed to HMRC.

Having been the good guy with AssetCo, HMRC now became the villain. At the time of its acquisition, Legion had outstanding PAYE and VAT liabilities which the directors, based on correspondence, had thought would be settled by a payment plan. However, on receipt of the £1.5 million payment, HMRC issued a winding-up order – causing Legion to be in breach of its banking agreement with Lloyds TSB. Administrators were appointed in August 2010 and immediately sold the business to OCS Group UK Limited for an undisclosed sum. Like other firms in this chapter, this was a decent company. Under other circumstances it could have provided a respectable return to shareholders. It was another loss for the AIM Fund and one to put down to experience: all the research under the sun cannot always unearth financial problems that might be lurking under the covers.

The National Lottery is regulated by the National Lottery Commission, established by the government of John Major in 1994. One of its main aims was to provide funding for enterprises that might have difficulty obtaining finance from conventional sources. It was decided that the total receipts from the lottery would be divided as follows: 50% in the prize fund; 28% to 'good causes'; 12% for UK government duty; 5% to the retailer; 4.5% to cover costs; and 0.5%

as profit to the operator. The enterprise has been a huge success, even though the odds against winning the big prize are astronomical.

A company called Chariot (UK) plc was formed in 2003 and raised £9.6 million on AIM in February 2004, with a view to offering a competing lottery designed to provide funding for charities. It signed up 70 partners, including Barnardo's, British Heart Foundation, British Red Cross, DEBRA, Macmillan Cancer Support, Rainbow Trust, War Child, Whizz-Kidz and WWF. The idea was that each week five charities would be nominated and ticket purchasers could select the one of their choice. In return, the charities were expected to market the service to their donors. Purchases could only be made over the internet. The organisers claimed that there was a 27× better chance of winning the jackpot than with a National Lottery ticket. There were to be two consecutive draws on a Monday evening; if no one matched six numbers, the players with the nearest numbers would win. Unfortunately, due to poor support from the charities and high advertising costs, sales were always below breakeven. The business assets ended up being sold in January 2007. The company delisted in June 2008 when net cash balances had dwindled to £350,000. It was not my usual type of investment and the holding only accounted for 0.5% of the fund.

All of the companies mentioned in this chapter were held in the Cavendish AIM Fund on 15 May 2006. In several cases, good-quality companies came unstuck and perhaps tighter regulation might have avoided some of the accidents. Thankfully, I sold a large number of these situations before the final nail was hammered into the coffin, and I was relieved to have held many more winners than losers. I was thankful that amongst these holdings, the only one owned in the Opportunities Fund was Langbar, where I was hoodwinked by the official announcements from the company.

The next chapter covers blow-ups that occurred in the last ten years, of which there were three in the Opportunities Fund and four in the Cavendish AIM Fund. My Select Fund, launched in May 2010, did not have any complete catastrophes.

20

More Down the Plug 'Ole

At the time of the Lehman crisis I managed to buy shares in Barclays, Lloyds and the Royal Bank of Scotland near the bottom of their trading ranges. A less happy story was Northern Rock. I bought shares in this company after the price had more than halved, only to scramble out with a fair-sized loss.

Northern Rock was formed in 1965 but had a much longer heritage. It was the result of a merger between Northern Counties Permanent Building Society and Rock Building Society, established in 1850 and 1865 respectively, and was headquartered in Newcastle. It then expanded through the acquisition of more than 50 small building societies. Demutualisation was effected by the issue of its shares to those members who had savings accounts and mortgages. The shares were introduced to the main market in 1997 and the company entered the FTSE 100 in 2000, where it remained until 2007.

The problem with Northern Rock was its business plan, which failed when the Lehman crisis caused a collapse in demand for secondary (subprime) loans. Basically, Northern Rock borrowed money on international money markets to provide funds for customer mortgages. The mortgages would then be packaged together and sold to investors in the form of a loan stock. When the market for these mortgage-backed loans dried up, Northern Rock had a problem. Some of the past loans were maturing and the bank did not have sufficient funds required to refinance. This necessitated an emergency loan from the Bank of England and depositors, afraid that the bank would go bust, queued outside branches to withdraw money. Support, totalling nearly £27 billion, was provided and the British government was forced to take Northern Rock into state ownership. Subsequently the bank was split into two parts: assets and banking. Virgin Money bought the bank for £820 million in 2011 and benefited from a refinancing package, part of which has now been repaid.

The origins of HMV stretch back to 1890. The name and logo derive from 'His Master's Voice', a painting by Francis Barraud of Nipper, a black-and-white dog captivated by the sound of his deceased owner's voice playing through the horn of an old fashioned gramophone. HMV opened its first shop on Oxford Street in 1921, eventually building up a national chain of 320 specialist music shops. Expansion into bookshops occurred when it bought Dillons in 1998, followed by the purchase of Waterstone's the same year. HMV folded Dillons into the Waterstone's brand, doing the same to Ottakar's after purchasing it in 2006. A further departure from its traditional music-selling business came with the acquisition of the MAMA Group, an operator of live-music venues – the best known being the Hammersmith Apollo. To take advantage of rapid changes to the music industry in the wake of digital music, HMV also purchased a stake in 7digital plc in order to provide download services and build a digital audiobook service for Waterstone's.

HMV listed on the London Stock Exchange in May 2002, with its shares offered for sale at a price of 160p. I acquired a holding for the Cavendish Opportunities Fund in the summer of 2009 at various levels (ultimately my average cost price was 90p). At the time it seemed a great idea – there appeared to be a string of positive factors. Zavvi, a competitor, had gone bust, removing some pricing pressure from the music market. More importantly, the Beatles were about to release a 15-CD digitally remastered boxset featuring all of their recordings between 1962 and 1968. It would retail at £120 and was too expensive to face competition from supermarkets. The sudden death of Michael Jackson also led to higher CD sales. In the run-up to Christmas, DVDs were likely to see decent sales and I expected that demand for games packages might be boosted by the launch of new models of PlayStation consoles by Sony. An exciting list of forthcoming book titles was also seen as a positive for Waterstone's. However, everything went pear-shaped when the decline in CD and DVD sales turned out to be much greater than expected and computer games had poor Christmas sales. To make matters worse, book retailer Borders UK went bust and the market became saturated with cheap books. After I had disposed of my holding at a small loss, HMV sold Waterstone's for £53 million and the Hammersmith Apollo for £32 million. This did not improve the underlying problem and administrators were finally appointed in January 2013.

A company called EBC Group (originally Exeter Building Contractors) was formed in 1939 to repair bomb-damaged properties. The firm's name changed to Rok after Garvis Snook became chief executive officer in 2000. Under his leadership, the company grew organically and by acquisition to become a diverse building company with activities ranging from construction to maintenance and building improvements for social housing. One interesting area was the provision of a service for insurance company claims. Rok had the authority to undertake repair work under a specific value without the need for it to be approved by insurance assessors. Thus claims could be met cheaply and in a timely fashion. The process worked particularly well in areas affected by storm loss, where a large number of properties might have suffered a similar type of damage. To provide this facility the company established a presence throughout the UK and called itself "The nation's local builder". It grew from a handful of offices to 60 locations, providing work for more than 3,800 employees.

In the early months of 2010, severe weather conditions hit the UK. This created a problem for Rok: a large proportion of its immense direct workforce was actually unable to access customer properties. The government's cost-cutting measures also meant that local authorities had cut back on repair and maintenance work on social housing. Even worse, there were issues with the firm's Plumbing, Heating and Electrical (PHE) division. As a result, the company turned in a loss of £3.8 million for the six months to 30 June 2010. Still, cash flow looked strong at £5.9 million and a dividend of 0.5p (cut from 0.75p) per share was declared. Banking covenants had not been breached and average net debt for the period was £64.2 million compared with committed bank facilities of £81 million.

A review of the PHE business was commissioned. On 30 September 2010 it was announced that the division's problems lay in the scaling back of subcontracting work from the private housing sector, together with weak operational, commercial and financial controls in that part of the business. With its high level of fixed costs, any fall in workload would have a magnifying effect on profitability. In September 2010, revenues fell 30% below budget. With little improvement in sight, joint administrators were appointed in early November 2010. It was a shock to everyone: only a month earlier, Snook and three fellow directors had invested a near-six-figure sum in the shares. I had faith in the company and was invested in the shares at the bitter end.

Now to the AIM-listed failures of this period. Probably the most disappointing was Shieldtech plc. The company came to the stock market in June 2007 via an AIM listing which raised £10 million. It had been incorporated in 1990 as a supplier of protective equipment to UK police forces. Its main product was protective armour incorporating a patented stab-protective material named BKT (for ballistic, knife and trauma). Initial orders were received from English and Danish police forces in 1997; by 2006, the company had orders from 24 police forces. A major breakthrough occurred in 2005 when Shieldtech won an initial £1 million order from the MOD.

There was a barrier of entry when it came to competing with protective equipment like that made by Shieldtech: the products needed UK Home Office accreditation. Shieldtech had achieved such accreditation, but a revision of the ballistics measurement standards in 2007 caused orders to be delayed. When the process was completed in 2008, the company received an order covering protective gear for 22,000 officers from nine UK police forces. In autumn 2009, the Metropolitan Police Service was expected to release a body-armour contract for tender. Winning this would be essential for procuring future orders from other UK police forces. Shieldtech was in a strong position, having raised £1 million from the issue of loan notes and renegotiated its working capital bank facilities. In the meantime, major contracts were won from the MOD and UNICEF.

Shieldtech had to wait until May 2010 before it was successfully appointed to the Metropolitan Police Authority National Framework Agreement, with potential access to orders worth £33 million, over a four-year term, covering at least 30 out of the 53 UK police forces. However, the British government was looking to make large public expenditure cuts and the tendering process had ground to a halt. To make matters worse, the banks did not allow Shieldtech access to proceeds from a fulfilled order from Turkey. This caused working capital problems – and in October 2010, the company was forced to appoint administrators. I would have been happy to subscribe to a rights issue – something the company stockbrokers suggested – but they were unable to obtain funds from other investors. In the end, the firm's trading subsidiary – a decent business that could have been saved – was sold for a small sum. Shortly afterwards, the ordering pattern returned to normal, a contract was awarded, and former shareholders missed out on a huge growth opportunity. I was extremely disappointed to have lost money in the shares and am sure that today the company could have been saved. Unfortunately, in 2010 economic circumstances meant that even institutional investors were unprepared to back companies by making an equity investment.

Birkwood Castle in Lesmahagow, South Lanarkshire, is reputed to be the most haunted premises in Scotland. It dates from 1860 and was the home of the McKirdy family until 1923, when the 86-acre estate was donated to the local authorities and the building became a mental asylum for children. Psychic reports detail a variety of alleged phenomena at the site, including a cigar-smoking spirit; the ghost of a man stabbed through the neck; strange smells; lights turning on and off; sounds of a young girl laughing and singing. A boy called Michael is rumoured to haunt the main spiral staircase – purportedly the place where he died. A doctor who died of a heart attack has been seen at one of the windows. The gothic mansion has been empty and in increasing disrepair since 2002. A £7 million development scheme was underway when, in July 2015, the west wing wall mysteriously collapsed. Locals blamed it on ghosts upset by the refurbishment.

The project – part of a scheme for the whole 83-acre site – was being undertaken jointly by Envestco and Birkwood Estate. These were companies owned by Chris Naylor, who had already successfully undertaken a similar scheme, and Jo Lloyd who had owned the property since 2012. Previously the property was owned by Eatonfield Group plc (Eatonfield), a company where Jo's father, Rob Lloyd, was a principal shareholder and chief executive. Eatonfield had acquired the site in May 2008 for £1.5 million and sought planning permission for a development worth up to £40 million. This was gained in May 2009 when South Lanarkshire Council granted permission for a hotel plus 160 houses and sports facilities.

I acquired a holding in Eatonfield when the company placed shares at 125p on AIM in 2006 to raise £10 million, giving the company a market value of £28.8 million. The company was formed by Rob Lloyd in 1998 and had become a successful developer of commercial and residential properties. In 2007, one year prior to the Birkwood acquisition, Eatonfield purchased the 87-acre Corus Rail Site in Workington, West Cumbria, for £2.6 million; in 2009 it received planning permission to build 650 houses, a retirement village, a hotel, public house and recreation facilities on the site. When the UK banking crisis struck, Eatonfield ran into trouble. Demand for residential property was hit by falling house prices, a collapse in commercial property values restricted the company from obtaining additional debt and the market in properties dried up. Its share price had peaked at 200p in 2007 – but at the time of the banking crisis property values collapsed and the company required additional capital. The share price tanked and in October 2009 the company was forced into raising £6.9 million through a share placing at 5p. Even this proved insufficient. Subsequently working capital was covered by a further issue of shares at the price of 1p. An agreed sale of some Welsh properties might have saved the day but the deal was terminated in May 2011 and a liquidator was appointed in July 2011. This was a company with significant potential that had just become financially overstretched at the wrong time. I was hopeful that the company might have survived and had a small holding in the AIM Fund.

Coal has been mined in Britain since before Roman times, but the invention of the steam engine in the Industrial Revolution really kicked off growth in the coal-mining industry. There was also a need to replace wood with an inexpensive product for domestic heating – and before gas and nuclear power, coal was also the main source of fuel used in power stations. By 1952, there were more than 1,300 deep coal mines in the UK, and nearly 100 surface mines, producing 228 million tonnes per annum. Clean energy initiatives in 2009 were responsible for a decline in demand and by 2013 UK mines were only producing 13 million tonnes of coal per annum. Opencast mining as a commercial practice commenced in 1940. Today it involves the use of large hydraulic excavators and off-road dump trucks to strip an area of land, exposing coal seams for mining. Once the coal has been extracted the land is restored to its previous state. A Scottish opencast mining company called ATH Resources raised £22 million when it floated on AIM in June 2003. Half of the proceeds were used to pay down debt and the rest to provide working capital.

At the time of the AIM listing, ATH was believed to be the third-largest producer of coal in the UK and had two mines at Skares Road and Garleffan near New Cumnock, East Ayrshire. Total reserves were estimated to be 3.3 million tonnes. Production was about 1.6 million tonnes per annum, most of which was pre-sold. Replacement of reserves was expected from other coal-mining projects estimated to contain a total of 11.5 million tonnes. Total UK production from all companies in 2003 was 28.8 million tonnes, of which 12.3 million tonnes was from opencast operations, with 6.9 million tonnes coming from mines in Scotland. In 2003 coal was used to generate 34.7% of the UK's electricity needs and 79% of ATH's production was sold into that market. The balance of income was derived from sales into the higher-margin domestic and industrial markets.

May 2005 saw the company acquire two further sites in East Ayrshire, containing reserves of 4.1 million tonnes, financed through a £16.8 million rights issue at a price of 173p per share. Expansion was not cheap. It involved the purchase of dump trucks, bulldozers, excavators and other mining equipment for a cost of £25.3 million. The next move to grow the company was the acquisition, in June 2006, of A. Ogden and Sons Ltd – a Doncaster-based coal-washing and processing business, for a net consideration of around £10 million. ATH was an extremely cash-generative company. It reported a near-doubling of net cash flow to £19 million for 2006 and £24 million for 2007. The granting of planning permission at Muir Dean, Fife, gave the company access to 1 million further tonnes of reserves. By 2012, the company had increased reserves to 7 million tonnes and in the six months to April 2012 had achieved an average selling price of £56 per tonne.

However, a time bomb was now ticking.

One of the main expenses in coal-mining is energy costs. Coal-gas prices had risen sharply in the UK but the North American mining industry had access to inexpensive supplies of natural gas. A mild winter in 2011 led to an oversupply of coal and international coal prices fell by 30% in the first six months of 2012. UK oil prices also fell and cheap imports increased the supply of coal going into power stations. The company was still forecast to generate cash and had borrowings in place until May 2013. However, in December 2012 its lender BECAP Capital Coal Limited (BECAP) demanded immediate repayment of debt totalling £12.5 million and when this could not be achieved, appointed administrators. The debt was secured on the assets of the company, which were sold to Hargreaves Services plc (Hargreaves) for £5 million. Hargreaves then purchased £10.4 million of mining assets – potentially containing five million tonnes of reserves – to be paid for by cash and settlement against the secured debt. Thus, 230 mining jobs were saved, but the ordinary shares became valueless. As in the case of Eatonfield, potentially valuable assets were forced to be sold when the owner became financially distressed.

Fridays are the worst day of the week for company announcements as they often include profit warnings or downgraded expectations. Part of the reason is that Friday news is seldom picked up by the weekend press and might be overlooked or forgotten about by the retail investor. This could lessen the impact of bad news on a share price. Most regulated news appears on the news services between 7 am and 7.30 am and it is most unusual for a significant announcement to appear at any other time. (An exception would be GlaxoSmithKline plc, which announces results at noon to cater for its large number of overseas investors.) Christmas Eve and New Year's Eve are the only days of the year when, to coincide with banking hours, the London Stock Exchange closes at 12.30 pm. Look carefully at announcements on those days – especially if they appear near the close of business.

At five minutes past 12 on Friday 23 December 2011 (functioning as Christmas Eve in this case because it was the last working day before Christmas), a company called Environ Group (Investments) plc announced interim results for the six months to 30 September 2011. Five minutes later it gave details of its intention to cancel its listing on AIM. The reasons given for the delisting were: lack of meaningful liquidity in the shares in the prevailing economic climate, reduced ability to raise finance due to losses and poor stock market conditions, the cost of maintaining the listing and regulatory requirements, and the existence of methods of raising funds not available to companies listed on AIM.

The part of the statement that stuck in my gullet was the proposal that 51% of BGC Limited (BGC), a wholly owned subsidiary, would be sold for £1 to a company owned by Mark Sims, the chief executive officer of Environ. To make matters worse, Environ would be granted an option to buy back 20% of BGC for £1 million. I was incensed by the timing and substance of the announcement and used my press office to send out a release. Fortunately, it was picked up by a reporter from *The Times* and I was able to get coverage in the business section. The news was missed by many and the price did not collapse until the stock exchange reopened.

An announcement giving further details of the arrangements appeared at 16:48 on 9 January 2012 after the stock market had closed. In that period, the three-year option cost to buy back 20% of BGC had been changed from £1 million to £500,000. It also came to light that Environ was proposing to sell 51% of its Fenham subsidiary for £1, with a three-year option for Environ to buy back 20% for £500,000. Paul Richardson, a director of Environ and Fenham, was also a director of the potential purchaser. Both companies were involved in the installation and maintenance of gas central-heating systems. In the seven months to 31 October 2011, BGC produced an unaudited loss of £30,000 and Fenham made a loss of £200,000. BGC owed the parent company £1.9 million and Fenham was owed £1.4 million. Both of these inter-company balances were to be written off.

To me, the Environ deals looked unattractive. BGC had been acquired in August 2007 for an initial consideration of £4.3 million, of which £3.3 million was in cash; an extra £2.3 million performance fee could also be paid over the next three years. Fenham had been bought in August 2008 for £3.8 million, with £3 million in cash – there was also an earn-out clause. Mark Sims had formed BGC in 2002 and Fenham, formed in 1990, was Paul Richardson's family company. It seemed wrong that both individuals would gain a controlling interest in these companies for £1. Environ would also see a net £0.6 million written off company balances. Looked at another way, if the Environ options were exercised in the next three years, the indicated value for each subsidiary would be £2.5 million.

The independent directors, having consulted the company's nominated advisor (NOMAD), considered the terms to be fair and reasonable – but I raised the matter with the stock exchange. Things moved quickly. On 23 January 2012 the shares were suspended and the AGM to ratify the deals was adjourned. The NOMAD resigned one week later and administrators were appointed on 8 February 2012. I sometimes wonder whether it would have been better to have a little bit of something rather than a whole lot of nothing. However, it would have been galling to see the proposed deals go through.

The delisting of a company listed on AIM is usually contentious. Often the reasons given are to save running costs, to make it easier to restructure without having to publish lengthy documentation or sheer frustration at the stock market valuation for the company. I am generally against delisting as it makes it difficult to value a company. There may be an unofficial market where buyers and sellers are matched, but shareholders cannot freely deal in shares. It is also more difficult to follow a company that does not have a stock exchange listing. There is an exceptional circumstance when I can favour a delisting: it occurs if a company is up for sale and the stock market value of the shares is detrimental to the price of a deal.

BNS Telecom group plc (BNS) listed on AIM in November 2005 when shares were placed at a price of 54p. To provide competition in the fixed-line telephone market, legislation was introduced to compel British Telecom (BT) to sell its services to independent providers at a level where they could profitably resell to their customers. BNS was such a reseller and, at the time of listing, had approximately 6,000 corporate customers. It devised a novel way of selling, by entering into agreements with regional corporations who would provide a package to their own customers. The attraction was that a customer's bill could be reduced without them having to change provider. Even better, the customer would receive a portion of the incoming call charges. However, the market was to change with the introduction of the internet to provide competitive telephony services. From 2007, BNS delivered a broad range of internet protocol (IP) products in a single package combining voice, data and other services between fixed-line and mobile devices. There was considerable potential to exploit the opportunities from the customer list, which now totalled 10,000.

When the decision to delist was made in April 2009, the IP business offering was growing strongly but BNS had been reporting pre-tax losses. Contracts were up to seven years in duration with an element of cash paid upfront. Accounting regulations meant that the profit could not be acknowledged immediately, but had to be recognised over the life of the contract. The directors found this very frustrating and felt that the stock market price did not take into account this guaranteed revenue stream. A decision had also been made to seek a buyer for the company but the low stock market valuation would have an unfavourable influence in takeover negotiations. More than 95% of the shares were in the hands of 15 shareholders, which led to a lack of liquidity and a depressed share price. On this occasion, I could see the logic of delisting as a way of achieving a decent value for the Cavendish holding. It was a risk worth taking as the company was bought by Daisy Communications at 20p per share – more than double the price at the time of delisting.

An even more attractive example of a company which created value through a delisting is Spectrum Interactive plc (Spectrum). The company listed on AIM in April 2005 and operated 9,300 payphones and internet terminals across the UK and Germany. It had acquired an estate of payphones from Mercury Communications in prime locations. Agreements were signed with Travelex to locate automated teller machines (ATM) and with Clear Channel for advertising in the payphone booths. Money was also made from the sale of pre-paid cards for use in the payphones. Due to the growth of mobile phones, the traditional business went into decline, and the German subsidiary was eventually placed in administration when no buyer could be found.

Growth came instead from the provision of internet desks and Wi-Fi installation. Agreements were reached with BAA for internet units in its airports and with Travelodge for exclusive Wi-Fi services for its hotels. By 2010, 62% of the company's revenue came from this source – but falling usage of payphones still caused profits to decline. It was decided to take the company private and shareholders were offered 7p per share, a 14.3% premium over the prevailing market price. There was the option to remain invested in the company: those who followed that course were rewarded when Spectrum was bought by Arqiva Broadcast Holdings Ltd at a price of 78.32p per share. It is nice to have ended this chapter with the story of a true ten-bagger.

21

The Zookeeper and the Penguins

It can be seen from the preceding chapters that an investment in equities can be a tricky business. Even after years of experience and hours of analytical work, investment mishaps can still occur. Once again, I would reiterate that a spread of investments in a portfolio is a good way of protecting against the impact of something going wrong. At any one time, I am holding shares in up to 200 different companies and closely monitoring a greater number. The obvious questions are:

- How can this be achieved?

- What does a fund manager do?

- How can a fund manager overcome the mental pressure of being responsible for managing other people's money?

To answer these questions, it seems sensible to first examine the workings of a fund manager. In this respect, I can only answer from personal experience, having worked in two boutique-type fund management companies. The Cavendish funds under my control comprise around £225 million of equity shares. My standard-sized investment in a company for the AIM Fund is around £500,000; it is up to £2 million for each of the other two funds. This means that my investment universe covers companies that are too small for larger institutions to consider. The other advantage is that anomalies can be found in smaller companies, which are often under-researched. I also have the freedom to make my own investment decisions. Frequently fund managers from large institutions can only buy from an approved list of company shares and, before dealing, need to check whether anyone else in the organisation has orders pending.

Because of the large number of companies that I follow, it is essential to keep abreast with corporate news. Most UK companies report results twice yearly, but between these times can also produce trading statements to give an update on progress. Press comment and movements of overseas stock markets can influence short-term investment decisions. Company regulated announcements hit the news channels from 7 am and are, therefore, in the public domain before the London stock market opens one hour later. As such, I make a point of being at my desk by 6 am. It is a bit inconvenient as it means leaving home at five and not staying up too late at night.

The effort is worth it, though: by 7.30, I have been able to look through the newspapers, make myself aware of overnight changes in China, Japan and other Far East stock markets and trawl through UK corporate news. With most companies, the headlines and outlook comments are sufficient to get an initial impression on how a share price might react to an announcement. Where I have a holding, it is important to study results more thoroughly. Fortunately, I have followed many companies for several years and know what information to look for.

Most stockbrokers have early morning meetings to discuss the latest news and any recommendations that their analysts might come up with. I will start receiving calls from my stockbroker contacts before the stock market opens. The salesperson can act as a catalyst but will not necessarily adopt their firm's view on a company. This can sometimes be awkward when a company in question is one of their corporate clients.

I am fortunate as I have a good relationship with my stockbroker contacts. This is where the zookeeper analogy alluded to in the title of this chapter comes in. Because I pass my own orders and do not have a separate dealing desk, I can respond quickly and efficiently to an investment idea. With other larger organisations, the fund manager has to place an order with his dealer, who might not even place the order with the firm that generated the original idea. (A broker's salesperson is remunerated by the amount of commission they produce.) Consequently, an order from me is well received and I feel that Cavendish is further up the early morning call list than larger firms with deeper pockets. In order to maintain a strong relationship, my brokers try to ensure that they filter the daily ideas and only put forward the best ones. I am like a zookeeper and the stockbrokers are the penguins: an order placed on the back of a good idea is the zookeeper throwing sardines to them. There is the added advantage that, once I have bought shares through a broker, they will follow that company on my behalf. Consequently, I seldom miss news flow on my holdings and the penguins receive their fair share of sardines. Of course the penguins are not puppets and have their own original thoughts on companies and markets – I should know as I was a penguin once. I feel privileged in having a strong rapport with my broker contacts.

It is essential to keep in contact with stock market moves and company announcements. There is no point going on holiday for two weeks and being out of touch. Many opportunities can be missed. For an active investor, investment decisions need to be made on a daily basis. Most of the time, this involves adding or reducing holdings in order to take advantage of share price movements, but there are occasions when more drastic action needs to be undertaken. For example, a company might produce a profit warning where a quick response is essential.

Thanks to modern technology, even when I am away I am still linked to my phone and have direct access through a laptop to all of my office functions. Consequently, I still retrieve the 7 am company announcements – being away is no different to sitting at my desk in the office. The only slight problem is that I am unwilling to stray far from the UK time zone, as getting up in the middle of the night would not go down too well with the family. Another solution might be to delegate responsibilities. This can work for some funds, but, as far as I am concerned, not in the case of those based on a stock picker. Certainly, I would not contemplate anything other than a hands-on approach.

One sunny morning, on the first week of a holiday, I was strolling along the promenade in Barcelona when I received a call from the executive chairman of Lighthouse Group plc (Lighthouse), which had earlier announced its intention to delist from AIM. When I read the 7 am announcement, I immediately rang the company broker to say that I was very much opposed to the move and intended to instruct my press department to publish a comment to that effect. The call that I received on my mobile was designed to convince me to change my mind.

Lighthouse had been incorporated and admitted to AIM in 2000 and, by the time of the delisting proposal in July 2012, was the only quoted independent financial advisor (IFA) company. It was explained to me that the company would be better placed as a private company ahead of new legislation to regulate financial service companies. The new rules – known as the Retail Distribution Review (RDR) – would take effect from the beginning of 2013 and were designed to make charging more transparent and to bring fairness to the investment industry. IFAs would no longer be able to obtain a commission from the funds their clients invested in, but would have to charge the client for advice upfront instead.

Advisors would be required to reach and maintain certain standards of competency. A large number of IFAs would be required to attend courses in order to obtain the necessary qualification. To Lighthouse and others, this created a huge amount of uncertainty. Commissions had to be replaced by fee income and several older IFAs would retire rather than undertake a retraining programme. Against this, there were numerous opportunities.

A further point put to me was that by delisting, a higher price would be achieved in the event of a takeover or trade sale. On the day of the announcement the mid-price of the Lighthouse shares fell from about 4.3p to 3.1p and finished at 2.6p the following day. After finishing my conversation with the Lighthouse chairman, I rushed out a press release canvasing support for retaining the AIM listing. Other shareholders rallied to the cause and the delisting vote ended in our favour. A new non-executive chairman was appointed and the company entered the brave new world of RDR as a public company.

Lighthouse has subsequently introduced new activities and products and looks to have an exciting future. When the company turned down a bid approach at 13p per share I felt justified that we had done the right thing. Had I been out of contact with the markets during my two-week holiday, the delisting could have gone ahead and I might not have benefited from the uplift in value. Being unlisted could have some advantages, but these would be outweighed by the transparency gained from being a publicly quoted company.

When the newspaper headlines read "billions wiped off shares" or "FTSE races to record highs", the impression given is that there has been frantic trading pushing shares higher or lower. In reality, much of the movement can be determined at the market opening. Between 7.50 and 8 am, stockbrokers and market makers are able to input orders to the London Stock Exchange computer price systems. At the opening, buyers and sellers are matched and the initial index is struck. It can often happen that the FTSE 100 is down by, say, 100 points at the opening and finishes the day down 75 points. That could be perceived as a weak market – whereas, during the day, buyers have actually pushed the index up from its opening level. The same might apply when the market rises, in that much of the gain is determined on the opening quotes. However, share prices can be subject to large fluctuations over the course of a day. I have the benefit of being in charge of my own destiny and constantly monitor share price movements throughout the day. I can place orders when I want and thereby take advantage of share price volatility.

By 8.15 am, most of the early activity has occurred and I will then have meetings with up to four companies. Cavendish's offices are situated about half an hour's journey from Central London. From my point of view, it is ideal as I can commute to work by car or, better still, motorbike (a bonus is that there is a readymade excuse for not attending group corporate presentations and broker lunches). It means that I will always have access to company directors on a one-to-one basis. Due to the travel time, most company meetings will be in the morning or late afternoon with a last start time of 3 pm. A presentation will normally last one hour and cover both financial and operational updates.

As, to my knowledge, I manage the only designated AIM Fund, there is excellent access and availability. Not every meeting is devoted to company results. I sometimes meet the management of companies coming to the market, or others might be seeking advice on takeovers, fund raising or other corporate issues such as directors' remuneration packages. Any spare moments are taken up following share prices, reading stockbroker research and completing onerous paperwork. Dealing with hundreds of daily emails probably takes up the most time. Stockbroker research material will now come through email attachments and can cover many areas, from economic factors and in-depth sector comments to individual company research. All can be useful. Even a stock picker has to pay attention to the economic picture so as to avoid mistakes.

Reports on such sectors as property, housebuilding, mining, retail, oil and gas, aerospace and food retailing can make interesting reading. However, analysts can be too close to their sectors and a lot of the time in-depth research is extremely good – only to be ruined by the wrong conclusions. Stockbroker reports on companies have three fundamental problems. First, the writer may have an axe to grind and is trying to convince the investor to be proactive in the shares in order that the penguins can earn commission for the firm. Secondly, a report might be about a corporate client – making it difficult to produce a note advising sale of the shares. Finally, the broker comment might just be a rehash of the company results without original ideas to give added value. Being a value hunter, contrarian stock picker, I will always view any research with some scepticism.

Another aspect of my job is to help the marketing team, which involves giving presentations to IFAs, talking to the press and doing the odd radio or television spot. Strangely, it is an aspect of the job which I quite enjoy. As a firm, we have not sought to make substantial sales to the large multi-asset managers. The idea is to have a quality and well-spread shareholder list of IFA clients so that our funds under management can grow without jeopardising performance by becoming too large. In making presentations, I do not use a series of marketing slides and often speak on whatever subject I want. To do the job thoroughly would take about two hours; when I am presenting with other speakers on the platform, I am usually allocated 20 minutes. On one nationwide tour, I was actually able to give different presentations at each of the nine venues. Marketing is not too disruptive to my work as I am still in contact via the mobile phone and laptop. On these occasions – as when I am on holiday – the penguins are still eager to earn their sardines.

It might sound from the above that I am a workaholic – but if one enjoys one's work, one does not have to work. The great joy I have is that every day is different. I get a huge amount of adrenaline from my job. Besides, I don't actually work all the time. Coping with the 1973 crash taught me that fund management can be a stressful occupation. Today, I make a point of neither staying late in the office nor, apart from reading Saturday's *Financial Times*, reading the weekend newspapers. Every week is a fresh start and brings its own rewards and challenges. One appreciates life as one gets older; time is precious and needs to be well spent. Consequently, I try to occupy myself as much as possible with interests outside the home.

One such interest is the card game bridge. In this country, bridge is administered by the English Bridge Union, which awards master points to those who finish in the top third of a competition. The points accumulate and are used to give the player a ranking from Club Master up to Grand Master. I have achieved the second-highest rank of Life Master. I have been playing for more than 40 years, but still find new points of interest. As a stock picker, it is a relaxing pastime – but also helpful in training one to make dispassionate judgements. With investment management, the timing of a purchase and sale of shares is as important as stock selection – the key thing is to be patient and not to make hasty decisions. In bridge this is equally true. A mishap at the table can be sorted out at a later time and arguing with a partner will only be a distraction in the bidding or play of the next few hands. (I once saw two 50-year-old bridge partners at a national competition fall into dispute and end up rolling around on the floor fighting.)

Also, in investing, as in bridge, it is better never to overvalue one's hand.

22

Footie not FTSE

When I was young, my parents allowed me to buy two comics on a regular basis. The more serious one was a publication called the *Eagle*, the front page of which featured the stories of spaceman Dan Dare and his sidekick Digby as they went up against green-coloured aliens from Venus named the Treens, led by the Mekon, a super-intelligent being with a tiny body and a huge head. It was also the first UK magazine to serialise *Tintin*, the stories of a boy reporter and his dog, Snowy, created by Hergé (Georges Remi), a Belgian cartoonist. Other strips in the comic followed the adventures of PC 49, Harris Tweed and Jeff Arnold, while articles of scientific interest were also included as well as the odd biography. Sadly the comic is no longer published, but my other comic of choice – the *Beano* – is still going. Perhaps its most famous character is Dennis the Menace, but Minnie the Minx, Pansy Potter, Biffo the Bear and Lord Snooty are other names I remember well. The *Beano* was first published in July 1938 and has produced more than 3,800 issues. Both comics – along with the *Dandy, Topper, Roy of the Rovers, Bunty, Buster, Twinkle, 2000AD* and *Valiant* – featured in a special stamp series issued by the Royal Mail in March 2012.

One series in the *Beano* was called Cardew the Cad, which featured the illustrated misadventures of a character created and played on television and radio by actor Cardew Robinson, who was six-foot tall, very thin and wore a schoolboy cap, short trousers and a trademark long scarf. He made many film, radio and television appearances – including in *The Last of the Summer Wine* and *Carry On... Up the Khyber*. Much to my surprise, I found myself seated next to him on at least 20 occasions in each of the years between 1986 and 1992. This happened when I took an interest in association football. As a boy, I had followed Dorking, my local amateur football team, which had a ground near where I lived in the middle of the town. There were numerous amateur teams in that part of the country, including Leatherhead, Redhill, Horsham, Guildford, Sutton, Carshalton and Kingstonians, but no professional club within easy reach. I would go every week and even attend away matches, visiting far-off places such as Worthing and Eastbourne in the team coach.

I did not follow the professional game too closely but was impressed by the dominance of Tottenham Hotspur and Liverpool in their glory years. One game I did attend was West Ham's 2–0 victory over 1860 Munich, in the European Cup Winners' Cup Final of 1965, at a packed Wembley Stadium. It was supposed to be a classic match but I was seated far from the pitch and found it boring. Seven years later, I watched Fulham produce a 0–0 draw at home in an Anglo-Italian Cup match on a cold foggy evening. This completely put me off watching live professional soccer – but like a true stock picker, I later performed a U-turn. In 1986, Wimbledon won promotion to the First Division (now the Premier League) and, as the ground was within driving distance from my home, I decided to invest in a season ticket. My idea was to watch the teams I had seen on *Match of the Day* rather than to support Wimbledon FC, of which I knew very little. I was convinced that the team would only stay in the First Division for one season and decided to watch in style by acquiring a season ticket in the executive area. How wrong I was. Wimbledon FC stayed in the top division – and then the Premiership – until relegation in 2000.

In the first game of the 1986/7 season, Wimbledon lost 3–1 playing away at Manchester City in front of a crowd of more than 20,000. I eagerly awaited my first home game against Aston Villa and expected it to produce a similar scoreline. The match was played at Wimbledon's home ground, Plough Lane, which had a capacity of a little fewer than 15,900. There was open standing behind the goals and the away end was not covered. My seat was in the directors' box on the halfway line – and who should be sitting next to me, wearing his trademark scarf, but Cardew Robinson. Wimbledon was his second team, having been a lifelong Arsenal supporter and season ticket holder. On occasions, he would attend Brentford games – but he rarely missed a Wimbledon home fixture. Wimbledon wore blue strips with a touch of yellow and Cardew enjoyed matches against teams wearing red such as Arsenal, Liverpool and Manchester United. It was great to be able to exchange banter with a person who was more knowledgeable than me about the game.

Wimbledon had knocked Aston Villa out of the FA Cup in the previous season and it was therefore a grudge match with both sets of supporters extremely vocal. In fact, I can still remember taking my seat before the match and being overwhelmed by the noise coming from both ends of the ground. The 6,000-odd crowd sounded like ten times that number. Apart from Dennis Wise, signed from Southampton, Wimbledon retained the squad which had won promotion. The club had risen from the amateur ranks in 1963 to the top division on the back of small crowds and a tight budget. Dave Beasant, the Wimbledon goalkeeper, had not missed a match since the 1981/2 season and had played in all four football divisions. He would arrive at matches on a motorbike and his unbroken run in goal would extend until October 1990. Another player from the club's days in Division 4 of the Football League was Alan Cork, who was signed by the club in 1978 and played 430 matches, scoring 145 goals by the time he left in 1992. He was already a club legend and the supporters' chant which amused me the most went:

Alan Cork, Alan Cork, Alan, Alan Cork
He's got no hair, but we don't care
Alan Cork, Alan Cork.

Aston Villa was a former European champion and most people, including myself, expected them to comfortably win. In an incident-packed first half, Wimbledon scored after ten minutes and Villa equalised, having been awarded a penalty against Nigel Winterburn, who later had a successful career at Arsenal FC. A Villa player was then sent off for punching the Wimbledon left-winger and John Fashanu put Wimbledon ahead in injury time. The action continued in the second half – both sides scored in the last three minutes of the game. I started the game as a neutral supporter and ended up wanting the underdog to win. Wimbledon won the next four matches and occupied the number one spot in Division 1. This initial success was not to last, though; Wimbledon had one draw and five losses in the next six games. Nevertheless, the team finished in sixth position at the end of the season.

Cardew said that, in many ways, he preferred watching Wimbledon to his other teams as there was much more goalmouth action. Unlike today, goalkeepers were allowed to pick up the football when passed to them by their own players. So, typically, the ball would often be passed back to Dave Beasant, who would then lob it towards John Fashanu and Alan Cork in the opponents' end. I also believe that Dave Beasant was among the first goalkeepers to take free kicks in most areas in his team's half of the pitch. To me, the game was exciting to watch – but the football purist hated this type of play. Teams such as Arsenal, Liverpool, Manchester United and West Ham were noted for their free-flowing football, where several passes would be strung together before a shot was taken on goal. To be fair, these teams were attractive to watch and had their deserved share of success.

In the 70s and 80s, Liverpool FC was the dominant force in football and won the First Division title 11 times. The club had some great players and was one of the most attractive teams to watch. In the 1987/8 football season Liverpool came top of the league, losing only two games and finishing nine points clear of Manchester United in second place. Wimbledon finished the season in seventh position and both teams faced each other in the FA Cup Final at Wembley

Stadium. This was my second season as a Wimbledon season ticket holder and I was excited at the prospect. Unlike my 1965 visit to the West Ham final, I was actually going to watch a team that I now supported and wanted to win. I expected my team to lose, but the Liverpool side was always worth watching. An added bonus was that the Wimbledon team coach drove past as I walked towards the ground. Bobby Gould, the Wimbledon manager, was seated next to the driver and gave me a wave.

Wimbledon had the reputation of being a tough team that enjoyed the role of underdogs and giant-killers. Vinnie Jones played 254 matches between 1986 and 1989 and 1992 to 1996, scoring a total of 23 goals. He was signed from Wealdstone for £10,000 and became a hero when he scored the only goal in a 1-0 victory over Manchester United. It was Vinnie's second game for Wimbledon and Sir Alex Ferguson's third game in charge of Manchester United.

On the day of the FA Cup Final, Vinnie and the rest of the team played their usual aggressive game. Wimbledon scored through a headed goal by Lawrie Sanchez in the 35th minute and Liverpool looked to have equalised, but the goal was disallowed as the referee had blown his whistle for an earlier foul. It was now a question of hoping that Wimbledon could hold on to the slender lead. Disaster looked to have struck when, in the second half, the referee awarded a dubious penalty kick to Liverpool. No goalkeeper had ever saved a penalty in a Wembley cup final, but Dave Beasant pulled off a thrilling save. Wimbledon held on well and the cup was theirs – creating a record of being the only team to win both the Amateur Cup and the FA Cup. The former was played in front of 45,000 at Wembley Stadium in May 1963 while the Liverpool game saw an attendance of 98,203.

Sadly, one year later, 96 Liverpool FC fans died in the Hillsborough disaster, with many crushed against perimeter fencing. An urgent report on ground safety was commissioned by the government and overseen by Lord Taylor of Gosforth. Among other things, the Taylor Report concluded that by August 1994 clubs in the top two tiers of English football should have all-seater stadiums. Some famous terraces such as the Stretford End at Manchester United, Arsenal's North Bank and Spion Kop at Liverpool were to be replaced by seated areas. For a club like Wimbledon, which survived on a shoestring budget, there was a huge dilemma. As it was difficult and costly to redevelop Plough Lane, the club entered an agreement, in 1991, to share Selhurst Park Stadium, the home of Crystal Palace. As I lived in Redhill, the situation was fine by me – but east/west public transport meant a difficult journey for those coming from Wimbledon.

When Wimbledon started to play its games at Selhurst Park in the 1991/2 season, I decided to relocate from the executive area on the halfway line to behind the goal. A disadvantage was not having an equal view of both ends of the pitch, but the action at the near goal was closer and much more exciting. Equally, the atmosphere was better. It was considered poor etiquette in the executive area to jump up from one's seat and anything apart from applause was frowned upon. Those behind the goal would rise from their seats when action approached their end and were not afraid to voice their opinion about the players, officials and incidents in the game. Sitting in the main stand at Plough Lane I had the benefit of serious comment from Cardew. The 'behind-the-goal brigade' would give more biased comments, but offered valid opinions on tactics, team formation and selection. Some of the fans lived and breathed football and had followed teams since they were toddlers. As I was a relative newcomer to the game and did not attend many away games, I respected their ideas but had the advantage of being a spectator without rose-tinted glasses. To be fair, though, supporters of teams such as Manchester United and Liverpool would applaud a team which had outplayed and beaten them.

Unfortunately, Wimbledon were relegated from the Premiership in 2000 and, after a change of ownership, relocated to Milton Keynes, where they played at the National Hockey Stadium. I retained my ticket for one season as the journey between my home and the stadium was a reasonable one, despite being a round trip of some 170 miles. When the owners changed the name to MK Dons, I decided to call it a day. In May 2002, the loyal Wimbledon supporters, who had seen their club hijacked and transplanted to a ground some 56 miles away, formed AFC Wimbledon. It was allowed to enter the ninth tier of the football league and, having been promoted six times, now plays in League Division 1. It was the first club formed in the 21st century to achieve promotion to the football league and holds the record set in 2003/4 for playing 78 consecutive games without defeat. MK Dons rose as high as the Football Championship, now playing in a purpose-built 30,500-seater stadium in Milton Keynes. Strangely they also now play in Division 1.

In the final few years at Selhurst Park, I held Wimbledon season tickets for myself and my three daughters. We were in the family enclosure where they could play videogames and have refreshments at half-time. When the move to Milton Keynes came to pass, I decided to find another football club. There were numerous London clubs, but tickets were either too expensive or there was a waiting list. I wanted to watch Premiership football but instead decided on Fulham FC, then playing in Division 1. Part of the reason was that there was still terraced standing behind the goals and I wanted my daughters to experience this. I am not sure that they were too impressed, but they could run around before the game. Great in the summer, but "We are freezing, can we go home now?" was sometimes heard at half-time on a cold winter afternoon. Fulham's football ground is situated on the banks of the River Thames and from Putney Bridge is reached by a walk through Bishop's Park. My children were still young enough to use the play area and therefore had some compensation for suffering the cold. In our first season, Fulham won the league in some comfort and I achieved my wish to watch Premiership Football. The club then retained its premiership status for 13 consecutive seasons starting from 2000/2001.

After I had given up going to see Wimbledon at Milton Keynes, I also bought a season ticket for Crawley Town FC. The ground is within easy driving distance from my home and the team had just been promoted to the Conference League, one level below the Football League Division 2. It is a modern stadium, but still has open standing behind both goals. In the first couple of seasons, supporters would change ends at half-time. There was some rivalry but never any crowd problems. This is hardly surprising when the average attendance was around 2,000 people. It is still a friendly club and opposing supporters mingle in the Redz Bar before the kick-off. Crawley also won promotion and now play in Football League Division 2, having reached Division 1. My seat is near the halfway line and the crowd is generally very quiet, but not without humour. On one occasion the referee booked a Crawley player for a dubious foul and the crowd chanted, "You don't know what you're doing". About two minutes later the referee awarded Crawley a penalty kick. The witty response was, "We were only joking".

Football is a strange game as it attracts a wide variety of supporter. At the top is the owner who these days needs to be extremely wealthy to finance operations. Often the owner is also the chairman of the club and a figure who can be praised or come into extreme criticism. There is then the fair-weather supporter, who will purchase a season ticket when a club is promoted and leave when it is relegated. The remainder are hardcore supporters who follow a club through thick and thin. Age groups vary, but today most clubs have a family following. I have always felt happy to take my children and granddaughters as I have never seen any crowd trouble or racial abuse. It is interesting to watch the reaction of individual supporters during the game. Some get very animated when a decision goes the wrong way and can hurl abuse at officials. One thing that is common to all supporters is that everyone will rise from their seats when their team scores a goal. When the opposing team scores, the fans are silent. An exception is Crawley, where the home supporters will politely applaud a spectacular goal scored by the opposite side. Crawley fans will also clap the away fans when the attendance figures are announced during the match.

It must be great to support a team that wins week in week out and is always near the top of the premier division. As the achievements grow, so do the ambitions and top of the list is to win the Champions League, where some of the very best continental teams compete. The most successful teams are expected to beat the likes of Wimbledon, Fulham and Crawley Town and it must be fairly galling to lose to such teams. By the same token, to me, beating a bigger club can seem like winning the cup final. How many teams are like Crawley and still celebrate the five-year anniversary of being beaten 1-0 by Manchester United at Old Trafford in a FA Cup game? On 25 October 2003, I travelled by coach with my girls to watch Fulham play Manchester United with the idea of visiting the huge modern Old Trafford Stadium and to soak up the atmosphere. We were impressed by the stadium and when Fulham unexpectedly won 3-1, it felt as good as Wimbledon winning the FA Cup.

When attending games, I do not sing, chant or wear replica football shirts. As a rule, I seldom go to away matches, but have on occasions been invited to the hospitality areas at Arsenal and Tottenham Hotspur. Both have great grounds, as do Liverpool at Anfield, which I have also visited. I guess that I picked my football teams the same way that I pick my stocks. In the stock market, it is very satisfying to find a winner in a sector that is out of favour with investors. There is also my contrarian attitude; I like to swim against the tide in stocks as well as in not choosing a team that every football supporter would follow. Watching football is a distraction from portfolio management and provides a good escape at the weekend. I would hasten to add that the more civilised sports such as rugby, tennis, cricket and athletics would provide a similar stimulus.

23

Other Distractions

My daughters reawakened my interest in music. I wanted them to play a musical instrument and paid for guitar lessons but they did not have sufficient enthusiasm to become musicians. It was a great pity and the reason why there is not a pop group called Mumford and Daughters.

To encourage them, I took them to see live performances. One of their favourite bands is the Manfreds. The group had a string of hits between 1962 and 1969 when they were called Manfred Mann, named after their leader who subsequently left to form Manfred Mann's Earth Band. I did not follow the group in the 60s. When the band reformed in the 90s, the line-up included most of the original group (absent Manfred Mann himself): vocalists Paul Jones and Mike d'Abo, lead guitar Tom McGuinness, keyboard Mike Hugg, saxophone and flute Mike Vickers, bass Benny Gallagher and Rob Townsend on drums. I was persuaded to see them by a stockbroker and it was probably the only decent recommendation that he ever made. Between 1969 and 1992, the band members had had separate careers and their three-hour shows as the Manfreds would therefore cover a wide variety of numbers from the different groups. I was most surprised that the early Manfred Mann recordings covered a huge number of rhythm-and-blues numbers that had not appeared as singles. This was a bonus and introduced my girls to the type of music I most enjoy.

There are an incredible number of music venues in the UK. Most cities have a theatre capable of showing major entertainment shows and virtually all towns feature pubs or clubs with live entertainment. Then there are the outdoor music festivals which can accommodate substantial-sized audiences. I have never attended Glastonbury or the Isle of Wight Festival but have been to a concert at Hyde Park. The atmosphere at these events seems fantastic but I prefer to watch them on television. Shows at the London Arena, O2, Royal Albert Hall and similar venues can be extremely good but in some respects gigs at smaller locations are even better. Dotted around London are several clubs and pubs that cater for events for up to 500 people. Most famous of these is 100 Club, situated in the basement of 100 Oxford Street. It has featured live music since 1942 and was originally a jazz club, with artists such as Glenn Miller, Benny Goodman, Humphrey Lyttelton, Ronnie Scott and Johnny Dankworth performing. Punk featured in the 70s and 80s and today there is jazz, blues and rock. The Rolling Stones held two impromptu performances there in the 80s and the club has been kept open with the support of Paul McCartney and fellow artists. Those visiting the club today might be in for a culture shock – it has not changed since the 1970s.

My introduction to small venues came from a work colleague who recommended a group called the Zombies, who were appearing at the Boom Boom Club at Sutton United FC. I did not know what to expect, though I knew the group's 1964 UK and US hit 'She's Not There'. The football club was founded in 1898, but has never achieved football league status; the team plays at a compact ground with a capacity of 5,013. The Boom Boom Club is situated in a 50-year-old club building next to the stand. At the time of my first visit, about ten years ago, there was no air conditioning and the temperature was regulated by huge ceiling fans which merely shifted hot air round the room. However, the acoustics were good – it was like having a live band in one's living room. Air conditioning has subsequently been installed in the premises and there are no longer problems with the room temperature. Apart from this, the venue still retains its old-fashioned football clubhouse appearance and atmosphere.

I would guess that the Boom Boom Club has a capacity for no more than 300 people. It draws good crowds for tribute acts for the likes of David Bowie, Queen and the Rolling Stones and some original bands that have built up a following. Other unknown artists might only attract an audience of 60 followers. The club is one of several run by Pete Feenstra, who has his own radio show and is passionate about live music. As most of the performers are established musicians, the audience is generally quite old – a pub with live music might attract the younger age group. To me, smaller venues are music's equivalent to the AIM market and are a place to search for undiscovered talent. Ticket prices vary between £10 and £15 for a few hours' live entertainment. Nowadays it is possible to get a preview of a little-known band by downloading a clip from YouTube.

There are numerous good bands that play around the country at smaller venues. It is a pity that they do not always get the recognition that they deserve. The bulk of the music-buying public is under 25 and it is understandable that it follows younger groups. Television, radio air play and publicity are the main factors that influence the music market. Without these, even the biggest international stars can go unnoticed. Take, for instance, Troyal Garth Brooks. Who? Brooks was born in Tulsa, Oklahoma in February 1962. He is an American country and western singer with a commercial rock/pop component to his songs. He has released 77 singles and 20 albums and, with more than 70 million album sales, has outsold Elvis and the Beatles and is thought to be America's bestselling artist. Apart from country and western enthusiasts, very few people in the UK have heard of him.

As a stock picker it is rewarding to find the little-known names. There are three artists or groups I have come across over the years that I think deserve to be ten-baggers of the pop music industry but who – for whatever reason – have been overlooked.

{ The first is singer/songwriter Robert Anthony Noonan, born in June 1948 and performing under the name Willie Nile. He was taught classical piano from the age of eight until his early teens and wrote songs from an early age. His career influences were Elvis, the Everly Brothers, Fats Domino and Buddy Holly, and consequently his music has a folk-rock lilt to it, as well as witty lyrics and original sound. There may be a little bit of Bob Dylan and Bruce Springsteen thrown into the pot too. Willie mainly plays electric guitar and fronts a four-piece band of talented musicians. Some of his songs are like anthems which, with the right promotion, could have been massive hits. I first saw him in 2010 at the Boom Boom Club and subsequently at other UK venues, including the 100 Club. He is an artist who loves to entertain an appreciative audience. Wealdstone Football Club is the home of the Tropic at Ruislip club. Willie Nile appeared there for the first time in 2010 in front of an audience of 23 people. At the end of the act, he immediately asked when he could play there again – amazing when considering that he is often watched by well-known musicians and Bruce Springsteen has been known to make an impromptu appearance with him on stage. Of his many songs to choose from, I would select 'American Ride' as the best example of his music.

{ My next potential ten-bagger of the music world is Roadhouse, a UK band with more than one vocalist. It has been in existence for over 25 years, having been founded by Gary Boner who writes most of the band's material. He created the band after being asked to provide entertainment for a wedding and having approached several gifted musicians. There have been a few changes in the line-up over the years – at one stage, in addition to Gary, the group featured three female singers, but now comprises two. It has produced 12 CDs, mainly in the rocky/blues genre. A new CD was cut in April 2016. The band has a reasonable-size following and appears at smaller venues and festivals in the UK. 'Telling Lies' is a recording which typifies the type of music played by the band.

{ The last would-be ten-bagger I would like to mention is Dana Fuchs, who was born in January 1976 just about the time that Willie

Nile was starting his musical career. Dana worked for MTV in the 90s and played and wrote songs for two films. She also featured as Janis Joplin in a stage musical. She certainly has that type of voice – but possibly sounds more like Tina Turner. I saw her at the Boom Boom Club in 2015 and immediately bought her three studio-produced albums. In my opinion, the mark of a great artist is when you hear them once and feel compelled to buy their CDs. It is also a compliment to the artist when their performance covers completely original songs. Fuchs would not be everybody's cup of tea but I would suggest 'Lonely for a lifetime' as a representative number. Strangely, Dana Fuchs has a large following in Germany – and the same applies to Willie Nile in Spain.

At the age of 12, Dana Fuchs started to sing in the First Baptist Gospel Choir. Many entertainers have been similarly influenced by gospel music. Rosetta Nubin was thought to be the first black gospel singer to break through into commercial recorded music. She was born in Arkansas in March 1915 and started performing with her family at the age of six; the first of her three marriages occurred when she reached 19. It only lasted for four years, but she adopted a derivation of her husband's name to become known on stage as Sister Rosetta Tharpe. She toured Britain in 1957, but I only became aware of her when she appeared in a live outdoor concert on television in 1964 at a disused Manchester railway station. What was memorable, and impressed me the most, is that Sister Rosetta played an electric guitar while strutting down the platform singing 'Didn't it rain'. Both Little Richard and Johnny Cash named her as their favourite singer, while Chuck Berry, Elvis Presley, Jerry Lee Lewis, Aretha Franklin and Tina Turner cited her as an important influence on their careers. Sister Rosetta died in 1973 and is known as the 'Godmother of Rock and Roll'.

Having been around at the time, I was aware of the American music scene and its various influences on British pop music. With the gospel influences in particular, it seemed incredible that something with so much passion could emerge from a church service. After my near-death experience mentioned earlier – when I nearly electrocuted myself in the bath – I felt that I really should be attending a church. The problem was that, to me, the services were dated and rather boring. However, I was convinced that there was some purpose in life and that death was not final. In 1991, my eldest daughter was moving into secondary education and there was an excellent school about 200 yards from my home. The problem was that being a joint Anglican/Roman Catholic School, parents had to be committed churchgoers. This was quite understandable, but my daughter had been a member of religious groups at school and a committed Christian. Due to the school entry criteria, I decided to start attending church on a regular basis. I found a convenient one and started taking my three daughters to Sunday school classes.

In the event, my eldest daughter failed to get accepted into the school and I protested with the help of the local press, my member of parliament and other sympathetic parties. I also purchased books on mathematics, science, geography and history which covered the GCSE curriculum so that I could teach my daughter at home. Before leaving for work, I would set homework which could be marked in the evening. Thankfully, this was only necessary in the autumn term as the school eventually capitulated and offered my daughter a place, which was gratefully accepted. Happily the church I attended had a progressive vicar who supported Manchester United and would bring football banter into the service. Needless to say, Fulham were sometimes on the receiving end. I actually enjoyed attending church, which I found quite uplifting. Although it was a traditional Anglican church, I was surprised that many of the congregation were casually dressed. Also the average age was much younger than I had expected. Part of the reason was that several parents wished to meet my daughter's school's entry criteria and consequently the congregation turnover was higher than it might otherwise have been.

After 20 years of attending the church, and following a change in personnel, I decided that I had fallen too much into a routine and would look for an alternative place of worship. This brought me to Holy Trinity Church in Redhill. The family service commences at 9.15 am on a Sunday morning and finishes at 10.30. It is always packed with parents and young children attending Sunday school classes. There is a small band featuring piano, drums, guitar and sometimes strings or brass. Occasionally, hymns are sung, but most of the time the service covers half a dozen modern songs with words featured on various screens dotted round the church. Different members of the congregation are involved in running proceedings, including two singers instead of a traditional choir.

The 11 o'clock service caters for the more traditional churchgoers and includes hymns as well as newer songs. It is appreciated that many youngsters and parents have sporting commitments on a Sunday morning and, for these, there is a four o'clock family service. Teenagers are not left out. At 7 pm there is a service with a six-piece band – three guitars, drums, keyboard and strings. All ceremonies are well attended by more than 500 men, women and children. The sermons are also amusing and relevant to modern culture. An added bonus is that the vicar attends Fulham football matches with his son, using his motorbike for the journey. My wife and I attend regularly and like the congenial atmosphere. It may not be a gospel stomping ground, but it certainly brings religion into the 21st century. People are not obliged to attend and numbers do not drop significantly in school holidays. Perhaps there are other similar churches elsewhere in the country; I hope so.

My other interest in the summer months is horse racing. After work, I will drive to Windsor for the Monday evening meetings at Royal Windsor Racecourse, where horse racing first took place in 1866. The course takes the appearance of a figure of eight, which means that in middle-distance races horses have to negotiate both right and left-handed bends. There are often theme evenings, where companies sell their products from tents pitched on the lawn between the paddock and the parade ring. It was here that I discovered, much to my surprise, how many varieties of sausage and different-flavoured cider brands there are in existence. There is an Irish night and a ladies evening plus roving jazz bands and, dotted round the place, individual musicians performing popular songs. Sometimes, a tribute band will put on a performance at the end of the final race. The course is easy to get to and has the bonus of free public parking. Those coming from Windsor have the option of travelling to the racecourse by boat on the River Thames.

Royal Windsor Racecourse lives in the shadow of Ascot Racecourse, where the first meeting occurred on Saturday 11 August 1711. At that time, Queen Anne was on the throne and pinpointed an area at Ascot Heath as being "ideal for horses to gallop at full stretch". The inaugural race was Her Majesty's Plate, featuring seven English hunters carrying 12 stone and run in three heats, each over four miles. There is no record of the winner, but the prize fund was 100 guineas – in those days a massive amount of money. A building which housed 1,650 people was constructed in 1794 and was in use over the next 50 years. An Act of Enclosure, to make Ascot Heath a permanent racecourse, was passed by Parliament in 1813. Today, the racecourse is best known for its Royal Ascot Meeting, which is high on the calendar of annual social events. The opening race is the Queen Anne Stakes, named after the royal founder, and the highlight of the meeting is the Ascot Gold Cup which was first run in 1807.

Until 1939 there was just one royal meeting, attended by the ruling monarch, but there are now several flat and national hunt meetings held during the year. Prize money is greater than that on offer at Royal Windsor and racing is therefore of a much higher standard. It is like comparing Manchester United with Fulham or a FTSE 100 company with a small cap. There are numerous smaller courses that might be considered the Crawley Town or AIM equivalent. To my stock-picking instincts, Royal Windsor is ideal. It is possible to unearth horses that have dropped down in class and make winning bets. Like bridge and the stock market, there is a challenge waiting to be taken. I will only attend if I think that there is a good chance of finding winners, and rarely come away from an evening out of pocket. I have built up a modest amount of money which is used as a racing bank.

In 1890, when King Edward VII was Prince of Wales, he opened Lingfield Park racecourse and gave permission for the Prince of Wales's feathers to be incorporated in its logo. Meetings have been held there every year since, apart from during the Second World War when the 450-acre site was requisitioned by the War Office for use as a prisoner of war camp for Italians. It is a standard circular course, with both a grass and an artificial Polytrack, which enables racing to take place in most weather conditions. In middle-distance races, the horses are ridden down a hill to negotiate a left-hand bend before entering a straight run to the finishing post. The track is similar to the Epsom racecourse and the principal event on the calendar is the Lingfield Derby Trial. Racing is of a similar standard to that at Royal Windsor and the racecourse also provides entertainment through tribute bands after evening meetings. As the racecourse is near where I live, I will sometimes attend on a warm summer evening.

My home is surrounded by many other racecourses, including Epsom, Sandown Park, Kempton Park, Brighton, Plumpton, Fontwell Park and Goodwood, which are all within striking distance. As in football, the largest venues attract the better-known singers, groups and bands. I occasionally visit these courses but not as often as Royal Windsor and Lingfield Park. Otherwise I do not follow racing closely and only have a bet when I am at a race meeting where I have had time to study the form of the runners. The best advice that I can give to anybody that gambles is to keep a record of winnings and losses. If the overall result is a loss, stop – there is no point throwing your money away.

Most people enjoy watching television and I am no different, but, due to time limitations, am very selective. One of the problems about getting up at four in the morning to be in the office by six, is that, apart from when I am playing bridge, I always have to go to bed at a reasonable time. Besides sport, the only programme I make a point of viewing regularly is a quiz show called *The Chase*, where four contestants attempt to win money from one of five experts. Questions can be very difficult and it is extremely hard to win the competition. Otherwise my preferred viewing is drama. Fortunately, it is now possible to record these series rather than watching them at inconvenient times. I also acquire DVD box sets of television dramas that have been shown over the last few years. I guess one could call it a stock picker's approach to watching television.

Salvatore Albert Lombino was born on 15 October 1926 and before serving in the US Navy, attended Evander Childs High School, later majoring in English and psychology at Hunter College. He legally changed his name to Evan Hunter in 1952 and also used the names Curt Cannon, Hunt Collins, Richard Marsten, D.A. Addams, and Ted Taine. He was an author and not a safe cracker or any other sort of criminal – the pseudonyms were used up until 1960, while writing books on differing subjects. Between 1956 and his death in 2005, writing under the name Ed McBain, he produced more than 50 books in the *87th Precinct* series, following the fortunes of the detectives of a New York police department. As Evan Hunter, he also published 14 books featuring a lawyer called Matthew Hope. Had it not been for this author, the idea of 'rock 'n' roll' might not have emerged as quickly as it did. Under the name Evan Hunter he wrote the screenplay for the film of his book *Blackboard Jungle*. It was released in 1955 and focused on juvenile crime in a New York School. It kickstarted the career of William John Clifton Haley. 'Rock Around the Clock' by the said Bill Hayley and the Comets was featured in the film and immediately reached the top of the hit parade, becoming a classic of its genre.

C I cannot remember how I found my first Ed McBain book, but I discovered that the *87th Precinct* series made light reading and it was interesting to follow the development of the various detectives, not all of whom lived to survive the series. It also inspired me to read novels that follow one main character and, in this respect, I have been hooked on the Jack Reacher stories by Lee Child. Quite by accident historical novels have also hit my to-read list. Of particular note are the five-part story of Julius Caesar by Conn Iggulden and the *Eagle* series of Roman military fiction by Simon Scarrow. Numerous great novels covering various periods of history have been written by Bernard Cornwell, most famed for his *Sharpe* series. Science fiction can be interesting but I have not strayed beyond John Wyndham. I am not averse to occasionally reading the odd autobiography. I find reading an enjoyable pastime – but, unfortunately, there are too few hours in the day. However, I will pick up a book when there is a spare moment. Holidays are a bonus as I can read several books in a short space of time. I am not sure that it helps the stock-picking process other than to provide a healthy distraction.

One thing that is missing from my life is participating in sport. In my younger days, I played a lot of tennis and, by rights, should take up golf. Several years ago, I gave it a bash and bought a set of golf clubs at a local auction. The idea was to practise in the garden. Rather than smashing the windows in my neighbour's house, I bought some plastic dummy golf balls. It was all very frustrating as I found it impossible to hit the balls into the air and, in the attempt, managed to ruin my lawn. I could have gone for coaching but decided to give it up as a bad job. Taking up squash was another alternative, but I do not possess the competitive edge for such strenuous exercise.

Now is the customary point in a book to produce a final chapter bringing all the points together, but I have concluded that we would then be in the land of repetition, waffle and hypothesis. At the end of the day, it does not matter too much what others think. The only advice that I can give is to enjoy life to the full and let stock-picking help to achieve a satisfying journey.

Will I be classed as a football-supporting rocker slob or a churchgoing, bridge-playing snob? Neither, I hope: a 'stock-picking moron' will do just fine for me.

INDEX

N

THANKS
FOR READING!

Our readers mean everything to us at Harriman House. As a special thank-you for buying this book let us help you save as much as possible on your next read:

If you've never ordered from us before, get £5 off your first order at **harriman-house.com** with this code: `mfd145f`

Already a customer? Get £5 off an order of £25 or more with this code: `54425m`

Get 7 days' FREE access to hundreds of our books at **volow.co** – simply head over and sign up.

Thanks again!
from the team at

Codes can only be used once per customer and order. T&Cs apply.